Teachers' Unions and the Politics of Education in Japan

SUNY series in Japan in Transition

Teachers' Unions and the Politics of Education in Japan

Robert W. Aspinall

State University of New York Press

Published by
State University of New York Press, Albany

Printed in the United States of America

For information, address State University of New York Press,
90 State Street, Suite 700, Albany, N.Y., 12207

Production by Kelli Williams
Marketing by Patrick Durocher

Library of Congress Cataloging-in-Publication Data

Aspinall, Robert W., 1962–
Teachers' unions and the politics of education in Japan / Robert W. Aspinall.
p. cm. — (SUNY series in Japan in transition)
Includes bibliographical references (p.) and index.
ISBN 0-7914-5049-X (alk. paper) — ISBN 0-7914-5050-3 (pbk. : alk. paper)
1. Teachers' unions—Japan—History. 2. Teachers—Japan—Political activity. 3. Nihon Kyōshokuin Kumiai—History. I. Title. II. Series.

LB2844.53.J3 A86 2001
331.88'113711'00952—dc21 2001020145

10 9 8 7 6 5 4 3 2 1

For my Parents

CONTENTS

LIST OF ABBREVIATIONS AND JAPANESE TERMS

Abbreviations

CCE	Central Council on Education (Chūō kyōiku shingikai)
CEC	Central Executive Council [of Nikkyōso], (Shikkōbu)
DSP	Democratic Socialist Party (Minshū Shakaitō)
JCP	Japan Communist Party (Nihon Kyōsantō)
JHS	Junior High School (Chūgakkō)
JSP	Japan Socialist Party (Nihon Shakaitō)
LDP	Liberal Democratic Party (Jiyū Minshutō)
MITI	Ministry of International Trade and Industry (Tsūshō Sangyōshō)
MOE	Ministry of Education (Mombushō)
MOF	Ministry of Finance (Okurashō)
PKO	Peace Keeping Operations
SCAP	Supreme Command for the Allied Powers
SDF	Self Defence Forces (Jieitai)
SHS	Senior High School (Kōtōgakkō)

Japanese Terms

Bunkai	School-based branch of teachers' union
Dōmei	Federation of private sector unions
Dōtoku	Postwar word for moral education
Genba	The actual site as which education is delivered (i.e., schools, universities, etc.)
Jichirō	Local Government Workers' Union
Juku	Private exam preparatory schools attended by children part-time
Kokurō	Japan National Railway Workers' Union
Keidanren	Federation of Economic Organisations
Nikkyō	Japan Educators' Union
Nikkyōso	Japan Teachers' Union
Rengō	Combined federation of public and private sector unions formed in 1989
Rinkyōshin	Ad Hoc Council on Education
Shunin	Teachers serving in positions of responsibility (e.g., head of department, head of career guidance, etc.)
Shūshin	Prewar word for moral education
Sōhyō	Federation of public sector unions
Tokyōkyō	Council of Tokyo Municipal Educational Personnel Unions
Yobikō	Private exam preparatory schools attended by children full-time usually after they have finished formal school education
Zendentsū	Telecommunications Workers' Union
Zenkyō	All Japan Teachers' Union
Zenrōren	Left-wing national union federation (alternative to Rengō) formed in 1989
Zoku	Unofficial cliques of LDP Diet members sharing an interest in a particular area of public policy

ACKNOWLEDGMENTS

I would like to begin by thanking my two academic supervisors at St. Antony's College, Oxford, Dr. Roger Goodman and Professor Arthur Stockwin, for all the help, advice, and encouragement they gave me in the preparation of the thesis that was the foundation for this book. I would also like to thank the Economic and Social Research Council, whose generous funding made the study possible. Thanks also go to my examiners, Professor Ian Neary and Dr. David Phillips, for their valuable comments on my thesis.

In Japan I am grateful go to all the people who helped me in my research. In particular I would like to thank Professor Ogawa Masahito of the Education department of Tokyo University, who provided invaluable assistance in setting up many of the interviews. I would also like to thank Yoshizumi Kaori of Kawaguchi Nishi High school, who helped me with my research in Saitama and gave me many insights into teacher unionism at the school level. Thanks also to Professor Horio Teruhisa for his advice and encouragement, and to Okada Akito, Chris Hood and Gareth Jones for all their help. Special thanks go to Karatsu Rie for her help and support. In Nagoya I would particularly like to thank Professor Ueda Takeo for his help and advice, and also Tan Mitsugu and Mutoh Makiko.

I would like to thank Jerry Eades and SUNY press's three anonymous readers for their suggestions and comments.

Finally, thanks go to all those friends and colleagues, too numerous to mention, in Oxford, Tokyo, Saitama, and Nagoya whose support, advice, and encouragement have helped sustain me along the course of study and research that has culminated in this book.

NOTES ON STYLE

Throughout Japanese personal names are given with the family name listed first. In general, union organizations, both local and national, are referred to by their abbreviated Japanese name. Thus, the Japan Teachers' Union is referred to throughout as Nikkyōso, except when quotations are made from authors who follow different conventions. Japanese political parties and ministries are referred to by the initial letters of their English names. Thus, the Ministry of Education is referred to as the MOE and the Japan Socialist Party as the JSP. Although the JSP changed both its Japanese and its official English names during the 1990s,* the original name is used throughout this book for the sake of clarity. A list of the main abbreviations and Japanese terms used is included for the benefit of readers more familiar with different conventions.

*In 1991, the official English name of the party was changed from Japan Socialist Part to Social Democratic Party of Japan, although the Japanese name, Nihon Shakaitō, remained the same. In 1996, the Japanese name was changed to Shakai Minshūtō and the English name was modified to Social Democratic Party.

INTRODUCTION

In the closing weeks of 1989, Nikkyōso (the Japan Teachers' Union)[1] finally broke in two after over two years of heated argument, factional maneuvering, and bitter infighting within its ranks. This schism marked the end of an era for one of the largest unions in postwar Japan. The year 1989, of course, marked the end of other eras too. It was the year when the Berlin wall came down, heralding the end of the Cold War and the international ideological cleavage between capitalism and communism. It was also the year when the Liberal Democratic Party (LDP) lost control of the Upper House of the Japanese Diet for the first time since the party's formation. Such ideological and electoral watersheds have led observers of Japanese politics to talk about the end of the 1955 system (a system named after the year of the LDP's birth). The stability of the 1955 system had been based on the existence of two rival camps—the governing conservative camp led by the LDP and the left-wing opposition camp led by the Japan Socialist Party (JSP). Nikkyōso had always been a powerful and important member of the latter camp and therefore its decline in the 1980s, culminating in the schism of 1989, was inevitably accompanied by a decline in the strength and influence of the opposition camp as a whole.

Since its creation in 1947, Nikkyōso had always seen itself, along with its political allies, as fulfilling the vital role of defending the postwar democratic settlement against reactionary attack from the right. Reforms carried out during the American Occupation of Japan from 1945 to 1952 were regarded by some as liberating and democratic and by others as foreign impositions out of step with domestic traditions and customs. Nikkyōso, whose very existence was made possible by the

Occupation-era removal of constraints on the creation of free trade unions, was firmly on the side of those who wanted to defend and extend those reforms. Therefore, it very soon became the enemy of those conservative politicians and bureaucrats who were critical of foreign interference and nostalgic for traditional prewar Japanese values. In any long-term conflict over values and ideas, the way that young people are educated must inevitably become the subject of bitter dispute. Thus, the battle for control over the nation's education system was one taken particularly seriously by both opposing camps. Nikkyōso's position as one of the strongest members of the opposition camp and also one of the most powerful interest groups involved in the day-to-day running of the education system meant that it was at the heart of the political and ideological conflict inherent in the post-Occupation system. This is why the timing of the split in the union with the ending of the 1955 system is no mere coincidence. It is also why any full understanding of the ending of the 1955 system must involve a detailed study of Nikkyōso.

The splitting of Nikkyōso in 1989 not only provides us with a reason to study it more closely, but also offers an opportunity to get at aspects of the organization that were previously less transparent. This is because in the ordinary, everyday functioning of an organization it can be very difficult to recognize the key factors that motivate the individual members and leaders of the organization. Questionnaire surveys can, of course, be conducted, but how far can the honesty of the responses be evaluated? This can be especially true with studies of Japanese organizations, where a high value is placed on loyalty to the group and consensus within it. The *tatemae* or official opinion might disguise the *honne* or genuine one. Thus, individual members might give what they think is the "correct" response to questions about their own membership as well as the aims of the larger organization. However, when the organization is thrown into crisis and the individual member finds him or herself torn between rival claims on his or her loyalty (as well as the opportunity to leave the organization altogether), a more genuine expression of the member's position might then be arrived at. Furthermore, factions within the organization that previously kept their differences of opinion muted will, at a time of schism, go public with their criticisms of their rivals. Arguments that were previously conducted discretely behind closed doors will now be given a public airing, allowing interested outsiders their first real glimpse of what the different factions really think of each other. Like a quarreling couple who finally reach divorce court, the bitterness of many a private row at last becomes public, as well the specific contents of each spouse's grievances against the other.

The preceding discussion is an argument for the usefulness of examining any organization undergoing the process of splitting in two. In the specific case of Nikkyōso, however, there are further justifications. Although, for the purposes of clarity, scholars always refer to Nikkyōso in the singular, as a single, national entity, it soon became clear to anyone who examined it that Nikkyōso, before the schism, was an amalgamation of many separate and distinct local unions, each of which was an amalgamation of dozens of local, school-based associations. Although Nikkyōso leaders and members would often use the rhetoric of unity, it was clear that a certain amount of disunity was inevitable. The manner in which the events of the schism unfolded threw this disunity into stark relief, allowing the outsider a clearer view of the complexity of the relationships between the different groups that made up Nikkyōso. Before embarking on a study of Nikkyōso's breakup, it is first necessary to review the current state of scholarship on Nikkyōso, scholarship that was carried out mostly when the union was a united organization.

Studies of Nikkyōso in English

An interesting feature of the study of Nikkyōso as an area of objective, academic inquiry is that, to date, the only two book-length studies of the union have been written by Americans. By coincidence, both were published in 1973. *Teachers and Politics in Japan* was written by the political scientist Donald Thurston,[2] and *Japan's Militant Teachers: A History of the Left-Wing Teachers' Movement* by a professor of comparative education, Benjamin Duke.[3] Before discussing these books in more detail, we must consider why no *Japanese* scholar has undertaken a study of such an important subject. The distinguished Japanese professor of education, Ichikawa Shōgo, wrote in 1984 about the tendency for some controversial topics in Japanese education to be avoided by Japanese scholars. He singled out Nikkyōso, the radical students' organization, Zengakuren, the Juku industry, and university reform as four areas in which the most important academic work had been done by foreign scholars, usually Americans. Why have Japanese scholars avoided these issues? Ichikawa answers this question in the following way.

> One reason for the reluctance of Japanese scholars to explore these issues is that research on controversial topics tends not to be regarded seriously by Japanese pedagogists. In addition, taking sides on delicate questions can place Japanese scholars

> in an awkward position and may even have negative repercussions on their careers.[4]

In my own experience I have often encountered surprise from Japanese academics that I have chosen Nikkyōso as a topic for research. This does not mean that there is no writing in Japanese about Nikkyōso. Of course there is an abundance, and it will be surveyed in the next section. However, this writing tends to be either partisan, sensational, or merely descriptive. It is no exaggeration to say that the only serious, book-length academic studies of Nikkyōso available in Japanese are the Japanese translations of Thurston and Duke.

Of the two books, Thurston's is the more theoretically rigorous. Not surprisingly, because Thurston is a political scientist, it treats its subject in a thematic way rather than adopting the chronologically historical approach favored by Duke. It has sections on Nikkyōso's ideology and objectives, its organizational structure, and its influence on the educational bureaucracy and parliamentary elections. It also contains the results of Thurston's own questionnaire-based survey of Nikkyōso members that examines areas like union consciousness and the motives of rank-and-file union members. From the point of view of the broader study of Japanese politics, Thurston's most important conclusion was that, although Nikkyōso was almost completely excluded from national-level educational policy-making during the period in question, it was still able to have a significant effect on policy by its influence at the implementation stage (at the school or *genba*) and by the awareness in the minds of policymakers of the enormous potential the union had for disrupting the smooth running of the school system if extreme policies were forced on it. The left-wing teachers' union was therefore an important counterbalance to the right-wing dominated government and Ministry of Education. Thurston writes about the results of this standoff between the two sides:

> In the author's judgement . . . because JTU leaders at the top have adopted a non-subservient, non-obedient, anti-traditional posture, buttressed by a Marxist-oriented view of Japanese society, the net result of the existence and activities of the JTU on educational policy in postwar Japan has been positive. In fact, the existence of the JTU as an independent teachers' union has been indispensable to the democratization of Japanese education, a process that is by no means complete but that the JTU through its activities as a strong countervailing power to the heretofore absolute Ministry of Education has greatly assisted.[5]

The more precise details of how Nikkyōso influenced, and continues to influence, educational policy will be dealt with in later sections. For now, the part of Thurston's conclusion that must be emphasized is his point about Nikkyōso's role in the "democratization of Japanese education." The assumption here must be that if a strong, independent, left-wing union had not been in existence, then the conservative government and Ministry of Education would have been able to sweep away the democratic reforms of the American Occupation and return the education system to something like it was before 1945. This is an historical counterfactual question that cannot be answered within the context of this book. However, one question that will be addressed is whether or not Nikkyōso's schism and the resultant weakening of the teachers' movement in Japan have given the ministry and the government the kind of powers that authors like Thurston were afraid of. Has the decline in power of the teachers' union removed the main impediment to total right-wing control of education policy in Japan? This important question, inspired by Thurston's classic 1973 work, is one of the main focuses of this study.

Although Thurston's book is regarded by Japanese and foreign scholars alike as the most important political study of Nikkyōso available, this does not mean that it has not come in for criticism. In 1975, one of its reviewers, Yoshimitsu Takei, criticized it for its survey methods (Thurston's questionnaire was only completed by 222 teachers) and its total lack of a comparative perspective. For example, Yoshimitsu points out that Thurston's conclusion that for most Nikkyōso members economic issues are more important than political ones is "a fairly common phenomenon" for other labor unions in Japan and elsewhere.[6]

Sixteen years after *Teachers and Politics in Japan* appeared, Thurston published an article entitled "The Decline of the Japan Teachers' Union" that brought his research on Nikkyōso up-to-date.[7] However, Thurston's approach still lacked a comparative perspective. Instead he concentrated on a detailed analysis of the forces that led Nikkyōso into decline in the 1980s. (In 1973 the future prospects for Nikkyōso had seemed to Thurston to have been much brighter.) As such, Thurston's 1989 article is an excellent account of the particular circumstances of Nikkyōso's decline, but shares the shortcoming of the same author's earlier book in that it does not apply its findings to general political theory.

Just like Thurston's book, Duke's study also does not try to apply its findings to a more general body of theory, be it political or comparative education theory. Instead, Duke became interested in studying the history of Nikkyōso because he realized that "a knowledge of the role of Nikkyōso is essential for the comprehension of postwar Japanese educational developments."[8] In other words, both Duke and Thurston are concerned primarily with the analysis of a particular organization operating within a specific historical time frame. They do not try to provide generalizations or contributions to theoretical debates that are going on beyond these self-imposed limits. Thus, Duke's only nonhistorical chapter is the final one (chapter eight), which is concerned with an analysis of the causes of Nikkyōso's militancy. This chapter tries to explain the reasons for the high level of militancy displayed by Nikkyōso's leadership during the period in question (1947–1967). It could be argued that such an inquiry would benefit from comparisons with other unions within Japan and abroad. However, in keeping with the historical approach characteristic of the rest of the study, Duke chooses to explain Nikkyōso's militancy by reference to the personal biographies of the union's leaders (whose training in prewar normal schools had led them "to be dogmatists"),[9] and the "*peculiar* set of circumstances prevailing within Japan during the prewar, the American Occupation, and independence periods."[10] (emphasis added). Both the strengths and weaknesses of Thurston's and Duke's studies arise from this attachment to Nikkyōso as the product of "peculiar" circumstances. Both studies are strong in the thoroughness of their approach to empirical detail. They are rigorous in their explanations of Nikkyōso as a particular, complex organization operating within a specific time frame and dealing with a particular set of external circumstances. Weaknesses arise from an unwillingness to extend the frame of reference to encompass Nikkyōso within a broader theoretical debate. One of the purposes of the present study is to analyze Nikkyōso with the tools supplied by various modes of political analysis and theory, and to thus provide the broader theoretical context lacking in earlier studies.

Studies of Nikkyōso in Japanese

The reluctance of Japanese scholars to tackle the subject of Nikkyōso has already been noted. There is no book-length study of Nikkyōso by a Japanese academic on a par with the works of Thurston and Duke. There are, however, many books and shorter articles in Japanese about Nikkyōso of less objective, academic worth, written by a variety of different types of people, for a variety of purposes. These publications can be divided into three categories: those written by, or on behalf of, Nikkyōso and its affiliated organizations; those written by opponents of Nikkyōso; and those written by people in the education world wishing to inform a specific audience about what is going on within Nikkyōso. We will now deal with these in turn.

Publications Written by, or on Behalf of Nikkyōso and Its Affiliated Organizations

This category includes official histories of Nikkyōso. Both the national union and most of the prefectural unions publish their own histories, usually updating them every ten years. These will often be written by a committee rather than an individual author. To the outsider, one of the most surprising things about these texts is the amount of space in each one devoted to national and international events that seem to have no direct bearing on the fortunes or concerns of the organization that is the subject of the history.[11] In addition to the histories of local and national unions, the histories of specific campaigns, (e.g., the campaign for peace education) are also published at ten-year intervals by Nikkyōso.[12]

Also included in this category is the abundance of official reports, whether regular ones about national conventions and the annual Education Research Conference or special ones like the report of the 21st Century Vision Committee (the most important report to emerge from post-schism Nikkyōso).[13] There are also official union newsletters and journals published both by the national and prefectural unions. The most useful of these for indicating the official party line of the national organization is the monthly journal *Education Review* (*Kyōiku Hyōron*).

Finally in this category are the books by officials or retired officials of Nikkyōso that are usually written in the form of personal memoirs or messages to the union membership. An example is *Rebirth of Nikkyōso: A Message to Colleagues* (*Nikkyōso Saisei: Nakamatachi e no Messeeji*), written by Yokobori Shōichi in 1988, an official of the Chiba affiliate of Nikkyōso.[14] He uses the book to give his own opinions about the various challenges facing Nikkyōso at that time, both educational and organizational. Another example of this genre is *Behind the Scenes of Nikkyōso's Struggle* (*Nikkyōso Kōsō no Ura no Ura*) by Mochizuki Muneaki, an ex-member of the union's executive leadership.[15] In this book, published on his retirement in 1987, he called on Nikkyōso members to stop blaming government repression for the stagnation of their movement. He urged them to place greater emphasis on Nikkyōso as an education movement, rather than a labor movement. Both books are useful for giving an insight into the debate going on within the union shortly before the schism, but it is not the intention of either author to make a contribution to scholarly knowledge about trade unionism or politics in Japan or the wider world.

Books and Articles Written by Opponents of Nikkyōso

The often bitter confrontations between Nikkyōso and the education authorities have left their mark in the form of an antipathy toward Nikkyōso that stretches far wider than just the politicians and officials who were in the front line of conflict against the union and its allies. A modern nation's education system is a set of institutions that, by definition, influences every citizen living there. Those who have disappointing or distressing experiences at school, whether as a child, parent, or teacher, will often look for someone to blame. One of the less edifying phenomena of the long years of confrontation between government and union in the postwar era was the habit of each side to blame the other for the ills of the education system. The kind of publications referred to in the previous section (i.e., those written from a pro-union standpoint) would often criticize the government and the Ministry of Education. In reply, politicians would often make speeches denouncing Nikkyōso (bureaucrats tended to be more circumspect).

As well as government sources of anti-Nikkyōso opinion, there is also a more marginalized body of writers who have come to the conclusion that Nikkyōso is bad for the nation's education. One example is Takihara Toshihiko, a university professor who wrote, in 1981, *Can We Entrust our Children to Nikkyōso?* (*Nikkyōso ni Kodomo o Makaserareruka?*).[16] In this book he accuses Nikkyōso of, among other things, being responsible for ruining the Japanese education system and putting the interests of its members before those of children. Another example of this genre is the work of Ishikawa Sachiko, an ex-schoolteacher from Sapporo who wrote a book entitled *Nikkyōso's Day of Destruction* (*Nikkyōso ga Kuzuresaru Hi*) in 1985.[17] In this book she attacks Nikkyōso for allowing school education to deteriorate while it pursues political and ideological struggles. She believes that Nikkyōso has been hijacked by the Japan Communist Party and has, as its goal, the ambition of turning children into political revolutionaries. Therefore, the education of Japan's children will only be improved by the removal of Nikkyōso and a reestablishment of patriotic education. Ishikawa is not a spokesperson for a political party or a government institution, but she is a member of a small group called the

Group for the Normalization of Japan's Education (Nihon no Kyōiku Seijōka o Negau Kai). There are many such small nongovernmental groups in Japan. Any education or political group on the right in Japan will automatically be anti-Nikkyōso, and the more extreme ones (not the one that Ishikawa is a member of) have been involved in bomb threats and harassment of Nikkyōso officials and meetings.[18] As with the publications under the previous category, the publications of these anti-Nikkyōso groups are useful insofar as they articulate a body of opinion critical of Nikkyōso and its aims and tactics. They also, however, share the same weakness of the publications in the other category—that is, they are not intended as a contribution to scholarly debate on trade unionism, comparative education, or political science.

"Neutral" Publications About Nikkyōso

It would be wrong to assume that all books in Japan written about Nikkyōso are either written by union insiders or people whose main goal is to attack the union and even destroy it. There is a third category of publication by more neutral people in the education world who write about Nikkyōso to make a contribution to the debate going on within Nikkyōso or to inform non-union administrators and other involved people about Nikkyōso-related issues. An example of a book in this category is *Nikkyōso Will Not Die* (*Nikkyōso Shisuru Kotonakare*) by professor of education Sagara Tadaichi, written in 1986.[19] Professor Sagara's aim in writing this book is to help Nikkyōso shake off its (from his point of view) narrow-minded opposition to the government and transform itself into a more positive and neutral educational pressure group. He is critical of Nikkyōso's past history, but, unlike the opponents of Nikkyōso, his aim is not the destruction of Nikkyōso.

In this category, journals like the *Board of Education Monthly Report* (*Kyōiku iinkai geppō*), *Education Law Quarterly* (*Kikan Kyōikuhō*), and *School Management Research* (*Gakkō Un'ei Kenkyū*) must also be included. These are journals for professionals working within the education system. They contain detailed accounts of ongoing debates, along with analysis that is aimed to help in the practical day-to-day tasks of administrators and managers. The people who write for these journals, and their intended audience, are those whose work brings them into contact with union members on a regular basis. The journals are not necessarily sympathetic to the problems of Nikkyōso, but equally they are not designed to be union-bashing organs. Thus, they are a potential source of neutral data about Nikkyōso.

"Neutral" publications about Nikkyōso suffer from the same problems as publications in the other two categories—that is, the aims of their authors are particular to the specific problem being addressed. They are not designed to be works of political science or comparative education.

Political Studies That Incorporate Nikkyōso Within a Wider Perspective

The political science literature on Japan has developed substantially since Thurston and Duke published their studies of Nikkyōso. Although David Williams in *Japan and the Enemies of Open Political Science* has warned about the "monist fallacy" of assuming that Western social science can adequately explain the growth of Japan to economic superpower status,[20] it is not the purpose of the present study to carry out a philosophical inquiry into applicability of "Western" social scientific methods in a non-Western context. Instead, my purpose is to build upon the scholarly work already done by Western and Japanese social scientists operating within existing paradigms of social scientific method in order to develop our knowledge about contemporary politics and education in Japan.

Two studies of Japanese politics that emphasize the crucial role played by Nikkyōso in the postwar Japanese political system are *Education Reform in Japan* by Len Schoppa and *The Enigma of Japanese Power* by Karel Van Wolferen.[21] Schoppa's arguments about education policy making will be dealt with in detail in chapter four. For now it is important to stress what he has in common with Van Wolferen. Both authors see Japanese politics as divided into two: between those who have access to power and those who do not. Schoppa's dichotomy is between the progressive camp and the conservative camp while Van Wolferen's is between those who are in the system and those who are outside. For both authors Nikkyōso is a key element of the group of organizations, parties, and so on that is *excluded* from power. Both Van Wolferen and Schoppa were writing before Nikkyōso's schism. However, Van Wolferen added an epilogue to a later edition of his book that appeared after the schism had taken place. In it he laments that "the disappearance of Sōhyō, and the demise of Nikkyōso as a genuine teachers' union has all but finally taken away the intellectual base for reasoned political opposition."[22] This is quite an extreme view (it is highly questionable that Nikkyōso is no longer a "genuine" teachers' union as will be discussed in chapter six), but it does highlight the recent developments that, combined with the demise of the Japan Socialist Party, must have had a profound effect on the progressive camp of Schoppa's theory, as well as the group of organizations that lie outside Van Wolferen's system. The fact that Nikkyōso's schism was a key event at the center of these developments makes it such a valuable subject for closer analysis. The events surrounding the schism not only help us to understand why the decline of the progressive camp took place, they also are very informative about the nature of the new system that is emerging from the ashes of the old. It is the purpose of the present study, therefore, to analyze the internal developments within Nikkyōso that led to the schism and defined the characteristics of the two new organizations that emerged as a result, and to examine the place of these organizations within the new political system that is in the process of replacing the old Japanese postwar polity. How these general aims will be achieved is the subject of the next section.

Research Methodology and Aims of the Book

One of the main assumptions of this study is that a large social organization like a national teachers' union cannot be understood properly without reference to the environment within which it is located.[23] Furthermore, knowledge about the organization's place within its environment contributes to our understanding of the environment itself.[24] Therefore, this study of Nikkyōso incorporates studies of the links between Nikkyōso and other political and administrative institutions both at the local and the national level. To do this, it is also necessary to update the work of previous scholars of the union. A major part of this study, therefore, is devoted to building on the work of Thurston, by bringing the history of Nikkyōso up-to-date with the dramatic events of the schism and its immediate aftermath, and also enlarging on the work of Schoppa by updating Nikkyōso's position within the Japanese policy-making process. Another major task of this book is to analyze the broader significance of the politics of teacher unionism in Japan. In other words, we are not only concerned, as Thurston was, with the close analysis of the teachers' organizations alone, or, as Schoppa was, with their place in the specific arena of education policy-making in the 1970s and 1980s. Instead, we are interested in locating the place of the teachers' unions within the whole Japanese political system—not just one part of it. The carrying out of this exercise will also contribute to our knowledge of that political system.

Analyzing the place of Nikkyōso within the contemporary Japanese political system involves the use of various theoretical tools. Some, like those developed by Schoppa, are needed for locating Nikkyōso within the education policy-making framework. Others are needed for analyzing Nikkyōso's role as a union and its relations with parties and the government bureaucracy. Where necessary, therefore, each chapter will contain a discussion of the relevant theoretical background. It should be noted that this book is always concerned with the politics of Nikkyōso. The word "politics" here is subject to a broad interpretation. Politics is not only significant in its conventional sense (i.e., related to government, institutions of the state, political parties, pressure groups, etc.), but also in its more subtle sense—related to ideology, debates about education, small-group dynamics, and the use of power and influence at all levels of social organization.

The general aims of the study provide the parameters within which we address more detailed questions. Of paramount importance in this whole discussion is Nikkyōso's environment. The organization of this book is largely based on subdividing this "environment" into its most important parts and then using the events surrounding Nikkyōso's schism to examine contemporaneous and related developments within each part. The parts in question are as follows: the contemporary Japanese education system; the contemporary state of Japanese trade unionism; and the ongoing realignment in Japanese national politics. In the case of each of these areas, Nikkyōso's schism is used as a lens through which developments can be observed, both those internal to the area in question and those that involve connections and relations with other areas. Although, for the purposes of organization, the book is divided into chapters and sections of chapters devoted to one or other of the areas in question, I have not lost sight of the fact that all of these areas are closely related. In summary, therefore, the key questions addressed by this study are as follows.

1. How has Nikkyōso's schism affected the state of teacher unionism in contemporary Japan?

2. What does Nikkyōso's schism tell us about the nature of power and policy-making within the contemporary Japanese education system?

3. What does Nikkyōso's schism reveal about recent developments in Japanese trade unionism?

4. What does Nikkyōso's schism tell us about the ongoing realignment of Japanese politics?

It is the contention of this study that all these questions are related. The process of addressing any one of them will be of benefit in addressing the others. There will be no attempt to construct one all-embracing theoretical model to cover all four questions, but existing models will be used (and modified if necessary) to serve as tools of analysis for particular areas under consideration. In this respect, this study differs from many, more formal works of political science. Rather than adopting the approach by which a hypothesis is proposed, data is gathered, and the hypothesis is tested, this book takes as its starting point one particular historical event—Nikkyōso's schism—and uses it as a means of testing the validity of a variety of existing social scientific models. At the same time, the ability of these models to adapt to the changing political landscape of 1990s Japan will be tested.

The data necessary to test these theories were gathered from a variety of sources. Information about the aims, ideologies, and structures of the various groups, institutions, and organizations concerned were relatively easy to obtain from official journals, newsletters, or publications. As far as the unfolding of specific events is concerned I rarely found any disagreement about what actually happened. Instead, the disagreement, if there was any, usually involved the interpretation of what happened and apportionment of blame. This is why much of the analysis in the body of the book is devoted to ideology and policy. This study is concerned with analyzing developments at the level of prefecture and school as well as at the national level. To this end, detailed research has been conducted in Saitama and Aichi prefectures,[25] including interviews in both these prefectures as well as Tokyo. A wide variety of people were interviewed, ranging from relatively powerful bureaucrats and union officials to ordinary classroom teachers. The difference in social status of the interviewees necessitated a corresponding difference in the style of the interview. In the context of research into educational politics, Fitz and Halpin make the point that it is a lot easier to observe what goes on in a classroom than what goes on in the offices of top bureaucrats and politicians.[26] So, on the whole, it was not surprising that Ministry or local Board of Education bureaucrats were more careful about what they said to me and were happier to stick to the "official line" than those interviewees lower down the political and social hierarchy. Because of strict time limits on the interviews it was easy for them to procrastinate and avoid difficult issues (e.g., relating to the controversy surrounding the national flag and anthem). Teachers and local union officials were likely to make the time for a more in-depth discussion that could take place at a less hurried pace, sometimes over drinks and on one occasion over lunch at a local sushi restaurant. Christena Turner's study of worker participation in union activities makes the point that the motivations of ordinary union members cannot be easily categorized by superficial surveys.[27] Therefore, it made sense for my interviews to be aimed more at quality of data (through longer interviews and, where possible, repeat interviews) than through quantity. The interviews were also quite flexible in allowing the interviewees to talk to me about what they thought was important. When discussing issues like the breakup of the union, this flexibility enabled the interviewees to express their most important motives and values. A list of the interviews is given at the back of the book. For those interviewees who were not talking in an official capacity (e.g., as a representative of union or ministry department) I have not included their names or those of their schools.

Plan of the Book

Chapters one and two cover the history of Nikkyōso from its formation to the eve of the schism. The position of the union within the postwar political system is given special attention, as is its confrontational relationship with the Ministry of Education and the LDP. Reasons for the chronic decline in membership are examined, as are divisions within the union and fundamental disagreements over policy. These weaknesses eventually resulted in the schism that is examined in chapter three. Special attention is given to the case of the schism within Saitama and Aichi prefectures. Every prefecture has a different experience of the schism, but certain patterns and trends are identified. How this contributes to our understanding of educational politics at the prefectural level is considered.

Chapter four is concerned with power relations within the national education system. It examines Schoppa's theory of policy-making as well as Katō's theory of bureaucratic rationality in order to arrive at an understanding of how policy-making in the 1990s is organized and what the place of post-schism teacher unionism is within that system. Chapter five is also concerned with education, but this time with the debate on education reform in Japan. The differing positions of Nikkyōso and Zenkyō are analyzed in the context of the post-Nakasone great education debate. The identities of both unions are greatly influenced by the positions they take with regard to this debate.

Chapter six is concerned with Nikkyōso's position as a union within the postwar tradition of public sector unionism in Japan, a tradition that came under attack in the 1980s by the ideology of privatization. Nikkyōso is also analyzed as a case study of a teachers' union. New literature on the comparative study of teachers' unions around the world is drawn on to learn more about the nature of Nikkyōso as an organization representing the interests of its members.

Finally, chapter seven examines Nikkyōso's schism within the context of the realignment currently under way in the Japanese political system. As a key member of the progressive camp the weakening of Nikkyōso had important consequences for the camp as a whole and therefore the system as well. The interconnections between the decline of Nikkyōso and that of the JSP are examined. The importance of the formation of the new labor federation Rengō is also discussed. The implications of these developments for existing political science models of policy-making and pluralism are discussed and modifications proposed.

CHAPTER ONE

THE AMERICAN OCCUPATION, THE FIRST POSTWAR TEACHERS' UNIONS AND THE FORMATION OF NIKKYŌSO

To understand the pressures that pulled Nikkyōso apart in the 1980s it is first necessary to analyze the forces that brought it together in the 1940s. This chapter examines the decisive impact the American Occupation had on the birth and early development of Nikkyōso. It is also necessary to examine the far-reaching changes that took place in the Japanese education system as a whole at this time. This chapter is divided into three sections. The first will look at the overall context of Occupation education reform, with special reference to the ideological and political nature of the education debate of the time. The second section will examine the events, after the end of the war, that led to the formation of Nikkyōso. It will concentrate on the ideologies and programs of the organizations that combined to form Nikkyōso and will address the reasons for Nikkyōso's success in attracting a mass membership. The third section will analyze Nikkyōso's development from 1947 to 1952, a crucial period in which its relationship with political parties, the government, and other unions was defined in such a way that they were to change little between that time and that of the schism. Finally, we will summarize some of the internal characteristics of Nikkyōso that had been established by 1952 and that were to prove sources of weakness in the union's future development.

The Occupation Reforms and the Ideology of the Debate on Education

The American Plan

The American occupying forces in Japan saw their mission as nothing less than the transformation of a totalitarian state into a democratic one. To this end they supervised the introduction of a new constitution, a new set of civil rights, far-reaching land reform, plus freedom of organization, the press, and religion. The Americans wanted to ensure that the implementation of this hugely ambitious program was carried out mainly by the Japanese themselves under the supervision of American advisors. This way the occupying forces could leave Japan confident that all the reforms they had introduced would not be immediately dismissed by Japanese reactionaries as merely the alien impositions of a conquering army. Education, naturally, was a fundamental plank of the Occupation's democratization policy. A special division of the Occupation forces was devoted to education reform. Joseph C. Trainor, one of the leaders of the Education Division, describes its role as "primarily that of furnishing the Japanese educators with guidance, advice and assistance as they endeavoured during the Occupation period to achieve reforms in their educational patterns and to acquire increasing facility for handling the new types of problems which were presented by the very fact of the development of a democratic society in which the new education was expected to function and to contribute its part."[1]

The first task for the Americans was to remove those aspects of Japanese education that they considered anti-democratic or militaristic. They therefore removed all military officers from schools (since 1935 at least one officer had been assigned to each boys' school to conduct about two hours a week of drill training)[2] and banned all kinds of military training in schools (even including, for a while, judo).[3] A purge of right-wing teachers was also initiated. As a result, almost 120,000 teachers or education officials left their jobs.[4] At the same time, the use of ultranationalist or militarist textbooks was suspended while new ones, more in keeping with the new ideals for education, were prepared.[5] The paraphernalia of emperor-worship, the copy of the Imperial Portrait, and the Imperial Rescript on Education were removed from each school. This coincided with the emperor's renunciation of his divinity and the demise of state shintoism. The Imperial Rescript on Education was replaced by the Fundamental Law of Education that guaranteed the freedom of educators and stated that education should not be subject to "improper control," but should be "directly responsible to the whole people" (article X).

In March 1946, a study mission of education experts from the United States arrived. After discussions with a special Japanese Education Committee, they proposed the creation of a uniform 6–3–3–4 system (six elementary, three middle, three high school, and four university years) to replace the differentiated complex of prewar schools. They also recommended coeducation for all levels. To reduce the central control of the Ministry of Education, the creation of elected school boards, parent–teacher organizations, and independent teacher associations was proposed.[6] The Americans also sought to encourage the growth of individualism and respect for human rights at all levels of the educational process.[7] "'Citizens, not subjects,' was the goal. Teachers were to exercise their 'professional freedom' to tailor their teaching to foster the growth of independent, productive community members."[8]

Of course, the negative part of the American education reformers' program—the removing of soldiers, nationalists, and pictures of the emperor from Japanese schools—was much easier to accomplish than the positive part—the creation of a new, democratic education system. Besides the problems encountered by the Occupation authorities in dealing with a very different society from that of the United States, there were many practical problems caused by sheer lack of resources in a nation devastated by war. There was also considerable controversy over the reform program. Despite these problems, much progress was made and most of the American reforms were successfully implemented. However, this implementation was not the end of the story. The departure of the Americans in 1952 only intensified controversy between concerned Japanese groups and individuals, with many officials claiming that they had only gone along with the reforms because the Occupation authorities had made them. The door was opened for a backlash against the "foreign" reforms that had been forced on a helpless nation by a conquering power. The fact that many progressive groups in Japan welcomed these reforms—foreign or not—meant that confrontation over education was bound to follow. Schoppa argues that "[m]uch of the antagonism still hampering educational policy-making in the 1980s can be traced to the events of this crucial period [i.e., the Occupation]."[9] We need to examine more closely the controversy surrounding the Occupation-era debate on education. In doing so, it is important to recognize how profoundly political and ideological the whole debate was.

Ideological and Political Aspects of the Occupation-era Debate on Education

A remarkable amount of optimism underpinned the American approach to the huge task of reforming, root and branch, the education system of what was, after all, a very different country about which they knew only a little. The Army and State Department started drawing up plans about how to reform the education systems of both Germany and Japan as early as 1943.[10] Underlying these plans was the assumption that both the Germans and Japanese would be able to develop into democratic peoples if only they were given the chance. The two-pronged plan of, on the one hand, removing the poisonous mind control of fascism and ultranationalism and, on the other, providing a thorough grounding in the ideas and mechanisms of democracy was the result of this way of thinking. American optimism was vital in providing the energy that drove their reforms forward.[11] However, it also had the drawback of blinding many of those in the Occupation forces to the highly political and ideological nature of the domestic debate they were now embroiling themselves in. Some Americans seem to have hoped that once political extremists had been removed from the education system (first the right-wing purge removed the militarists and ultranationalists, then the Red Purge removed the most influential Communists), then the ensuing debate on education could proceed in a practical, nonpolitical way. This equation of extremism with politicization overlooked the highly political nature of many issues in Japanese education the controversial nature of which can be traced back to the Meiji reforms. We will now take a closer look at some of the specific educational issues of the day that were very highly politically and ideologically charged. Ideology and politics infused the discussions and plans concerning both the structure of the education system and the content of education. These will be dealt with in turn.

The Structure of the Education System. The Americans set themselves three goals for the reform of the institutions of Japanese education. First, they wanted to introduce more democratic accountability; second, they wanted to decentralize what they saw as an overcentralized system; and, third, they wanted to redesign a system that gave "one type of education for the masses and another for the privileged few."[12] With the last goal in mind the Americans drew up plans to create a uniform system of compulsory education and extend it beyond six years. The end result was the 6–3–3–4 system of which the first nine years would be compulsory. Some conservatives in Japan saw this as the imposition of an alien system. For example, some Japanese education officials at the time expressed the view that the Americans had already decided to impose their 6–3–3–4 system onto Japan and that the discussions and consultations that took place during the short duration (twenty-four days) of the Education Mission's main visit to Japan were merely a sham.[13] Politicians (e.g., Japan's later prime minister, Tanaka Kakuei) joined in this criticism of the 6–3–3–4 system and other education reforms of the Occupation.[14] Indeed, this theme of foreign imposition was to be a refrain of many right-wing critics of those reforms for many years after they were implemented. However, recent research by Gary Tsuchimochi into the previously unavailable minutes of meetings between Japanese and American education experts that took place during the U.S. Education Mission's main visit to Japan in 1946 has revealed that the Americans had originally proposed a 6–5 school system, *not* a 6–3–3 one. Actually it was members of the Japanese Education Committee who persuaded the Americans that a 6–3–3 system was preferable.[15] Against the objection of their own Ministry of Education, the Education Committee wanted to abolish the higher elementary schools and youth schools, which constituted the non-elite track, and establish a single-track system for all students.[16] Despite historical evidence like this supporting the view that many of the main reforms of the Occupation era were backed by Japanese educators and officials and in some cases initiated by them, it remains the case that, as Schoppa points out, "the importance of this history has less to do with facts than with perceptions."[17] However much historical evidence is uncovered, the right in Japan will continue to maintain that those reforms of the Occupation that they don't agree with were the product of foreign imposition.

In addition to their concern with addressing bias due to elitism, the reformers of the Occupation era also were concerned with gender inequalities. Official policy was to bring female education up to the level of that for males. The Ministry of Education, however, allowed cities, towns, and villages to implement this policy at their own pace.[18] Nevertheless, the door had been opened to allow for significant expansion in education for girls and women over subsequent years.

The most difficult and problematic structural reform of the Occupation was the creation of a system of elected boards of education. The Board of Education Law of 1948 ordered the immediate creation of elected boards in each of the forty-six prefectures as well as in five of the largest cities. The aim of this law was nothing less than the realization of the twin U.S. goals of democratic accountability and decentralization. The long-term aim of the U.S. Education Mission was actually to reduce the role of the Ministry of Education to that of an advisory agency.[19] SCAP (probably unwittingly) undermined this plan, however, by ensuring that conditions would remain favorable for the resurgence of the power of the ministry once the Occupation was over. It did this by using the existing central Japanese bureaucracy to administer its own reforms and failing to set up adequate mechanisms for local governments to finance their own programs independently of grants from the central government.[20] This reform ran into trouble because of genuine differences of perspective between the Americans and the Japanese concerning the political nature of the new boards. Marshall describes the SCAP officials as being both idealistic and naive in their hopes of creating American style, nonpoliticized boards of education in Japan.[21] That does not mean, however, that they did not try. Duke gives an account of how the Military Government in Tokyo tried to educate teachers about the American tradition of having laypersons, not educators, on school boards.[22] This advice, however, fell on deaf ears, and at the first school board election on October 5, 1948, fifty-four of the winners were teachers endorsed by Nikkyōso; twenty-three others had been sponsored jointly by Nikkyōso and other local organizations. Out of a total of 296 seats this was not a victory for Nikkyōso, but it was significant enough to worry conservatives about the danger of a left-wing takeover of educational administration. It also annoyed SCAP, and upset the American vision of a nonpolitical local education apparatus controlled by laypersons.

The Content of Education. The Occupation reformers did not merely want to remove the ultranationalistic and militaristic elements of Japanese education, they also wanted to promote the development of a new, democratic curriculum that would influence (in SCAP's words) the "attitudes, social habits and spiritual qualities" of Japanese children.[23] This involved thorough reform of the school curriculum, teaching methods, textbooks, and the relationship between religion and education. All these were areas in which the Americans simply had to have the full cooperation of as many practicing teachers and education officials as possible, if they were to hope to have any success. Comparing Japan with the case of occupied Germany, Tsuchimochi concludes that American reforms were successful in the former and unsuccessful in the latter because "[i]n both cases . . . the fate of post-war education reform rested with the recipients of the reform, and to what extent they themselves were receptive to initiating its implementation."[24] He goes on to argue that a likely explanation for the willingness of the Japanese to accept reforms proposed by a foreign power is provided by the success of their adaptation of foreign educational ideas during the Meiji period.[25] This argument could be further developed by pointing out that not only did the Meiji period establish the precedent for importing ideas and methods from abroad, but also that some of those educational ideas themselves were directly related to the Occupation-era proposals of the American reformers. In an analysis of educational ideas during the 1870s and 1880s, Mark E. Lincicome tracks the history of one particular pedagogical doctrine called *kaihatsu shugi* that he translates as "developmental education."[26] This doctrine was brought to Japan by Japanese educators who had been sent to American Normal Schools to learn about Western teaching methods. During the 1870s, developmental education was a major influence on the educational philosophy of the Tokyo Normal School, at that time the most important center in Japan for the development of elementary school teaching methodology and curricula. It brought to Japan the concept of the teacher as a professional, autonomous expert in his or her field as well as the idea that education should cater to the needs of children as individuals. Clearly these ideas had political as well as educational ramifications that were not lost on those in power in the new Meiji state. The rise of authoritarianism in the 1880s witnessed the triumph of statist ideology, and developmental education suffered accordingly. However, it did not die out altogether because of its usefulness in assisting in the creation of good classroom practice. Thus, it was able to flourish during the brief period of interwar Taishō democracy, only to be suppressed again as Japanese education came more and more under the control of militarists during the 1930s. This meant that when the Americans arrived in Japan in 1945 there was already in existence a legacy of educational doctrine very similar to their own. Indeed, Lincicome argues that the 1947 passing of the Fundamental Law of Education represented the transformation of developmental education from heterodoxy to orthodoxy.[27] Thus, it would be mistaken to see that law as the brand-new, foreign imposition of an alien creed. As noted earlier, however, historical *facts* were often less important than popular *perceptions* of history when it came to right-wing attacks on the "foreign" nature of Occupation reforms. The prewar history of developmental education also taught Japanese educators how deeply interconnected politics and education can be in Japan. Theories about how best to teach children and what the proper position and status of a teacher should be are not merely educational theories. They have ramifications that go far beyond the confines of the classroom.

There was more to the Fundamental Law of Education than just the passing into the law of the land of previously unorthodox views on how children learn and what the role of teachers should be, important though those developments were. The law was also very significant because it was consciously intended to act as a replacement for the 1890 Imperial Rescript on Education, the ideological centrepiece of the prewar education system. Marshall summarizes the main ways in which the new law differed from the prewar Rescript: "Philosophically, [the Law] constituted a stress on values that transcended such collectivities as the community or the state. Truth and justice replace loyalty and filial piety; individual and personality are privileged over group. There are also, of course, implications for social hierarchy in the call to 'respect labour' and for antimilitarism in the call for a 'peaceful state.'"[28] Left-wing Japanese educators and activists saw the law as not only representing a break with the past, but also as setting a blueprint for the future. The influential Japanese Professor of Education, Horio Teruhisa writes: "By stipulating the legal foundations and intellectual principles required to ensure the continued development of democratic values in Japanese society this law gave voice to an irreversible departure from the educational traditions of pre-war Japan and set forth the role it was hoped education would play in the reformation of Japanese national life."[29] Although a rearguard action had been fought by some senior education officials to save the Imperial Rescript in some form or another, they were unsuccessful in resisting the determination of the Americans and left-wing Japanese to sweep away all traces of the prewar imperial state. Combined with the new constitution, the emperor's declaration of his humanity, and the removal of his portrait from every school, it looked as if, as intended, the new Fundamental Law of Education really had set the tone for a new postwar, secular Japan. However, this did not mean that the nationalist right had given up the ideological struggle for control over the new education system. The prewar emperor system may be dead, but that did not mean that the right had to forsake the struggle for the particularly Japanese values they believed in. Nor did it mean that Japan had to cease being a strong, centralized, and disciplined state. Because they were powerless to prevent the passing into law and common currency of a new orthodoxy, they instead had to fight a new battle over the meaning and interpretation of the new language of the constitution and the Fundamental Law of Education. Lincicome has collected a very useful list of some educational terms over which there has been a hard fought battle of definition and interpretation since 1947:

> With democracy now the law of the land, phrases like "esteem individual dignity," "full development of personality," "esteem

> individual value," "imbued with the independent spirit," "respecting academic freedom," "cultivating a spontaneous spirit," respect for "the status of teachers," "fair and appropriate treatment" of teachers, and "political knowledge necessary for intelligent citizenship" have become common currency throughout the educational community, not just among reform-minded teachers and educational journalists, but among politicians, ministry and local officials, judges, and lawyers as well. Even so, the challenge still remains: who shall possess the authority to define these terms; whose interpretations shall prevail?[30]

All these phrases are direct quotations from the Fundamental Law of Education, yet all have ideological ramifications that go far beyond the field of education. The American Occupation authorities consciously hoped to mold Japanese society for the better through reform of the education system. They were both optimistic and ethnocentric in their view that any country would benefit if it adopted their own, American set of ideals and laws, and they were aided by many Japanese educators and teachers who shared these goals. However, there were also groups and individuals on both the left and the right who were opposed to the main thrust of the reforms, but wanted to exploit and influence them in ways that would further their own agenda. The resulting struggle, which was both ideological as well as a practical competition for control of political or labor organizations and institutions of state, had already begun before the Americans left in 1952. After 1952, it was destined to continue, following the basic contours established during the hothouse period of the Occupation. The teachers' union, Nikkyōso was destined to be a major player in this postwar educational struggle. It is to this organization that we now turn.

THE FORMATION OF NIKKYŌSO 1945–1947

Within the space of a few months, the unionization of Japan's teachers proceeded at such a pace that, from a starting point of almost nothing, one united union was successfully created encompassing the vast majority of the profession throughout the country. This national union was inaugurated on June 8, 1947, and by the autumn of that year the American authorities estimated that its membership stood at over 446,000, or 98 percent of the country's elementary school teachers.[31] The circumstances of this remarkable period of growth helped define the type of organization that Nikkyōso became. In analyzing this formative period, we will look first at the nature of this union's early leadership, and then at its program for action and the success it had in attracting hundreds of thousands of ordinary teachers to its cause.

Leadership and Programs of the Early Unions

In September 1945, the first fledgling teachers' organization started life in the home of Ono Shumichi who, although he had been the chairman of a government-sponsored teachers' association during the war, had also made contacts with several progressive, democratic teachers. Together they formed the Education Reconstruction League (Kyōiku Saiken Renmei). Many more prewar activists were attracted to this group and soon, in the words of Benjamin Duke,[32] "this group of teachers represented a broad spectrum of beliefs and political inclinations." Two of their number were to become prominent in the teachers' movement. These were Hani Gorō, a Communist Party member and historian who had been imprisoned for his opposition to the war, and Iwama Masao, a progressive teacher who soon became leader of the radical wing of the movement. On December 1, 1945, this group of activists established the All Japan Teachers' Union (Zen Nihon Kyōin Kumiai or Zenkyō for short). Its initial steering committee consisted of Hani and three other JCP members.[33] The specific demands of Zenkyō are summarized by Smethurst as follows:

> In the teacher welfare field, the union called for five-fold pay increases, relief for teachers who lost their homes in air raids, medical and unemployment insurance, and the right of collective bargaining with the Mombusho. In the political sphere, the union called for the abolition of the Greater Japan Education Association on the grounds that it was a "tool of the militarists," for the punishment of the "educators responsible for the war," the reeducation of "nationalistic" and "militaristic" teachers, the reappointment of "progressive" teachers, the abandonment of government compiled textbooks, the control of the schools by the union, election of school principals by the public, and the rejection of all officials appointed by the Emperor on the grounds that they were, because of the source of their appointment, automatically "despotic and corrupt."[34]

In addition to this official program, other statements made by leaders of the union gave outsiders an idea of what the union stood for even if they were not sanctioned by the leadership as a whole. The best example is provided by Hani Gorō who, in the first issue of the union's periodical, wrote that teachers, as members of the proletariat, should move forward in a common front with the workers of Japan, and that the emperor was a war criminal.[35] This kind of statement from one of the founders of the union, combined with the large Communist presence among the leadership, must have given rise to grave doubts in the minds of moderate or conservative teachers contemplating joining the union. Yet it was Hani and his left-wing colleagues who were successful in recruiting the vast majority of ordinary teachers into their organizations, and it was the rival moderate and conservative teachers' leaders who failed to attract a mass membership into their camp. We now turn to the reasons for this turn of events.

Union Membership and the Motives of Ordinary Teachers

After it came into being Nikkyōso was often referred to as a *tanchō zuru* or "red-crested white crane" reflecting the common perception that the leadership were very left-wing while the ordinary members were more moderate or apolitical.[36] Why then did the vast majority of ordinary teachers join an organization under the control of people whose political views seem to have been minority views? The answer to this question has several parts. First, the economic circumstances of teachers in the aftermath of the war contributed substantially to the success of unionization and to the willingness of previously uncommitted teachers to join a radical union. Of course, life was extremely hard for the vast majority of Japanese people in the final months of the war and its immediate aftermath.[37] However, statistics collected for SCAP from the period show that teachers and other government workers were particularly hard done by.[38] According to newspapers and other sources, teachers had to resort to finding second jobs just to survive and feed their families.[39] As well as the obvious extra job of private teacher there are also reports of teachers working at side jobs such as knitting, repairing watches, and even shining shoes (in this last job they would make sure that they worked well away from the catchment area of their school so that their students would not witness their destitution).[40] These conditions made Japanese teachers ripe for unionization. Thurston even argues that "the economic situation had the most prominent influence in the early post-war development of teachers' unions in Japan."[41]

It was not only extreme economic circumstances that led many ordinary teachers to willingly join a radical movement, it was also the peculiar political and ideological circumstances that surrounded the end of the war. As Thurston points out: "Psychologically shattered by the total failure of the pre-war Emperor-centred ideology, these ordinary teachers were disillusioned with the militaristic government and those forces in the society which had misled the country into the disastrous war; they were ready to join organizations that would represent their protest and their denunciation of the past."[42] After such a bitter experience of war and defeat, teachers distrusted the central government and were resentful of the control it had had over their lives. They were therefore very keen to support an independent organization that would protect them from this kind of intrusive control. This concern soon came to be connected with the related objective of securing and defending the professional autonomy of teachers. In these respects the "radicalism" of left-wing union leaders was very much in step with the needs and wishes of a large number of ordinary rank-and-file teachers.

Economic motives, combined with a distrust of the government, explain the widespread drive for unionization, but they do not, by themselves, explain why the union had to be left-wing controlled. If the majority of teachers did not share the left-wing sympathies of Nikkyōso's leadership, what was to stop them forming or joining a more moderate, but still independent, organization? The answer lies in the particular circumstances that accompanied the formation of Nikkyōso. Following the end of the war, the release of wartime political prisoners, and the lifting of restrictions on meetings and organizations, several rival groups claiming to represent teachers were formed. Initially, the two main organizations were Zenkyō and the Japan Educators' Union (Nihon Kyōikusha Kumiai or Nikkyō for short). It was a feature of the most important teachers' organizations of the time that they were formed at the top administrative level first, and appeals for rank-and-file support followed later.[43] Thus, both Zenkyō and Nikkyō went about trying to build a mass organization after they had already chosen their main leaders and worked out a basic platform of ideas and aims. An analysis of these platforms reveals, clearly, that Zenkyō was the more radical of the two,[44] and yet it was Zenkyō that prospered and went on to form the basis of Nikkyōso, while Nikkyō declined and eventually disbanded. The decline of Nikkyō can be attributed to two main factors. First, although Nikkyō demands were far more moderate and realistic than those of Zenkyō, the Ministry of Education was not any more willing to fulfill Nikkyō's demands than it was Zenkyō's. Thus, ordinary teachers in desperate economic straits soon learned that moderate courses of action were not getting them anywhere. Second, a fatal split occurred within Nikkyō in 1946 over the issue of whether to align with the moderate Sōdōmei labor federation or the Communist-dominated Sanbetsu federation. The union's main founder and leader, Kagawa Toyohiko, was dismissed as chairman and Nikkyō fell apart amid infighting and recrimination. The demise of Nikkyō did not, however, leave the field entirely uncontested for Zenkyō in its struggle to recruit members.

Another moderate alternative to Zenkyō came onto the scene on April 26, 1946, when three small groups in the Tokyo area came together to form the Council of Tokyo Municipal Educational Personnel Unions (Tōkyōto Kyōshokuin Kumiai Kyōgikai or Tokyōkyō for short).[45] Tokyōkyō attracted teachers who were disillusioned with Zenkyō because they did not like the Communist influence they detected there. Tokyōkyō's moderate posture also, however, attracted some support from the government that ended up doing it more harm than good. Smethurst argues that "the government's tacit support of the newly organised Tokyōkyō scared away many moderate teachers who feared government control of education more than they feared the leftist and allegedly Communist dominated [Zenkyō]."[46] Tokyōkyō ended up a poor second to Zenkyō in the drive to recruit members in the capital. Thus, the success of radical-led unions and the failure of more moderate ones in attracting "ordinary" members can be put down partly to division and disorganization among the moderate leadership, but also, and probably more decisively, to the fact that the perceived collusion between the moderate unions and the government acted as a powerful disincentive for many teachers. This is further evidence in support of the view that in the extreme circumstances of the period immediately following Japan's defeat in the war, the views of the left-wing leaders of the new teachers' organizations did not seem as extreme as they might have in more normal times.

Another reason for left-wing success lies in the realm of tactics and organization. If the moderate union leadership was found wanting in the drive for expansion after 1945, then the left-wing leaders were able to exploit this with a combination of greater organizational skill and tactical awareness. As noted earlier, the main unions began life in Tokyo with the formation of administrative and ideological centers, followed later by appeals for rank-and-file support across the country. Zenkyō was more successful than its moderate rivals in recruiting in the Tokyo area, and it proceeded to set up regional offices in Kobe, Kyoto, Nagoya, and Fukuoka in early 1946. However, it was frustrated in its efforts to attract the allegiance of the new, independent prefectural unions that had already been formed or were in the process of forming. It seemed that some of these prefectural unions were reluctant to affiliate with Zenkyō because of the perceived Communist domination of its leadership. Zenkyō responded to this image problem by reorganizing itself and changing its

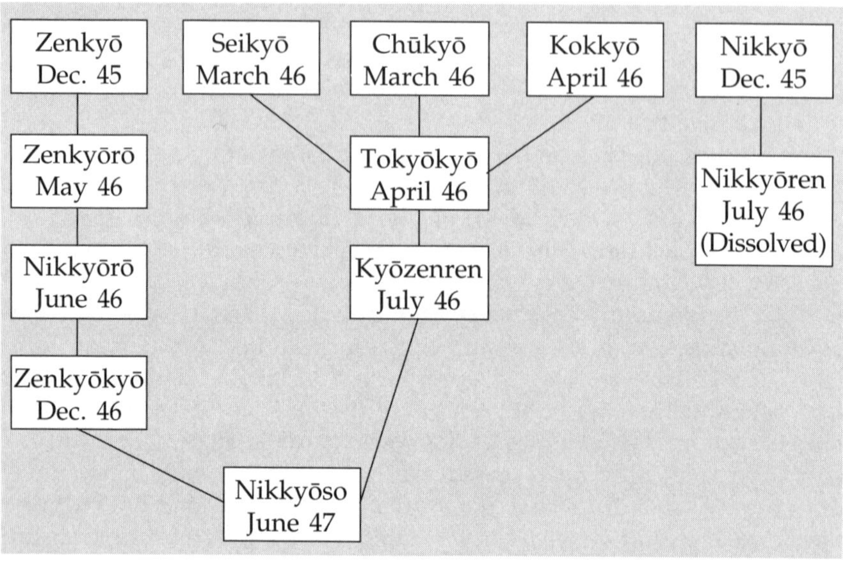

Figure 1.1 Evolution of Teachers' Unions in Postwar Japan, 1945–1947

(Name of organization is followed by date of establishment)

name. It first changed its name (in June 1946) to the Japan Educational Labour Union (Nihon Kyōin Rōdō Kumiai, or Nikyōrō), and later (in December 1946) it merged with powerful regional organizations from Hokkaido and West Japan and formed the All-Japan Conference of Teachers' Unions (Zenkyōkyō). This paved the way for the final merger in 1947 when Zenkyōkyō came together with the smaller moderate union, Kyōzenren (the name given to Tokyōkyō when it expanded beyond Tokyo in its recruitment drive) to form Nikkyōso. By means of the name changes and mergers of that time, the left-wing Zenkyō leadership was able to attract all the prefectural unions into an organization they controlled. In that respect they were very successful in their tactical game plan. However, it would be wrong to assume that the independently minded prefectural unions simply sacrificed all their independence on affiliating with Nikkyōso. Their continued inclination toward independent action has been shown time and again throughout the federation's subsequent history. Often, the success or failure of national campaigns would be determined by the extent to which the prefectural unions joined in the campaign. National headquarters would often be frustrated by the failure of some unions to follow the national line or the lack of wholehearted enthusiasm demonstrated by others. In this way, the specific circumstances of Nikyōso's creation helped determine an important feature of its basic organizational structure that has lasted down to the present.

The rapid expansion of left-wing teacher unionism was also helped by the very favorable political environment of the early months of the Allied Occupation. The Occupation forces at first seemed very sympathetic to the cause of an independent teachers' movement in Japan because they saw it as one safeguard against a renewal of militarism and ultranationalism in schools. Almost immediately after arriving in Japan the Occupation forces under the Supreme Command for the Allied Powers (SCAP) ordered the Japanese government to eliminate all control over workers, to reinstate protective legislation, and to remove all legal hindrances short of those that would protect the goals of the Occupation from union activity.[47] In the following month SCAP ordered the removal of all teachers "known to be militaristic, ultra nationalistic, or antagonistic to the objectives and policies of the occupation."[48] By the time this right-wing purge was complete (May 1947) 120,000 teachers, or 22 percent of the entire teaching corps, had been taken from their posts, most of them going voluntarily rather than waiting to be called before the various committees created especially for this task.[49] Besides serving the intended purpose of eliminating militarists from the classroom, this purge must also have removed a potentially powerful source of opposition to the left wing in the teachers' movement as they set out to put their stamp on the new organizations. The left were also helped in their initial drive to unionize Japan's teachers by the support and encouragement of the Occupation forces, especially those in the Labour Division of the Economic and Scientific Section of SCAP, who held the view that the working class and their unions were the only reliable base for democracy in Japan. However, fundamental disagreements about the form this democracy should take were soon to undermine the cooperative relations between SCAP and left-wing union leaders. SCAP visualized a liberal democracy on the American model, but the union leaders were more dedicated to Marxist or Socialist models of a democratic future. Thus, the union leaders did not believe that political activity should be confined to Parliament, and, if necessary, workers (including teachers) should take to the streets to further their demands and oppose their class enemies. Kobayashi points out the effect this had on the Americans: "Strikes and demonstrations by leftist groups led occupation authorities to rethink their policies, and moved some to understand and sympathise with the thinking of their more conservative colleagues in the Ministry of education."[50] This drift to the right by SCAP finally came out into the open in a dramatic way in January 1947 when General MacArthur intervened directly to order the cancellation of a general strike planned for February 1 by government office workers, railway workers, communications workers, and the more radical of the two main teacher unions (originally called Zenkyō, now—four name changes later—called Zenkyōkyō). This came as a great shock to the union leaders who had thought that SCAP was on their side and represents a watershed in SCAP–union relations.[51] The honeymoon in relations between the American authorities and left-wing teachers' organizations was now at an end, but it had lasted long enough to allow those organizations to expand their memberships dramatically. The left-wing leaders exploited to the full the first period in Japanese history when they were allowed, without any restrictions or interference, to organize, publish, and recruit. Even the ending of the honeymoon had some beneficial consequences, for MacArthur's cancellation of the general strike helped persuade union leaders that they would be better off presenting a united front to the authorities. This helped bring about the Grand Amalgamation Meeting in Nara on June 8, 1947, when Nikkyōso was formed.

Nikkyōso During the Occupation Period 1947-1952

By 1947, the goal of creating a single union representing the vast majority of teachers in Japan had been achieved. Once created, however, the union then had to define for itself a position vis-à-vis the other groups and organizations with whom it would have to work to achieve its aims and objectives. So an examination of Nikkyōso's relations with political parties, government bodies, and other unions will help us to understand what kind of an organization Nikkyōso was at the time of its inception and how it subsequently evolved. Before doing this, it is first necessary to examine Nikkyōso's position under Japanese law and how this changed dramatically in the first few months of its existence.

Nikkyōso's Legal Position

In December 1945, Japan's trade union movement won an historic victory with the passage of the Trade Union Law. This law clearly granted workers the right to form free and autonomous unions, the right to engage in collective bargaining with employers on an equal footing, and the right to strike. These conditions applied equally to public sector workers as well as those in the private sector, and it was under these conditions that Nikkyōso was formed. Nikkyōso saw itself unambiguously as the single representative voice of the entire teaching profession in Japan. It believed that the interests of teachers were best served by united, national campaigns, involving nationwide strikes if necessary. At the time of its creation, this position accurately reflected the legal status of the union. However, this position was destined not to last for long.

Following MacArthur's cancellation of the 1947 general strike, the Occupation authorities took further action to limit the newfound freedoms of workers and their organizations in Japan. In July 1948, SCAP took action that effectively countermanded the 1945 Trade Union Law: it banned all public service employees, including teachers, from striking. Two years later this ban was written into law as article 37 of the Local Public Service Law. The same article also stripped Nikkyōso's national leadership of the legal right to negotiate on behalf of its members.[52] This law was decisive in defining Nikkyōso's subsequent relations with the central government. Nikkyōso never stopped thinking of itself as a national union, conducting national, united campaigns. From the moment the law was passed, however, the Ministry of Education ceased recognizing any teacher' representative organizations at the national level. This view was shared by the governing conservative parties. This fundamental difference of the perception of the proper role of Nikkyōso set the scene for the confrontation that was to follow.

Relations with the Central Government

During the first months of the Occupation, conservative politicians and right-wing bureaucrats had been powerless as they watched the growth of left-wing teacher unionism take place all over the country. They failed in their attempts to encourage the development of a more harmless, moderate union, Nikkyō, which by the end of 1946 had ceased to exist, and their backing of another moderate union, Tōkyōkyō (which later became Kyōzenren) backfired when the association of this union with discredited government bureaucrats was a major factor in discouraging teachers from joining. During the Occupation, the central Japanese administration found itself powerless to influence teacher unionism so long as the Americans were on the side of the unions. That was to change, however, as American priorities changed. Actually, there had always been voices within the Occupation ranks who warned about the dangers of Communist and Socialist influence within the new, rapidly expanding union movement. For example, at the 1946 May Day labor demonstrations a manifesto was presented that contained, to American eyes, suspiciously Communist-sounding language. Some Americans (e.g., the U.S. chairman of the Allied Council for Japan, George Atcheson) even suspected Soviet involvement.[53] The following months witnessed a continued disagreement within the American camp over how to deal with the unions. The central dilemma was how to resist the twin dangers of industrial instability and Communist subversion, without returning to the prewar methods of coercion and authoritarianism. MacArthur's decision to cancel the proposed 1947 general strike was a watershed, indicating that from then on the Americans would be less sympathetic to the unions. From that moment, the attitude of the Occupation authorities to the unions hardened, although members of the labor Division of SCAP still tried to argue the unions' case.[54]

In addition to a hardening of the line on Japanese unionism, the American authorities also became intolerant of left-wing influence within the education system. This was to have serious consequences for teachers' unions. By 1948, some senior members of the Occupation authorities clearly believed that elementary and secondary schoolteachers were preaching communism to their impressionable pupils.[55] Then, on July 19, 1949, Dr. Walter Eells, the SCAP advisor on higher education, delivered a speech in which he argued that Communists should not be allowed to be university professors in a democratic country. At this time action was being taken against professors and teachers within America's domestic education system, and so it seemed only a matter of time before a similar purge would occur in Occupied Japan. So SCAP and the Japanese government used Eells's speech as the occasion to launch a purge of about 1,000 teachers, professors, and education administrators who were thought to be Communist party members or sympathizers.[56] This was in addition to about 20,000 other people who lost their jobs in government, information media, and industry.[57] Because the Red Purge was clearly a violation of the constitution, it had to be carried out under the pretext that it was an exercise to eliminate surplus employees.[58] Nikkyōso's national leadership was not touched, but the ranks at local level were severely depleted of left-wing activists.[59] It can be seen, therefore, that both the crackdown on political extremism in the teachers' union movement and the curtailment of the political activities of teachers were legacies of the American Occupation authorities. Once the Occupation was over, the Japanese central government was to continue willingly with this work.

Relations with Socialist and Communist Political Parties and Conflict over Party Allegiance

The elections of 1947 brought a qualified victory to the Socialist Party. A coalition government was formed by Katayama Tetsu, the first postwar Socialist prime minister, who selected Morito Tatsuo, a Socialist scholar, as minister for education. At the same elections the teachers unions moved into national politics for the first time. Both Hani Gorō and Iwama Masao won seats in the upper house without having formal ties to any party, and eight other Zenkyōkyō members won seats after campaigning as Socialist Party candidates (three in the upper house, including Araki Shōzaburō, Zenkyōkyō's chairman, and five in the lower). The moderate Kyōzenren also ran three successful Socialist party candidates in the upper house, including their chairman Kōno Masao.[60] (Having both unions led by Socialist Party members was one more contributing factor behind their merger later that same year.) With direct access to the government of the day, the teachers' unions developed a two-pronged strategy to attain their demands. Their political influence in the Diet was backed up by the threat of strikes in the schools and demonstrations on the streets.

The Japan Communist Party (JCP) did badly in the 1947 general election, and at that time most Communist Party sympathizers in the union movement kept a low profile. All that was to change, however, after the 1949 election, when, exploiting a mood of widespread dissatisfaction with the Socialists, the JCP were able to increase their number of seats in the Diet from four to thirty-five. The surge of popular support for the JCP that this expansion of its vote represented encouraged some Communist sympathizers within Nikkyōso to proclaim their allegiance unambiguously. In a joint statement Iwama Masao and seventy other union members declared their membership of the JCP. This did not really surprise anyone who knew these people well, but it was damaging for Nikkyōso's image with the non-Communist general public, and, of course, with SCAP. Non-Communists in Nikkyōso were also worried about the strength of Communist influence within their union, and they did not like the clandestine and highly organized nature of the Communist faction. It turned out that the JCP held direct control over the Communists within Nikkyōso through its education and culture department (Kyōiku Bunka Bu) and its labor department (Rōdō Bu).[61] Fearing a Communist takeover of the union, influential Socialist members organized themselves into a rival faction. Thus, 1949 witnessed the first open break between Communist and Socialist factions within Nikkyōso.[62] At that time the balance of power seems to have been quite even, with Communist control of the union's Central Executive Committee being countered by a firm anti-Communist stand taken by President Araki. The Communists were never again to be as influential within the top ranks of Nikkyōso as they were in the late 1940s. However, the stage had been set for a rivalry between Communist and Socialist factions that would continue right down to the schism in 1989.

The presence of a large Communist faction within the top ranks of Nikkyōso was also exploited by the union's enemies and used as a justification for anti-union activities. International events (i.e., victory for the Chinese Communists in 1949, followed by the outbreak of war in Korea in 1950) seemed to justify fears of a Communist takeover in East Asia. This brought the American Military Authorities and the old Japanese ruling elite, bitter enemies such a short time ago, together in a common cause. A "depurge" of thousands of individuals convicted during the immediate postwar right-wing purge was carried out, and Communists were now perceived to be more dangerous than rightists or militarists. After the Americans left, anti-Communist rhetoric continued to be used repeatedly to attack left-wing unions in general, and Nikkyōso (always either the largest or second largest union during the postwar period) in particular. For its part, Nikkyōso denied that it had any Communist influence. Instead, it claimed that it was merely trying to promote democratic education and the cause of peace. It claimed that the government was really using the excuse of anti-Communism as a means of reestablishing a police state in Japan. This war of words between government and union was also destined to continue well beyond the end of the Occupation.

Relations with Union Federations

The struggle for influence between Socialists and Communists was not confined to the teachers' unions. The rapid expansion of unions after the war bore witness to similar rivalries and conflicts in almost every area of working life in Japan as workers joined free unions for the first time in their lives, and activists competed for control of the new organizations. This competition for control went on at every level of union organization, from the branch or shop floor level up to that of the national federation. It is the latter that we will consider here. After the war, two main national centers for labor were created. These were Sanbetsu Kaigi (Zen Nihon Sangyōbetsu Rōdō Kaigi or the Congress of Industrial Unions of Japan) organized mainly by Communist activists, and Sōdōmei (Nihon

Rōdō Kumiai Sōdōmei or the Japanese Federation of Labour Unions) organized mainly by moderate Socialists. The two teacher unions that merged to form Nikkyōso were affiliated to these federations. (In July 1946, Nikkyōrō had joined Sanbetsu, and in the same month Kyōzenren had joined Sōdōmei.) Having different sections affiliated to different federations paved the way for Nikkyōso's role in organizing the creation of one large, united public sector federation. In 1949, the other two significant public sector unions, the railway and postal unions, were both split over the Red Purge and so it was left to Nikkyōso, the largest public sector union, to take a lead (with SCAP helping out behind the scenes).[63] The result was Sōhyō (Nihon Rōdō Kumiai Sōhyōgikai or the General Council of Trade Unions in Japan), which was formed on July 11, 1950. SCAP approved of Sōhyō because it was basically anti-Communist.[64] The Communist rump of Sanbetsu Kaigi was no longer a significant feature on the industrial relations landscape and it withered and finally died in 1958. However, this did not mean that Sōhyō would be a compliant servant of American or right-wing Japanese interests. The newly born Sōhyō began to change its line in less than a year with a move toward closer ties with the leftist faction of the Japan Socialist Party.[65] It soon became the most powerful federation of unions in postwar Japan and an important player in organizing major anti-government campaigns. Thus, the dissolution of Sōhyō in 1989 was a very significant event in the history of unions in Japan. The role of Nikkyōso was to prove just as decisive in the death of Sōhyō as it had been in its birth thirty-nine years earlier.

Conclusion: Nikkyōso in 1952

By the end of the Occupation the defining characteristics of Nikkyōso had all been formed. It had established itself as a national organization representing the vast majority of teachers in Japan. It was one of the strongest components of the powerful public sector union movement, and it had a strong influence on Socialists in the Diet. It also was an important voice on educational matters, fiercely defending the reforms of the Occupation, and, from 1951 onward, sponsoring annual meetings on educational research. It was also strongly pacifist, adopting the popular phrase "Never send our children to the battlefield again" as the official union slogan. With memories of the war so recent, this slogan struck a chord with the vast bulk of the membership.

Underneath this appearance of strength and unity, however, serious long-term weaknesses were also evident in 1952. Although it considered itself a national organization speaking with one voice for all of Japan's teachers, this was not how the government, or the law, viewed Nikkyōso. The prefectural teachers' unions were legal entities, but the national union was not. Because the most important education policy decisions in Japan are made at the national level, this was to have serious consequences for Nikkyōso's influence on policy-making in the years to come. The nature of Nikkyōso's left-wing leadership was also to cause it problems. One set of problems would result from the divided nature of the leadership, with two factions, one Communist and the other Socialist, clearly established by the end of the Occupation. While they would often unite against the common enemy of a conservative government and Ministry of Education, they would also be prone to internecine wrangling and conflict. Eventually this proved the undoing of the union.

Another set of problems caused by the left-wing nature of the leadership relates to the "red-crested crane" nature of Nikkyōso. The extraordinary circumstances of the immediate postwar period meant that radical activists and ordinary teachers had much in common. Once, however, a reasonable amount of normality had been restored, the allegiance of rank-and-file toward their radical leadership might be less forthcoming. A definition of normality here might be very difficult to arrive at, but it seems clear that once the majority of teachers had achieved reasonable economic security and freedom from excessive control over their teaching by the authorities, then they might be less inclined to follow the union leadership in political campaigns that they feel are remote or unnecessary. In other words, Nikkyōso was always in danger of becoming the victim of its own success. The better-off that ordinary teachers became, the less likely they might be to follow the radical lead of Nikkyōso's leadership. This development, combined with the fact that as time passed memories of the horrors of war faded, meant that Nikkyōso would always be challenged to adapt itself to changing circumstances. In 1952, Nikkyōso enjoyed the loyalty of the vast majority of Japan's primary and secondary school teachers. There were no guarantees at all that this situation would continue.

CHAPTER TWO

THE HISTORY OF NIKKYŌSO, 1952–1988

This chapter is concerned with analyzing the main developments that unfolded between 1952 and 1988, culminating in Nikkyōso's schism. Much of the chapter, which is divided into five sections, examines the chronic decline in size and influence of the union. The first section will briefly analyze the immediate post-occupation events that brought about the consolidation of the division of Japan's political actors into two camps, and Nikkyōso's part in this process. The second section will look at the main government policies since the Occupation that have been perceived by the union as being designed to weaken it. The third section will examine the causes for Nikkyōso's long-term decline in membership. The fourth section will look at the factional infighting within Nikkyōso's leadership. Finally, the last section will analyze two areas of irreconcilable difference between the left and right wings of Nikkyōso in the 1980s. These differences, combined with the split over leadership, brought about the schism of 1989. The details and events of the schism itself will be dealt with in chapter three.

NIKKYŌSO'S PART IN THE FORMATION OF THE 1955 SYSTEM

Once the official American Occupation of Japan was over in 1952, the Japanese government was left to its own devices as to how to handle dissent from the left. It was also now given a free hand to deal with the legislative legacy of the Occupation, and to modify or revise it according to the domestic conservative ideology of the day. This process became known as the "reverse course." In the field of education this took the form of attempts by the government in partnership with the Ministry of Education and local conservative elites to remove those parts of the Occupation reforms that were considered too foreign or liberal to suit the conservative image of what Japanese education should be. Thus, in the years immediately following 1952, Nikkyōso found itself pushed on the defensive as it struggled to preserve the Occupation reforms. In an almost ironic reversal of prewar roles, the progressives in the independent teachers' movement found themselves resisting change as the conservatives and traditionalists in government tried hard to push through educational reforms. In the process of resisting the reverse course, Nikkyōso came to involve itself in the wider struggle that was going on between the conservative government and its progressive opposition. This situation came to be known as the 1955 system (named after the year in which the JSP was reunited and the LDP formed) and proved to be the defining arrangement of Japanese politics until the LDP lost control of the lower house of the Diet for the first time in 1993.

In the field of education, one early example of an area in which battle between conservatives and progressives raged was the area of moral education or *shūshin*. Three successive education ministers in three successive cabinets of Prime Minister Yoshida Shigeru (the ministers were Amano Teiyū, Okano Kiyohide, and Odachi Shigeo) urged the reestablishment of moral education as a separate course, even though it had been deliberately banned by the Americans as a method of prewar ultra nationalist indoctrination. Nikkyōso fought back by establishing educational committees in almost every city, town, and village, and by cooperating with the Socialist Party and other unions to turn public opinion against the government.[1] Despite these efforts, however, the ministry succeeded in requiring one hour a week of moral education in elementary and junior high schools starting in 1958, although it did concede that the details of what would be taught in these lessons would be left up to individual teachers and schools.[2] The government was also careful with the terminology it used. The prewar word for moral education, *shūshin,* was dropped in favor of the more neutral *dōtoku,* and there was no attempt to reintroduce emperor-worship or the Imperial Rescript on Education. However, the battle over moral education was set to continue down to the present, with critics of the government pointing to the similarities between much of the content of prewar *shūshin* and postwar *dōtoku.*

Critics argued, and continue to argue, that it is not the role of a democratic government to determine what the norms of human conduct should be.[3] As was typical of many of the disputes between these two adversaries, Nikkyōso continued to be frustrated by its lack of access to central policy-making while the government's frustration lay in its very limited ability to enforce its policies at the *genba*.

Another extremely controversial issue over which the union and government did battle during this period of the "reverse course" was the issue of textbook control. In 1956, the government introduced a bill that would have strictly limited the number of textbooks that could be used throughout the country (about three in each subject area for each grade level), and would then have required a prefectural selection committee to choose one textbook from this list for a given subject for each grade level in the prefecture. On April 20, 1956, this bill passed the lower house. During its reading in the upper house, Nikkyōso organized a walkout of half a million teachers, plus protests and demonstrations involving other unions and sympathetic organizations. Efforts to defeat the textbook bill were successful. At the same time, however, the conservatives were able to pass through an act that replaced local elected school boards with appointed ones. During the passage of this act, exchanges between Liberal Democratic Party members and the Socialist Party (which contained a large block of Nikkyōso-supported representatives) grew so heated on the House floor that the police had to be called in to restore order.[4] Even the apparent victory for Nikkyōso over the textbook issue was soon undermined as the ministry switched tactics and decided to enforce a system in which it selected a number of books from which teachers were allowed to choose the one they wanted to use. It introduced this system without resorting to legislation. Although not as restrictive as the bill, it still meant that the ministry could at least make sure that books that were not acceptable were excluded from the list.[5]

The textbook and *shūshin-dōtoku* controversies, and the dispute over replacing elected boards of education with appointed ones, illustrate the struggle between Nikkyōso and the government in the immediate post-Occupation years, and show how, even with friends and supporters in the Socialist Party, the wider union movement, and the public at large, Nikkyōso was unable to wrest the initiative from its conservative adversaries. In this way, by the end of the 1950s, the battle lines had been drawn (which were to remain largely in place until the 1990s) with two camps—the progressive and the conservative—lined up facing each other in the area of education as in other areas. This period has been referred to as one of "warfare waged between the entrenched"[6] because it was characterized by uncompromising hostility between the two sides (at least at the national level) and a World War I style stalemate in terms of ground won or lost. For, despite serious efforts for education reform in both the 1970s and the 1980s, very little substantive change in the education system took place. However, to continue the World War I analogy, the ongoing war of attrition between the two sides had the additional effect of slowly but surely wearing Nikkyōso down. The rest of this chapter will examine the process of this decline, as well as the related processes at work within the organization that eventually pulled it apart.

Government Policies Perceived as Being Anti-Nikkyōso

Chapter one examined some of the ways in which the American Occupation authorities, after initially being supportive of unionization in Japan, turned against Nikkyōso and other unions that were perceived to be a threat to American interests in the region. After the departure of the Americans it soon became clear that the domestic government would continue this anti-union work. Whether or not "union busting" was ever a coherent and prioritized program of the government is a controversial question, nowever. Nikkyōso officials, for their part, claim that it consistently was an unspoken government policy to break their union. Furthermore, Schoppa makes the point that since Nikkyōso was the main force blocking government education policies, then "it had naturally become a corollary of these policies that the union must first be weakened."[7] Evidence supporting this point is provided by a series of government policies that had the effect of weakening the union. We will now look at the three main policies that were enforced during the period between the end of the Occupation and the schism. These concern the assessment of teachers, the training of teachers, and the assessment of pupils.

The Teachers' Efficiency Rating System

In July 1957, the government announced its intention to enforce, throughout the nation, a plan to rate individual teachers according to their efficiency. Teachers who received a low rating would be in danger of losing pay increases or being sacked. Nikkyōso regarded the plan as an attempt, by the government, to restore prewar style controls over teachers. In October of the previous year, elected boards of education had been replaced by appointed ones. Nikkyōso therefore regarded the enforcement of the teachers' efficiency rating system as the next stage in the government's plan to extend its power and control back down into the schools themselves, while at the same time make a direct attack on the union. The rating system required principals to rate the teachers in their schools and then send the results to the local board of education. Nikkyōso chairman, Kobayashi Takeshi, explained the union's opposition to the plan as follows:

> Our main concern is that the implementation of the rating plan will result in subservience to authority, characteristic of prewar Japan, thereby distorting education. Under the new system the local school principal must evaluate the teacher's performance. In this role the principal will become merely a representative of the controlling powers, that is the boards of education and the Ministry of Education. The resulting disastrous effect will be an emotional struggle between the principal, representing the entrenched power structure, and his teachers. The principal will then be able to coerce his teachers through the implementation of the rating system.[8]

This quotation highlights two of the main concerns of Nikkyōso during the first two decades of its existence. First they were worried that the government and the "entrenched power structure" were attempting to turn the clock back in order to recreate the prewar Japanese political and educational system. Second, they were highly conscious of the political nature of every educational or administrative reform. The Ministry of Education, for its part, argued that it was merely trying to increase the effectiveness of teachers by introducing the teacher rating scheme. Nikkyōso was suspicious of any rhetoric from the authorities that said they were acting out of apolitical, educational motives.

The campaign to prevent the implementation of the efficiency rating system constitutes, in Thurston's words (writing in 1973), "the strongest, most widespread, and most significant struggle of [Nikkyōso's] history."[9] At first the union adopted a policy of "absolute opposition by force," calling for a nationwide boycott of classrooms for September 15, 1958, not only by teachers but by pupils as well (Sōhyō joined in the struggle by ordering all its 3,500,000 members to keep their children from school on that day). The government responded by ordering all schools closed on the day of the boycott. However, only unions in seventeen prefectures complied with the national call for action.[10] Further days of national unified action were organized by Nikkyōso during the autumn and winter, but successful walkouts and strikes were often blighted by violent clashes between strikers and police or right-wing gangs.[11] Confrontation was much worse in some prefectures than others. The most serious struggles took place in Tochigi, Tokushima, Kagawa, and Ehime, prefectures in which militant union leadership clashed with determined conservative local governments. It has been argued that Tochigi was singled out for particularly strenuous anti-union activity by the government because it contained the Diet constituency of Moriyama Kinji, the LDP member most devoted to the anti-Nikkyōso cause.[12] With the danger of continuing disruption in many areas, and in the face of public criticism that it was too extreme in its use of pupils as pawns in the power game, Nikkyōso's national leadership climbed down and changed its policy from "absolute opposition by force" to one of "noncooperation"[13]. This did not mean, however, that the Ministry of Education had won. For Nikkyōso was able to effectively render the efficiency rating system meaningless when it was implemented at the school level. It did this by adopting the so-called Kanagawa formula (*Kanagawa Hōshiki*). This formula was worked out in early 1959 by negotiations between the Kanagawa board of education and the local prefectural teachers' union affiliated with Nikkyōso. (Kanagawa was a prefecture where the two sides were on reasonably good terms.) The compromise involved getting teachers to influence the grades they received through consultation with their principal.[14] The formula was adopted nationwide after Secretary General Miyanohara overcame the opposition of the Communist-supporting faction in Nikkyōso's Central Executive Committee. In some prefectures (Thurston gives the example of Iwate) teachers actually wrote out their own evaluations and together made sure that they all got uniformly high grades.[15] Principals would usually go along with this in the interests of keeping peace in their schools. The teachers had achieved their aim of preventing the reintroduction of government control into schools.[16] This success strongly influenced Nikkyōso's future tactics. "Absolute opposition by force" at the national level was counterproductive in the face of an unbending government and Ministry of Education. Therefore, a more flexible policy of noncooperation with government policy at the local and prefectural level was more likely to achieve results.

Teacher Training and Recruitment

In the early postwar years the debate about the reform of teacher training institutions was heavily influenced by the memory of prewar normal schools (*shihan gakkō*). Inspired by the French system of centralized, state-run normal schools, the Meiji government had set up its own system designed to meet the staffing needs of its new mass education system. The central government used the control it had over these new institutions to create a school regime that would produce the type of teacher it thought the nation needed. This included the introduction of military-style regimes, which were intended to develop patriotism, character, and moral leadership in the new generation of teachers.[17] Army officers were assigned to each school, and because most normal school students were boarders the schools soon took on many of the characteristics of army camps. The militarization of the 1930s removed any scope there might have been for free-thinking or the development of any ideas "not in accord with the national polity."[18] It is interesting to note that all of the first generation of Nikkyōso leaders were trained in such schools. Duke makes the point that because normal school students were "trained, as it were, to be dogmatic,"[19] then this helps explain the militancy of the early postwar union leaders. The shock of Japan's defeat combined with the guilt they felt for having urged so many of their pupils to sacrifice their lives for the state meant that many teachers switched their allegiance from emperor and nation to pacifism and democracy. In fighting for these new causes, they proved to be just as dogmatic and uncompromising as they had been when working for the old. Duke argues that this factor, combined with aspirations to improve the economic lot of teachers, was much more important than any abstract political ideology in explaining the militancy of Japan's teachers in the period that is the subject of his study (i.e., the end of the war up to the mid-1960s).[20]

Given the firsthand experience of Nikkyōso's leaders and members in the prewar normal school system, therefore, it is quite understandable that they would support the Occupation authorities in their reforms of that system. These reforms involved the replacement of normal schools with a system modeled on the contemporary American one, combining colleges of education and various teacher certification programs offered by universities.[21] The prewar central control of teacher training institutions was broken. The centralization inherent in the rest of the system, however, meant that the Ministry of Education still retained significant influence. Present-day Japanese trainee teachers, for example, tend to view the curriculum they are learning to teach as a given from the Ministry of Education, whereas their counterparts in many Western countries (e.g., the United States or Britain) would be encouraged to learn how to construct a curriculum.[22] Nikkyōso, for its part, believed that the whole process of teacher training and recruitment was used to undermine the union. They argued that, first, teacher trainees at the college level were subjected to anti-union propaganda,[23] and, second, new recruits into the profession were screened by their employees (usually the prefectural board of education) in order to eliminate potential union members.[24]

Because Nikkyōso was inclined to believe that its enemies in national and local government were always trying to use the training of new teachers as a weapon against it, it has been strongly opposed to any teacher training reforms emanating from the government or its advisory bodies. In the name of improving teacher quality, the Ministry of Education has repeatedly tried to increase training requirements. Nikkyōso has consistently opposed these attempts because it was afraid that increased course requirements would force many departments in regular universities to close, leaving teacher training increasingly in the hands of government run teacher training colleges.[25] The union has also been opposed to changes in the provision of in-service training for probationary teachers, most recently those proposed by *Rinkyōshin*. Because of the split it caused in Nikkyōso's leadership this will be dealt with in more detail in the final section of this chapter.

Assessment of Pupils

In 1961, the Ministry of Education announced that it would be conducting nationwide achievement tests in five subject areas for all second- and third-year junior high school students.[26] Nikkyōso was opposed to this for two reasons: first, they were against, on principle, the extension of ministry control over the content of education; and, second, they believed that the test results would be used to divide students (and their teachers) against each other. Having learned the lessons of the campaign over the teacher efficiency rating system, Nikkyōso decided to avoid direct confrontation with the government and simply ignore the tests when the time came to implement them. The resulting disruption had varying consequences according to the local balance of power within each prefecture and depending on the willingness of ordinary teachers to support the union's action. In Iwate, Fukuoka, Hokkaidō, and Kōchi most schools did not administer the tests in 1961. In other prefectures disruption was less significant.[27] By 1962, most prefectural boards of education had agreed to Nikkyōso's main demand that the names of students not appear on the answer sheets or the test scores on their academic records. In return, the union dropped its disruption of the tests.[28]

In the case of both the rating of teachers and the assessment of pupils, Nikkyōso was largely successful in opposing the main thrust of the Ministry of Education's reforms. This success, however, had harmful consequences because it allowed Nikkyōso's enemies to portray it as an organization dedicated to resisting government attempts to improve education. Nikkyōso would reply that it was dedicated to improving the performance of both teachers and pupils. Because the most newsworthy events of this period always had Nikkyōso in the role of *opposition* to change, however, the negative image was usually the more enduring one in the public eye.

There was another consequence of the battle over teacher rating and pupil assessment that was not lost on either side of the conflict. This was the fact that open confrontation between teachers and the authorities usually resulted in a loss of members for the prefectural union concerned. In the teacher rating struggle the two prefectures that witnessed the most bitter confrontations between militant local union leaders and intransigent boards of education were Ehime and Tochigi (Ehime had actually been used as a test case for the system before it was implemented nationally—it therefore endured the longest period of confrontation). By 1964, the percentage of teachers who were members of the Nikkyōso-affiliated prefectural union was 9.6 percent in Ehime and 3.5 percent in Tochigi (at that time the median prefecture, Akita, had a membership percentage of 77.2 percent and only six prefectures out of forty-six had membership percentages of less than 50 percent).[29] Nikkyōso's response to this situation was the previously mentioned shift in policy from one of "total confrontation" to "noncooperation." The lesson for Nikkyōso's enemies was that the union would always be weakened by a bitter or prolonged confrontation.

Decline in Nikkyōso's Membership

One of the clearest ways of measuring a union's strength or weakness is through its membership figures. Chapter one described the huge success Nikkyōso and its predecessor unions enjoyed in their initial recruitment drives, recruiting, for example, up to 98 percent of the country's elementary teachers, according to SCAP estimates. So long as Nikkyōso maintained a high national membership it could coordinate campaigns across the country that could seriously reduce the effectiveness of government education policies. Nikkyōso was able to make up for its lack of legal status as a national organization by its ability to structure these national

Table 2.1 The Decline of Nikkyōso Membership as a Percentage of Educational Personnel (1958–1987)[30]

1958	86.3%
1964	72.9
1969	56.2
1973	55.1
1977	55.2
1981	51.3
1985	49.5
1987	48.5

campaigns. However, these campaigns would only continue to be effective so long as Nikkyōso enjoyed a high level of membership. Since the 1950s, therefore, the inexorable decline in membership figures has been a constant cause of concern to the union leadership as well as an (unspoken) cause of satisfaction to its enemies. The figures in Table 2.1 have been collected by the Ministry of Education and clearly show the decline that had taken place.

What are the main causes of this decline? Two factors have already been alluded to: the screening out of potential union members in the recruitment process, and the loss of members caused by sustained disruption due to conflict between union and authorities.[31] In addition to these factors, Thurston, writing in 1989, identified three more causes for membership decline: high teachers' salaries, high union dues, and the rise of an apolitical generation of teachers who view Nikkyōso as irrelevant.[32] We will now look at these in turn.

High Teachers' Salaries

As we saw in chapter one, low pay was a significant factor behind the rapid mass unionization of teachers after the war. Since then, the pay of teachers has improved beyond recognition. The biggest single rise occurred with the Law Governing Special Measures for Securing Competent Educational Personnel in 1974 that delivered a 10 percent raise and committed both the Ministry of Education and Ministry of Finance to future increases. The passage of this law was a rare case of agreement and cooperation between the various actors involved in educational policy-making. Nikkyōso and its allies in the JSP were in favor because of the benefits the raise brought to union members, and the Ministry of Education and the LDP were in favor because they were able to introduce the new managerial scales of vice-principal and teacher-manager as part of the legislative package.[33] (These categories were seen by the right as a way of extending government authority into the schools.) But the raise in pay was also of benefit to the right (whether this was intentional or not) because it undermined one of the main motivations for union membership, especially among younger teachers who had no memories of the destitution teachers suffered in the 1940s. By the 1990s, Japanese teachers were among the best paid in the world, with their salaries 2.4 times the national per capita income (this compares to only 1.7 times for teachers in the United States).[34] It seems that by achieving these levels of pay Nikkyōso has been a victim of its own success.

Unusually High Union Dues

Thurston found that Nikkyōso charged higher union fees than other unions. The fees vary from prefecture to prefecture and are dependent on age and years of union membership, but, in 1986, Thurston found that some teachers were paying as much as 12,000 yen per month, with extra charges occurring at the biannual bonus months.[35] Saitama prefectural union charged only half this, 6,000 yen per month (less than 3 percent of a young teacher's take-home pay), but even this was given as a contributing factor behind some teachers leaving the union during the period of the schism.[36] Nikkyōso fees were (and continue to be) very high because of the financial support the union is obliged to give to a large number of teachers who have been dismissed, suspended, or had their salaries reduced by the government as punishment for striking illegally. In 1987, throughout Japan, 85,000 teachers or ex-teachers were receiving help in this way, at a cost of about eleven billion yen per year to the union.[37] Although no national opinion survey has been conducted on this matter, it is Thurston's impression, and my own, that the willingness to pay union dues has lessened. He wrote in 1989 that "[m]ost teachers are no longer convinced that the benefits they receive from the union are worth the high dues."[38] This decrease in enthusiasm among individual teachers to sustain a financial burden for which they may receive no immediate personal benefit is probably linked with the next factor behind the decline in Nikkyōso's membership.

The Rise of an Apolitical Generation of Teachers in Japan

Thurston believes that the coming into the profession of a generation of teachers who have no direct experience of the war or its immediate aftermath has led to less support for Nikkyōso's traditional goals.

> Young Japanese born during the 1960s have no memory of war or the early postwar years of hardship. Those who aspire to the teaching profession today also have little knowledge and no memory of the intense struggles of [Nikkyōso] to maintain the occupation-inspired egalitarian education system and preserve the independence of education from government control. With little understanding of the tight authority the prewar government exercised over education and teachers that contributed to the inability of the Japanese people to prevent the rise of militarism, few teachers today see the danger of an educational system increasingly controlled by the government and not by themselves.[39]

As shown in chapter one, the new teachers' union of the late 1940s, which was characterized as being a "red-crested crane" (i.e., having an "ordinary," moderate, membership and a left-wing leadership) was very much a product of those extraordinary times. The changes that occurred in Japan between the 1940s and the 1960s have, indeed, been drastic, and Nikkyōso, like all interest groups, was continuously subject to societal and generational factors that were beyond its control. Moderates among the leadership began to recognize that trying to appeal to a new generation of teachers using the slogans of the 1940s and 1950s was not proving effective. Nor was it enough to blame the decline in membership solely on government propaganda and intimidation (although these factors certainly made an important contribution).[40] New approaches would have to be worked out for dealing with the changing times. By proposing the revision of Nikkyōso's basic policies that this would entail, however, the moderates incurred the wrath of the left within the union, who regarded this kind of revisionism as a betrayal of Nikkyōso's principles. Thus, the decline in membership, as well as weakening Nikkyōso in its struggle with the government, had the additional effect of provoking an ideological battle between left and right within the union that was one of the main causes of the schism. In other words, the union's enemies not only benefited from its chronic, long-term, decline in membership, but also from its attempts to find solutions to this crisis. A series of arguments over how to reverse the membership decline was not the only cause of division within Nikkyōso's leadership, however, as will be shown in the next section.

Factions Within Nikkyōso

Chapter one covered the first open split between Socialist and Communist factions within Nikkyōso that occurred in 1949. Because this split was so enduring, it is tempting to regard the eventual schism of the union as an inevitability. Indeed, disputes between Socialists and Communists were often so heated and bitter over the forty years before the schism that it might seem surprising that it did not happen earlier. The truth of the matter is that there was always a combination of influences on activists of differing ideologies, some of which brought them together and others that pulled them apart. The situation was further confused by the existence of divisions *within* factions, and by the personal rivalry of ambitious individuals.

Socialists and Communists often joined together in a common struggle when they perceived it was in their interests to do so. This would usually happen when battle was joined with the Ministry of Education and its allies in local government. However, when it came to issues of power and influence within the union organization they would divide into separate factions. In this context the word "faction" is really a term of convenience because Nikkyōso factions were never as distinct or as open as, for example, factions within the LDP. The factional identity of union activists, however, would always come out into the open on two regular occasions. One of these was the election of the union leadership; the other was the passing of motions concerning which political party or parties to support.

The balance of power that existed in the late 1940s continued into the 1950s, with Communist control of the union's Central Executive Committee (CEC) being balanced by Socialist control of the chairmanship. This fairly evenly matched struggle went on until the national conference of 1958, at which a decisive struggle for hegemony of the union took place.[41] The struggle centred around the election of Nikkyōso's secretary general, the second most important position in the union. The contest was between the incumbent, Hiragaki Miyoji, and the challenger, Miyanohara Sadamitsu. The former was the de facto leader of the Communist faction (although he always denied being a Communist) and the latter was the leader of the more moderate faction, sympathetic to the Japan Socialist Party (JSP). Miyanohara narrowly won the contest, and a member of his faction, Makieda Motofumi, was elected vice secretary general. Miyanohara and Makieda proceeded to consolidate and extend their control, and in 1962 a reduction in the size of the CEC from sixty-six to forty-seven gave total control of that organ to their faction too, which from that moment on can be considered the mainstream faction (*shuryūha)* of the union. This faction's "gradualism" had superseded Hiragaki's tactics of absolute confrontation in most of the prefectural unions too by this time[42] (following the lessons learned during the campaign over the teachers' efficiency rating system previously discussed). At a special conference in 1961, Nikkyōso had voted to adopt a policy of giving exclusive support to the JSP (the assumption that association with the JCP was bad for the union's image help to swing the vote). From that year onward each annual conference witnessed an attempt by the anti-mainstream faction to overturn this decision and support both parties. Conference votes over this issue thus gave a rough idea of the relative strengths of the two sides each year.

The year 1962 saw Miyanohara become chairman and Makieda assume the position of secretary general. Their mainstream faction was now secure in its control of Nikkyōso (at the national level—the picture at the local level varied from prefecture to prefecture) but, as time went, by, splits began to emerge *within* this faction, mirroring similar divisions within the JSP. In 1971, when Miyanohara retired, Makieda became chairman, reinforcing the custom that the secretary general always succeeds to the chairmanship. By the time Makieda's own succession came up, however, this custom was to prove very problematic, because by then a clear split within the mainstream faction had emerged between left wing and right wing, and while Makieda was clearly on the right, his secretary general, Nakakoji Kiyoo, was equally clearly on the left.[43] To avoid Nakakoji's promotion to chairman, Makieda engineered (through a right-wing majority on the CEC) the promotion of fellow right-winger, Tanaka Ichiro, to the post of first vice-chairman (in 1980) and then chairman (in 1983). Nakakoji had been left in the post of secretary general and effectively passed over for promotion. He and his followers felt cheated by the breaking of union precedent. Furthermore, Tanaka was an extremely controversial choice for chairman because he had previously built up contacts with members of the government as well as LDP Diet members who belonged to the *bunkyōzoku*, or education "tribe." A survey of all the prefectural unions conducted in 1987 by the journal *Kikan Kyōikuhō* found that the most common reasons cited by these organizations for Nikkyōso's internal problems were all related to Tanaka's style of leadership.[44] Thus, by the mid-1980s relations between the two wings of the main faction were at a very low point. This meant that Nikkyōso was ill prepared to face what Thurston describes as "the most crucial question of its entire postwar history"[45]—the debate about whether to join in the creation of Rengō. This will be dealt with in the following section.

Splits over Policy: Irreconcilable Differences Within Nikkyōso

The existence of factions within Nikkyōso and splits within these factions had not previously become a threat to the union's unity for two main reasons. First, the existence of the "common enemy" (i.e., the LDP, Ministry of Education, and their allies) gave activists and leaders a good reason to bury their differences whenever possible in order to present a united front. Second, Nikkyōso's lack of legal status as a national organization gave a lot of leeway to prefectural unions to adopt policies of their own in defiance of national policy. For example, even though the national conference has consistently, since 1961, voted to endorse only the JSP at election time, some prefectural unions (e.g., Saitama) have openly defied this and thrown their support behind local JCP candidates.[46] Thus, even when activists failed to get their preferred policy endorsed by the national conference, they were still able, on occasion, to have the consolation of having their policy adopted by their prefecture.

The forces holding Nikkyōso together as a united organization, however, proved inadequate in the face of two major debates of the late 1980s. One of these concerned the question of whether to join in with the unification of Japanese labor under the new giant confederation Rengō. The other involved how best to respond to the large-scale educational reform initiated by Prime Minister Nakasone and his Ad Hoc Council on Education (*Rinkyōshin*). Differences of opinion over these two issues would prove to be irreconcilable

Disagreement over Affiliation with Rengō

In 1987, the two main Japanese union federations, Sōhyō and Dōmei, declared that they would merge to form one all-embracing federation—Rengō (the formal merger would take place in 1989). It can be argued that this merger brought about the effective privatization of the public sector unions—that is, it made public sector unions that affiliated with Rengō behave more like private sector unions. Throughout the postwar period, private sector companies in Japan had dealt with the perceived threat of an independent union movement by sponsoring the development of "second unions" within each company. By a process of sticks and carrots these second unions were able to grow at the expense of the original independent organizations until they became the dominant form of worker organization in the private sector. The main union officials in these unions were often indistinguishable from managers, and indeed after a spell working for the union would usually go into management positions in the company.[48] Independent unions in the public sector were suspicious of these kinds of company unions, which they believed were incapable of protecting the workers' interests in any serious dispute with management. Thus, the belief arose that the government's plans for the privatization of the railways—splitting up JNR into smaller private companies—was part of a scheme to smash the railway unions. The subsequent breakup and enfeeblement of the once mighty railway union Kokurō seems to give some credence to this view. The example of the railways is a clear example of the effects of privatization on one public sector union, but how applicable is this concept with regard to the teachers' unions who represent employees in a sector that was never considered appropriate for literal privatization? The answer lies at the confederation level. By merging the two existing confederations, Dōmei and Sōhyō—one private sector, one public—into one, the influence of private sector union practice could be brought to bear on public sector unions. This influence was manifested in Rengō's stated position of opposing strike action and also in its clear anti-communism. These two policy positions, as well as other Rengō statements about their position on educational issues, were decisive in influencing many on the left of Nikkyōso to oppose affiliation with the new confederation. Left-wing leaders, like the presidents of Tokyo Metropolitan Teachers' Union, and Osaka High School Teachers' Union, accused Rengō of collaborating with big business, and when the more moderate central leadership of Nikkyōso declared that they were in favor of affiliating with Rengō they were accused of betraying Nikkyōso's most basic and cherished principles. In reply, those in favor of affiliation said that the time had come for Japanese unions to look to the future and stop fighting old Cold-War-era battles. These kinds of discussions and disagreements were replicated at every level of the union. It was one thing for the central leadership to decide to affiliate with Rengō. It was quite another for them to persuade the local organizations and individual members to follow suit. The flexibility that allowed individual prefectural unions to follow different courses of action from the nationally decided one had often been one of Nikkyōso's strengths. Now, however, it was to prove its undoing. This was because the process of affiliation to the new confederation required each prefectural union to affiliate separately (the prefectural unions being the legally recognized entities). Thus, it was up to each and every prefectural union (and in each prefecture there would be at least two such unions—one representing teachers in compulsory education and the other representing teachers in high schools) to decide for itself whether to join the national leadership in affiliating with Rengō. The stage was set for the most damaging schism in Nikkyōso's history.

Disagreement over Education Reform

Coinciding with the historic changes taking place within the Japanese union movement, potential wholesale reform of the education system was also being debated in the mid-1980s. The Ad Hoc Council for Education (*Rinkyōshin*) was set up on the initiative of Prime Minister Nakasone in 1984. It was given the task of advising the government on "basic strategies for necessary reforms with regard to governmental policies and measures in various aspects, so as to secure such education as will be compatible with the social changes and cultural developments of our country."[49] (The content of *Rinkyōshin*'s proposals is discussed in more detail in chapter five.) As in previous national policy-making exercises, Nikkyōso was excluded from the policy-making stage of the proceedings, but the Ministry of Education's awareness of the union's power to disrupt reform at the implementation stage meant that it did have some influence. However, there were still elements in the final recommendations of *Rinkyōshin* that Nikkyōso was flatly opposed to. Of these, the two main bones of contention were the proposal for a new in-service education and training program for probationary teachers and the enforcement of the teaching of respect for the national anthem and flag. Nikkyōso was opposed to the first measure because they saw it as giving educational authorities greater control over new teachers (new teachers were to be placed under supervisors specially trained and appointed by local boards of education), and they were opposed to the second proposal because they saw it as an attempt by the right to bring back prewar style nationalism. Nikkyōso leaders were united by their opposition to these initiatives.[50] Splits arose, however, concerning the best methods to adopt in resisting them. In response to the teacher training program, left-wingers in the CEC (i.e., Communists and the left-wing part of the mainstream faction) called for a strategy of all-out opposition, resorting to open confrontation that would include demonstrations and (illegal) strikes. The right wing, however, argued that this approach would only weaken the union. Many within the union were worried about Nikkyōso's popular image as an organization that seemed opposed to all reform.[51] These people wanted to encourage negotiations with educational authorities at all levels to modify the program rather than reject it out of hand.[52] In a way, this dispute was nothing more than the old argument about direct confrontation versus noncooperation or negotiation, an argument about tactics that has been going on throughout Nikkyōso's history. The difference now was that the dispute coincided with a bitter disagreement over who should be the leader of the union, and an equally bitter fight over whether or not to affiliate with Rengō. Thus, the dispute over how to respond to *Rinkyōshin*'s education reforms was the final ingredient in a deadly cocktail that was to turn rivalry and disagreement into a full-scale schism.

Conclusion

The history of Nikkyōso between 1952 and 1988 is one of confrontation and conflict, not only between the union and its "enemies," but also within the union, between ideologically opposed groups of the left and right. The balance of power between left and right varied from prefecture to prefecture, but at the national level an uneasy alliance was maintained by the practice of sharing the top positions of secretary general and chairman between the rival groups. However, in the 1980s, this tradition of compromise was upset by the need to decide on whether to affiliate with the new national union federation, Rengō. The all-or-nothing nature of the decision about Rengō made it a question impossible to resolve in a way that would please both sides. The other problems that coincided with this issue—that is, disagreements over how to respond to the government's program of education reform and arguments over the personal opinions of chairman Tanaka—were problems that, by themselves, could have been resolved by compromise and consensus building. But, because they came along at the same time as the dispute over Rengō, they merely aggravated an already serious situation. Thus, it can be concluded that the dispute over the affiliation with Rengō was the primary cause of Nikkyōso's schism. In the next chapter we will examine the process by which the schism became a reality. We will look at the exact events of the schism at the level of nation, prefecture, and school.

CHAPTER THREE

NIKKYŌSO'S 1989 SCHISM: THE END OF AN ERA?

This chapter deals with the events of Nikkyōso's schism itself, starting with an analysis of the continuing factional dispute within Nikkyōso's Central Executive Committee (CEC) and the failure to arrive at a durable compromise. Then it moves on to describe the sequence of events that led to the breakaway of some prefectural unions to form an alternative national union that would not affiliate with Rengō. (A chronological table, Table 3.6, is included at the end of this chapter to summarize these events.) After this, two prefectures, Saitama and Aichi, are examined to show how the schism played itself out at the local level. Then the different outcomes of the schism in other prefectures are studied, using Rohlen's model of conflict within the Japanese education system as an analytical tool. Finally, there is an analysis of the ideological debate between the two sides that accompanied the schism.

Failure to Resolve Factional Differences Within the Leadership

Chapter two covered the origins of the split within Nikkyōso's JSP-supporting mainstream faction. Tanaka Ichirō, the chairman, led the right-wing group within this faction, and Nakakoji Kiyoo, the secretary general, led the left. They disagreed fundamentally over the union's approach to the proposed formation of Rengō and the stance that should be adopted to the reform proposals of Nakasone's *Rinkyōshin*. (The two issues were related by Rengō's favourable stance vis-à-vis Nakasone's reforms.[1] In other words, support for Rengō was incompatible with wholehearted opposition to Nakasone's reforms.) The dispute proved so intractable that Nikkyōso was unable to hold its national conference in 1986 or 1987. Tanaka, who was responsible for calling the conference, was unable to because of the danger of Nakakoji's group voting with the JCP-supporting anti-mainstream faction in order to block affiliation with Rengō. Out of a CEC of forty members, only seventeen could be definitely counted on by Tanaka. If the vote had gone against him, it is likely that Tanaka would have led his faction out of Nikkyōso to join Rengō by itself.[2] The story of Nikkyōso's schism would have taken a different course, but schism itself would not have been avoided.

The delayed national conference was finally called for February 1988. To make this possible, a compromise had been worked out between the two groups within the mainstream faction that involved the right-wing group giving up the chairmanship (to Fukuda Tadayoshi, who was neutral) in exchange for the left-wing group's endorsement of a positive policy toward unification with Rengō. The CEC endorsement of this policy was followed by approval from the February national conference. On the face of it, this compromise represents a considerable concession by the left-wing group on the issue of affiliation with Rengō. It is difficult to be sure about the motives of neutral members of the CEC and members of Nakakoji's left-wing group because they lacked the consistency of the right-wing group (who were always in favor of unification of Rengō) and the JCP-supporting faction (who were always opposed). Some of them may have been persuaded by the sheer size of the proposed national confederation, uniting, for the first time, private sector and public sector unions in Japan. Others may have had pressure put on them by colleagues in Sōhyō or the JSP who were more enthusiastic about the whole Rengō project.[3] There is also evidence that, for some, the move was purely tactical, designed only to prevent Tanaka's group from leaving the union. Nakakoji himself, for example, said at the time the compromise was worked out that "[i]t is not an overall statement. It is a provisional measure that was necessary in order to resolve an unusual situation. There was no choice but to reach an agreement in this form."[4] Nakakoji may have had a plan to try to reverse the decision on Rengō at the conference the following year. However, this idea soon came to be superseded by the plans of others. In the end it was left-wing leaders from outside the CEC who led their followers into a breakaway organization.

THE DECISION TO FORM A BREAKAWAY NATIONAL UNION

The professed anti-Communism of Rengō meant that JCP supporters within Nikkyōso had no option but to consider breaking away from the union once unification looked likely to proceed as planned (i.e., before the end of 1989). Nikkyōso was not the only public sector union to be placed in this predicament. In March 1989, left-wing members of Jichirō, the union of local government workers, formed a breakaway national union and at the same time called for the creation of a "class-conscious national center" to provide an alternative national federation to Rengō. Some leaders of Nikkyōso's prefectural organizations also decided that the time to act had come. It is at this point that the semi-independent nature of the prefectural unions that make up Nikkyōso started to work to the disadvantage of the union's unity. Because the prefectural unions are all separate legal entities, they have to arrive at individual resolutions whether to follow the national lead. Thus, in 1989, each prefectural organization had, at its annual conference, to decide whether or not to follow Nikkyōso into Rengō. Local left-wing leaders, Mikami Mitsuru (president of the Tokyo Metropolitan Teachers' Union) and Sayama Shigeru (president of Osaka High School Teachers' Union) decided not to attend the September national conference, but to set up a rival national organization instead. They organized a "union members' network conference" in Tokyo in July and then held a larger rally in August. These events were attended by representatives of thirty-three prefectural compulsory sector or high school unions. The official inauguration of the new union took place at a Conference in Tokyo held on November 17 and 18, 1989. Mikami was elected chairman and Sayama secretary general of the new organization that was given the official name of the All Japan Council of Teachers and Staff Unions, or Zenkyō for short. Zenkyō immediately affiliated itself with the labor confederation known as Zenrōren, the new militant JCP-supported alternative to Rengō. Zenrōren was the successor to the Council of Labour Unions for the Promotion of Labour-Front Unification—Tōitsu Rōsokon—a national organization that many moderate Socialists accused of being mainly a tool of the JCP. In 1997, both Nikkyōso and Zenkyō published fifty-year anniversary histories of the teachers' union movement in Japan. As might be expected, they give differing accounts of the events that led up to the schism of 1989. The Nikkyōso version accuses the leaders of the breakaway prefectural unions of working in concert with Tōistu Rōsokon and the JCP to actively bring about the schism.[5] The Zenkyō version for its part accuses Nikkyōso's

Table 3.1 After the Schism: Teachers' Union Membership in 1992

Prefecture	% *Nikkyōso*	% *Zenkyō*	% *Other*
Hokkaidō	45	10	8
Aomori	4	15	5
Iwate	55	0	10
Miyagi	32	0	5
Akita	38	10	10
Yamagata	54	0	8
Fukushima	29	5	14
Ibaraki	52	5	6
Tochigi	0.5	1	93
Gunma	16	11	8
Saitama	3	20	1
Chiba	41	3	9
Tokyo	18	23	20
Kanagawa	68	0	9
Niigata	62	2	9
Toyama	37	20	9
Ishikawa	62	0	2
Fukui	85	0	0
Yamanashi	57	0	32
Nagano	52	21	7
Gifu	1	8	22
Shizuoka	51	3	2
Aichi	49	6	2
Mie	83	0	0
Shiga	23	25	9
Kyoto	1	46	11
Osaka	30	28	13
Hyogo	43	11	8
Nara	26	28	7
Wakayama	2	51	4
Tottori	62	0	0

continued

Table 3.1 *continued*

Prefecture	% *Nikkyōso*	% *Zenkyō*	% *Other*
Shimane	3	13	28
Okayama	43	15	8
Hiroshima	48	6	12
Yamaguchi	3	16	35
Tokushima	4	0	67
Kagawa	0.5	3	62
Ehime	1	1	84
Kochi	7	21	15
Fukuoka	39	0	18
Saga	33	22	9
Nagasaki	16	12	4
Kumamoto	29	0	9
Oita	64	0	21
Miyazaki	22	0	24
Kagoshima	31	0	6
Okinawa	61	0	1
National Figures	**35%**	**11%**	**13%**

% = Percentage of total number of teachers in that prefecture who are members of prefectural organization affiliated to Nikkyōso or Zenkyō, or, in the case of "other," members of a local union that is not affiliated with either national organization. The residual percentage in each prefecture is made up of teachers who are not members of any union.

In 1992, there were 1,165,915 schoolteachers employed in Japan.

Source: Kyōiku iinkai geppō, June 1992.

JSP-friendly leadership of "surrendering" to the right-wing, anti-communist ideology of Rengō.[6] The two versions do not disagree about basic facts, names, dates, or places. More than anything, it is the *intentions* of the principal actors in this drama that are the subject of most dispute.

The formation of Zenkyō provided prefectural unions with a clear choice. Some local union conferences voted to stay with Nikkyōso and thus affiliate with Rengō. Others voted to go the other way and side with Zenkyō and Zenrōren. In many prefectures there was a large enough minority to break away from the main union and form a new, parallel organization. At a national conference held in March 1991, Zenkyō relaunched itself and united with Nikkōkyō, the national federation of senior high school teachers' unions that had previously been a branch of Nikkyōso. (This was indicative of how Zenkyō enjoyed proportionally more support among senior high school teachers than those in compulsory education.) At this time Zenkyō claimed a membership of 210,000.[7] Nikkyōso publications, however, put the figure at only 130,000.[8] Nikkyōso, for its part, claimed a post-schism membership of 430,000, a figure uncontested by Zenkyō.[9] Official Ministry of Education figures are close to the Nikkyōso interpretation of things.[10] The effects of the schism differed from prefecture to prefecture. In most cases, Nikkyōso-affiliated unions enjoyed greater support than their Zenkyō-affiliated rivals. In a smaller number of prefectures the reverse was the case. (See Table 3.1 for a detailed guide to what happened.)

As can be seen from the table, in some prefectures Zenkyō failed to have any impact. In Iwate, Miyagi, Yamagata, Kanagawa, Ishikawa, Fukui, Yamanashi, Mie, Tottori, Tokushima, five out of the seven Kyūshu prefectures, and Okinawa, they failed to get a prefectural organization off the ground. In other prefectures they were able to recruit more union members to their cause than Nikkyōso. In Aomori, Saitama, Tokyo, Shiga, Kyoto, Nara, Wakayama, Shimane, Yamaguchi, Kagawa, and Kōchi they outnumbered Nikkyōso affiliated members once the schism was over. How can such a variety of outcomes be explained? One of the purposes of this chapter is to address this question. Before moving on to explore whether any patterns can be discerned from the mixed set of results, the specific case of two prefectures, Saitama and Aichi, will be analyzed in detail.

The Schism: The Case of Saitama Prefecture

Saitama prefecture is to the north of Tokyo. Many of its 6.7 million population live in the south of the prefecture within commuting distance of the metropolis. This is where most of Saitama's forty-two cities lie and where its densely packed population continues to increase year by year. The administrative center of the prefecture is Urawa city, an old town that sits astride the Nakasendō, historically the alternative, northern route to the Tokaidō, the road between Tokyo and Osaka. Prefecture-wide organizations continue to have their head offices in Urawa, although since the expansion of the Shinkansen network made it an important transport hub, Omiya city to the north has now become the larger population center. At the time of the schism there was a process under way to merge the two cities (and a smaller one, Yono, which is sandwiched in-between) into one large city to be called Saitama city. Doing this would establish a population of over one million, and therefore will allow the new city to become a "designated city," receiving all the benefits that such status bestows.[11] Educationally, Saitama has a reputation for being a progressive prefecture. It has been in the forefront of national campaigns, such as the introduction of foreign language teachers to high schools as well as more flexible high school syllabuses. It has some excellent prefectural schools, but they have to compete with a higher than average concentration of private schools, both within Saitama and in neighboring Tokyo.

In 1947, the year of massive expansion of teacher unionism throughout the country, a Saitama teachers' union (Saikyōso) was established that included teachers from all sectors of the education system. This union affiliated itself with the new national union, Nikkyōso. When the backlash against left-wing unions occurred in the latter half of the Occupation a rival "anti-Nikkyōso" national organization called Zenkōkyo was formed with the intention of enticing senior high school teachers away from Nikkyōso. The Saitama affiliate of this organization was called the Saitama Prefecture Independent Senior High School Employees Union (Dokukōkyō). It was established in 1951. In response to this, Nikkyōso-supporting senior high school teachers formed a separate prefectural union called the Saitama Prefecture Senior High School Employees Union (Saikōkyō). This was created in 1953 and affiliated itself with the Nikkyōso-affiliated national federation of senior high school teachers called Nikkōkyō.[12] At the prefecture level both the Nikkyōso affiliates—that is, Saikyōso representing mainly elementary and junior high school teachers (in other words, teachers who taught children at the compulsory level of education) and Saikōkyō representing mainly senior high school teachers—coordinated joint campaigns through a special committee called the Saitama Education Employees Union Federation (Saikyōren). The separation of teachers into two organizations, one for the compulsory education sector and one for senior high schools, made sense because almost all senior high schools are administered directly by the prefectural board of education, while all elementary and junior high schools are administered by their local city board of education. Thus, this pattern became standard throughout most of the country.

The leadership of both Saikōkyō and Saikyōso had a reputation for being left wing, and had on occasion sanctioned the endorsement of Communist candidates at national and local elections. When Nikkyōso chairman Tanaka Ichirō attended a party in aid of LDP candidate Nishioka

Table 3.2 Teacher Union Membership Rates in Saitama[15]

Year	*Nikkyōso*	*Other*	*Zenkyō*
1964	77%	5%	—
1970	42	4	—
1973	41	4	—
1977	35	2	—
1981	33	1	—
1985	31	1	—
1988	29	1	—
1992	3	1	20%
1995	3	4	17
1997	3	4	16

(% = Percentage of teachers in the prefecture)
(Total number of teachers in the prefecture in 1997 = 50,073)

Takeo in April 1986, both Saitama unions joined in the wave of protest that followed.[13] The leadership of these unions was also adamantly opposed to unification with Rengō. From 1987 onward, both unions was also involved heavily in the campaign against the imposition of the *Hinomaru* and *Kimigayo* into school ceremonies. It was no surprise therefore that at a special conference in Urawa in October 1989 Saikōkyō decided to break from Nikkyōso and affiliate with Zenkyō. (Saitama, following the lead of Tokyo and Osaka, was one of the first prefectures to side openly with Zenkyō.) An overwhelming number of the delegates to the conference were in favor of this action. A motion to put the decision to a prefecture-wide vote was defeated, however.[14] This meant that the teachers in the schools and their school-level local organizational units (bunkai) were expected to go along with this decision now that it had been made. Individuals opposed to the decision therefore had to either "put up and shut up" or leave the prefectural union. The same process was simultaneously under way in the smaller Saikyōso.

Those Nikkyōso-supporting teachers who left their union now had to create two new prefectural organizations. In doing so they chose names for the new organizations that were identical to the old ones, except for the exclusion of the Japanese character for "prefecture" (*ken*). This led board of education employees to refer to the two rival pairs of unions as *ken ari* and *ken nashi* (with and without *ken*). Table 3.2 shows the consequence of the split in terms of proportion of teachers in the prefecture who belong to the rival groups. In 1988, the year before the schism, 29 percent of Saitama's teachers were members of the two Nikkyōso affiliated unions. By 1992, the year after the schism had ended, only 20 percent of teachers were in these unions and they had changed their affiliation to Zenkyō. Of those who had left, two-thirds had left altogether and one-third had left to join two new prefectural organizations affiliated with Nikkyōso

Saikōkyō's leadership called the setting up of the two new unions a reckless attempt to break up the unity of teachers in Saitama.[16] However, at the school level the parting of the ways that took place during the schism seems to have been, in Saitama at least, without animosity. Mostly it took the form of a small number of individual teachers leaving their local bunkai and forming a new one in the school. Often the new bunkai would only have one or two members. According to one of the participants, most of the members of this breakaway group were teachers in their late forties or early fifties, people who were at university at the time of the student disturbances (*funsō*), and remember the part played in those disturbances by Communists with strong beliefs. This experience left them with a strong suspicion of the motives of Communist activists and a deep unwillingness to take part in any organization that had Communists in control. From their point of view, the affiliation of Saitama teachers' organizations with Zenkyō represented nothing less than a cynical takeover of their unions by Communist activists.[17] This did not mean, however, that all those teachers who remained in Saikōkyō and Saikyōso were committed Communists. Rather, it seems that the majority of teachers followed the lead of the head of the bunkai, the bunchō in their particular school. Since the decision to affiliate with Zenkyō had been properly arrived at by conference, the bunchō were bound to follow the official line. It took an act of personal determination for an ordinary teacher to break from this consensus and leave his or her bunkai to form a new rival one within the same school when, as in the vast majority of schools in Saitama, the teacher would only be accompanied by one or two colleagues. Thus, the majority of union members in Saitama's schools followed the line of least resistance and stayed with their existing union.

The Schism: The Case of Aichi Prefecture

Aichi prefecture is located in the center of Japan. With a population of 6.9 million it is the main population center in that region. In contrast to

Table 3.3 The Schism and Teachers' Unions in Aichi and Nagoya

Before the Schism (All Unions Affiliated to Nikkyōso)

1. Aichi ken kyōshokuin kumiai (Aikyōso)—union for teachers in the compulsory sector in the whole of Aichi prefecture (including Nagoya).
2. Aichi ken kōtō gakkō kyōshokuin kumiai (Aikōkyō)—union for teachers in high schools in Aichi prefecture (excluding Nagoya).
3. Aichi ken shiritsukōkō kyōshokuin kumiai rengōkai (Aichishikyōren)—union for teachers at private high schools in the whole of Aichi prefecture (including Nagoya)
4. Nagoya shi kōtō gakkō kyōshokuin kumiai (Meikōkyō)[19]—union for teachers in high schools administered by Nagoya City.

After the Schism—Unions Affiliated to Nikkyōso

1. Aikyōso
2. Meikōkyō
3. Aichi kōtō gakkō kyōshokuin kumiai (Aikōso)—new union that broke away from Aikōkyō

After the Schism—Unions Affiliated to Zenkyō

1. Aikōkyō
2. Aichishikyōren

Saitama, Aichi has a reputation for being politically and educationally conservative.[18] The situation regarding teacher union organization is also different there. Although Saitama was in the process of establishing a designated city at the time of the schism, Aichi already had one in the form of Nagoya. In Japan a designated city has many of the functions and duties of a prefecture. Thus, a high school teacher working in a school administered by a designated city is an employee of the city, not the prefecture. As with prefectures, a designated city employee will normally spend his or her entire career working within institutions administered by the city. This arrangement means that Nagoya City high school teachers belong to a union distinct from the one that Aichi prefecture high school teachers belong to. At the time of the schism each union had its own decision to make about which direction to take. The affiliations of the different teachers' unions in Aichi and Nagoya are summarized in Table 3.3.

In 1989, the executive committees of the various Aichi and Nagoya unions had to decide whether to stay with Nikkyōso or join the newly founded Zenkyō. As with Saitama, local as well as national considerations came into force in the decision-making process. The story of what happened to the Aichi prefecture high school teachers' union, Aikōkyō, has parallels with the case of its equivalent union in Saitama, Saikōkyō.[20] In both cases a clear majority decided to take the side of Zenkyō and a small minority left the union to form a new Nikkyōso-affiliated organization. In both cases, also, the name of the new breakaway union was almost identical to that of the existing union. However, for the sake of clarity, the chosen abbreviated names were clearly different. In Saitama the original union Saikōkyō faces a rival calling itself Saitama Kōkyōso, while in Aichi, the original Aikōkyō faces a rival called Aikyōso. Another similarity is that, at the level of prefectural organization, the original union and the new breakaway union are unable to cooperate with each other. The chairman of the Executive Committee of Aikōkyo, Takahashi Sanaru, declared that "since the new union is so small there is no point in talking to it's representatives [at the prefectural level]."[21]

Similarities between Aichi and Saitama disappear, however, when the decisions of other teacher unions are examined. Aikyōso, the union representing compulsory sector teachers in Aichi (the biggest union in the prefecture), voted to stay with Nikkyōso and teachers within that organization who may have been sympathetic to Zenkyō decided not to form a new breakaway organization. Also, the union for high school teachers employed by Nagoya City, Meikōkyō, voted to stay with Nikkyōso. The case of Meikōkyō is particularly interesting because of the closeness of the vote in 1989—the decision to stay with Nikkyōso was carried at the union's Central Executive Committee by just one vote. This meant that there was a large number of teachers in the union who were very critical of Nikkyōso's shift to the right. They decided to remain with the union, but to fight for their ideals from within. The current chairman of Meikōkyō, Mori Jun, said that "we managed to avoid a split or an internal quarrel, but some of our members say it is very shameful to be in Nikkyōso."[22] Although these dissident members lost the very important vote of 1989, they subsequently achieved some smaller victories. For example, they prevented Meikōkyō from affiliating with the newly formed prefectural branch of Rengō in Aichi. This was despite the fact that Meikōkyō had been affiliated to that organization in its previous guise as a branch of Sōhyō.[23]

When this table is compared to the one for Saitama it can be seen that the movement to form a breakaway union organization in Aichi was not so successful. This may confirm Aichi's reputation as a "conservative" prefecture and Saitama's reputation as a "progressive" one. Labels like conservative or progressive, however, when applied to geographical

Table 3.4 Teacher Union Membership Rates in Aichi (including Nagoya)[24]

Year	*Nikkyōso*	*Other*	*Zenkyō*
1964	82%	0%	—
1970	74	0	—
1973	69	0	—
1977	62	1	—
1981	62	3	—
1985	59	3	—
1988	57	2	—
1992	49	2	7%
1995	48	2	6
1997	47	2	6

(% = Percentage of teachers in the prefecture)

(Total number of teachers in the prefecture in 1997 = 51,753)

areas can be less than helpful in an analysis of what actually happened during a complex event like Nikkyōso's schism. A survey of what occurred in the other prefectures will also reveal the problematic nature of simple labels or monocausal explanations.

The Schism: Other Prefectures

In Saitama and Aichi prefectures the schism unfolded in a particular way. Other prefectures had comparable experiences. However, the fact that so many more prefectures had completely different experiences is indicative of the variety of the types of organization that made up Nikkyōso. It has already been pointed out that Nikkyōso's national leadership had difficulty whipping the prefectural organizations into line on many occasions. It should also be noted that the local balance of political and administrative forces also varied from prefecture to prefecture. Although the Japanese system of educational administration has a reputation for centralized control, scholars like Thomas Rohlen, Steven Reed, Purnendra Jain, and Muramatsu Michio have thrown considerable light onto the possible diversity of local, prefecture-based politics.[25] Although constrained by regulations from the center, local politicians, officials, and other actors do have some discretion about prefectural education policy. Reed pointed to the crucial importance of the prefectural balance of power between teachers' unions and conservatives in determining the nature of local educational politics.[26] One of the contentions of the present study is that this balance of power helped determine the outcome of Nikkyōso's schism at the prefectural level. Before developing this theory further, it is first necessary to get a clearer view of the different types of outcome that occurred. This will be done by dividing these outcomes into five categories.

1. **Nikkyōso unchallenged,** that is, the failure of Zenkyō to form any prefectural organization at all. (Fifteen prefectures: Iwate, Miyagi, Yamagata, Kanagawa, Ishikawa, Fukui, Yamanashi, Mie, Tottori, Fukuoka, Kumamoto, Oita, Miyazaki, Kagoshima, Okinawa.)

2. **Nikkyōso dominant,** that is, those cases when Nikkyōso won at least twice as much support as Zenkyō. (Twelve prefectures: Hokkaido, Akita, Fukushima, Ibaraki, Chiba, Niigata, Nagano, Shizuoka, Aichi, Hyogo, Okayama, Hiroshima.)

3. **Evenly divided,** that is, those prefectures in which neither rival was able to gain the upper hand. (Eight prefectures: Tokyo, Gunma, Toyama, Shiga, Osaka, Nara, Nagasaki, Saga.)

4. **Zenkyō dominant,** that is, those cases in which Zenkyō won at least twice as much support as Nikkyōso. (Eight prefectures: Aomori, Saitama, Gifu, Kyoto, Wakayama, Shimane, Yamaguchi, Kōchi.)

5. **Both decimated,** that is, those cases when the combined membership of both unions was less than 5 percent of the prefectural teaching force. (Four prefectures: Tochigi, Tokushima, Kagawa, Ehime.)

To develop a theory about what happened at the prefecture level in Nikkyōso's schism, we must first review existing (i.e., pre-schism) theory about the balance of power within the educational establishments of Japanese prefectures. Thomas Rohlen's analysis of conflict at the three levels of the education system provides a very useful model for studying this kind of balance of power. We will now examine Rohlen's theory as it applied to the pre-schism education establishment and then apply it to the post-schism situation. In so doing, we will arrive at a set of possible explanations for the five different categories of prefecture previously described.

Rohlen's Theory of Power and Conflict Within the Education System

Anthropologist Thomas Rohlen wrote a paper in 1984 entitled "Conflict in Institutional Environments: Politics in Education." He was interested in how institutions adapt to accommodate a situation of continued conflict between parties located within those institutions. The coexistence of high-profile national disputes over education with the smooth running of the vast majority of Japan's educational institutions seemed to be a paradox that needed to be explained. In his research Rohlen discovered that the type of political conflict to be found within the Japanese education system varied considerably, depending on which administrative level was being examined. He drew the following conclusions about the three most important levels of the system: the school level; the prefectural level; and the national level. We will look at these first before moving on to an analysis of the effect of the schism on Rohlen's theory.

The School Level

"Centrist" leadership usually emerges in most schools because everyone realizes that simple majority rule is not sufficient for the smooth functioning of a small institution that routinely brings teachers into face-to-face contact with each other. In this kind of situation one often finds principals subverting the Office of Education's authority and union leaders tempering directives from union headquarters to minimize disruption in the day-to-day life of the school. In other words, "the school, rather than the administration or the union, becomes the main focus of loyalty."[27] (Exceptional schools are "union castles" in which the local union branch is very active and politicized.) It seems that most teachers are as distrustful of union "interference" as they are of government "interference." Often they like to play one off against the other, so they respect local leaders who are centrist and can strike a balance. Rohlen concludes that "the very nature of most school-level conflict is so local and particular in origin that it cannot be generalised."[28]

The Prefectural Level

The strength of Nikkyōso in the prefecture (or designated city), the politics of the school board, and the history of interaction between these two are the leading forces shaping the character of conflict. For example, punishment of strikers varies greatly from prefecture to prefecture. "During the *shuntō* strike of 1975, for example, nearly every teacher who went on strike belonging to Shiga prefecture's very weak union received some kind of punishment [from a school board appointed by a conservative governor]; whereas only nineteen union leaders out of more than ten thousand strikers were punished in Tokyo where the school board [was] appointed by a governor backed by the Socialist and Communist parties."[29] When strong mainstream unions and determined offices of education (e.g., those in Hokkaido, Fukuoka, and Kagoshima) confronted one another over the imposition of the *shunin* system in 1976, the conflict became very intense (see chapter five for more details about the *shunin* system).

Rohlen concluded that the prefectural level of conflict was characterized by the following three traits:

1. Considerable independence from national authority

2. A distinct set of institutional and organizational interests separate from the school and the national levels

3. Limited authority over, but great reliance on, school-level responses

The National Level

Rohlen agrees with the conventional view that postwar national educational politics is best characterized as "warfare between the entrenched" and concludes that "the intensity of the conflict waxes and wanes but remains essentially political. There is less reason to compromise at the national level, since responsibility for the normal functioning of school lies elsewhere."[30] Both sides are geared for conflict and their normal public postures are hostile. Maintaining this kind of position for any length of time would be very difficult at the prefecture level and impossible in schools. The LDP regards fighting the union as an aspect of dealing with the political opposition. This is Rohlen's explanation for the apparent postwar contradiction of the coexistence of a highly volatile and confrontational national situation alongside smooth, efficient, educational provision in the vast majority of cases at the local level. Thus, "the majority of Japanese schools are more independent and less political than anyone would predict from events at the national level."[31]

The Schism and Rohlen's Theory

The pattern of conflict has been changed by Nikkyōso's decision to end its national strategy of opposition and noncompliance in favor of one of conciliation and compromise. Rohlen points out that it is unusual for a state of conflict to persist for so long in one institution.[32] So, according to this argument, the ending of (large-scale) confrontation in the Japanese education system is not really as remarkable as the fact that it persisted for so long (almost forty years).

In his article Rohlen points to one of the long-term factors that would eventually take the fight out of Nikkyōso: "A few . . . prefectural unions have a feisty leadership, but as a general rule aggressive moves by such weak unions lead to further declines in teacher enrolment rates."[33] There seems to be a "critical mass" in the membership of a union above which it makes sense for individual members to join or maintain their membership for the simple reason that that is "the done thing" that the majority of the people around them are also doing. One new teacher I interviewed at a Nagoya City high school said that she "joined the union [Meikōkyō] because everyone else was a member. Actually I'm not very interested in politics."[34] At that school, and indeed at most Nagoya City high schools, union membership runs at 90 percent—a union density rate that is rarely achieved in the rest of the country and harks back to the heyday of Nikkyōso.

In times of serious conflict, the support and camaraderie of a large membership around the individual is comforting, and quitting the struggle or the union will be difficult to do because of feelings of betrayal to the group and worries about ostracism. However, when enough people *have* left the local union, the temptation to join them will become very strong for all but those who are very ideologically committed to both the aims of the particular struggle in question and the tactics their union (both local and national) is using. After a large enough number of teachers have quit it becomes very risky for the leadership to lead the remainder into a divisive or difficult struggle for fear that they too will jump ship. This concept of critical mass seems to have consequences at all three of Rohlen's levels. As noted in chapters two and three, it certainly looks as though one of the motivating factors behind Nikkyōso's change of course in the late 1980s was a concern that their national posture of confrontation was losing them members at an unsustainable rate. Learning from the examples of militant prefectural unions in analogous circumstances, they decided that, for them, discretion was the better part of valor. Warfare between the entrenched was over and Nikkyōso's leadership called for an armistice.

The decision of Nikkyōso's national leadership to end its posture of confrontation does not, of course, mean that conflict within the education system is now a thing of the past. Indeed, the recent schism within the union brought about by this change of heart has actually *added* a potentially new dimension to the conflict in the form of Nikkyōso versus Zenkyō rivalries and disputes. We will now examine this new type of conflict and how it affects all three levels of the system.

The School Level After the Schism

As Rohlen rightly points out, this is the most difficult level to generalize about, and the recent union schism has made the picture even more messy. Now, besides the split between union members and nonmembers, there is the addition of another group of union members who will have a separate leader, separate meetings, separate directives from their prefectural or national headquarters, and a separate set of norms, perspectives, and aims.

In Kobe, where Rohlen did most of his primary ethnographic research, he found four types of school situation (there are twenty-eight public senior high schools in Kobe).

1. Union castles—that is, schools where most of the staff are active members of the union (three or four schools)

2. Schools with totally dormant union chapters (two or three schools)

3. Schools with a small but dedicated local union that has a limited influence over the rest of the staff, and where there is a dedicated group of anti-union teachers (about eight schools)

4. Schools where the staff are very reluctant to take "political" action, but will act in support of the union over issues that will benefit the school as a whole (the majority of schools in Kobe)

Theoretically, a post-schism list would be longer and take into account the existence of a second national teachers' union, Zenkyō.

Post-Schism School Types

(a) Union castles—Nikkyōso only

(b) Union castles—Zenkyō only

(c) Union castles—Nikkyōso and Zenkyō combined

(d) Schools with totally dormant union chapters

(e) Schools with no union members at all

(f) Schools like Rohlen's category (3)—Nikkyōso

(g) Schools like Rohlen's category (3)—Zenkyō

(h) Schools like Rohlen's category (3)—Nikkyōso and Zenkyō

(i) Schools like Rohlen's category (4)—Nikkyōso

(j) Schools like Rohlen's category (4)—Zenkyō

(k) Schools like Rohlen's category (4)—Nikkyōso and Zenkyō

It should be stressed that this is a theoretical list. The number of types of post-schism category will vary from prefecture to prefecture. In sixteen prefectures there will be no Zenkyō affiliates because there is no prefectural organization affiliated with Zenkyō (see Table 3.1 for the full list of what happened in each prefecture). In other prefectures, because of the way decisions were made about who to affiliate with at the time of the schism, it will not be possible to have two different unions at the same school. It is even possible that some of the categories do not exist in reality anywhere. Category (3), for example, may not exist because of the small number of schools in each prefecture that are union castles and the tendency of members in a strong school-based union to follow that union's leadership. In all categories (except for the dormant one) the affiliation of the school branch will be important in determining the levels of conflict and management–teacher relations in each school.

What will conflict be like in these new categories? Because Zenkyō's stated aim is not to abandon the struggle against the old enemies, it can be assumed that in Zenkyō-only schools the situation will be very similar to what it was like pre-schism. I found one junior high school in Saitama where this was certainly the case.[35] Thus, Rohlen's categories 1, 3, and 4 will correspond to post-schism categories (b), (g) and (j). In the corresponding categories in which Nikkyōso is substituted for Zenkyō—that is, (a), (f), and (i)—the situation will probably be different, although it should not be assumed that just because a local branch has decided to stay with Nikkyōso instead of breaking off and joining Zenkyō, that this means they will necessarily be less confrontational than they were before. Exactly as Rohlen points out, local branches can be highly selective about which national or prefectural directives they choose to follow and which they choose to ignore.

Yet another variable has to be considered in those schools that have both a Zenkyō and a Nikkyōso affiliate. That variable would be the degree of cooperation between the two groups. One school in Saitama prefecture, a commercial high school where I conducted research, can probably be regarded as post-schism category (k). At this school twenty years ago 80 percent of the teachers were in the union. Now the figure is more like 40 percent—that is, twenty-five teachers, of whom three are in the Nikkyōso affiliate and the rest are in the Zenkyō affiliate.[36] The three who left the branch union to form a new branch that would maintain their allegiance to Nikkyōso did so because they hated the Communist Party and distrusted the national Zenkyō leadership whom they suspected of taking over the teachers' union for political purposes. They had no quarrel, however, with their colleagues in the school who remained in the Zenkyō-affiliated branch. In all matters relating to the interests of the school or fellow members of staff the two groups are able to work together.[37] I was told, however, that in other schools in Saitama there was intense rivalry between the two groups. It is probable that situations like Rohlen's story about the bitter staffroom dispute that erupted over the volleyball coach's request to allow his team to miss the annual ski trip in order to get in more practice for an important tournament[38] could develop an extra dimension as petty personal rivalries and grudges can now be played out, not only on a union—anti-union axis, but also on a Nikkyōso–Zenkyō axis. If they do occur, these kinds of petty disputes are likely to drive even more people out of membership of both unions.

Another school in Saitama at which I conducted research is an academic high school. Fifteen years ago it could have been classified as Rohlen category 4—that is, not a center for political activity but a school with a fairly large union membership (about 60 percent) who would act in defense of school or staff interests if they needed to. However, because the school is a very high status school in the prefecture they usually had few quarrels with the Board of Education. Today the union situation is more like "dormant" with only ten members (about 17 percent of the total staff). All of them are in the Zenkyō affiliate. A decline in the strength of the union has made little difference to this school that has been without serious internal conflict for most of its history.[39]

Clearly, what is required now is more detailed ethnographic research of the kind Rohlen conducted in the 1980s to bring our knowledge of school-level power relations in the post-schism education system up-to-date. More detailed and extensive research in other parts of the country should help us to arrive at more of an understanding of the accuracy of the suggested post-schism categories of school-level conflict and also give us an indication of the frequency of occurrence of each particular category. For this kind of knowledge, there is no substitute for actually visiting the schools themselves and conducting ethnographic research. Only by this method will a true picture of power relations within Japanese schools be arrived at. In the absence of more detailed school-level research, however, we can posit some general conclusions about the effects of the schism on power relations at the local level. Just before the schism, Thurston noted that "the decline in effective leadership at the national level has contributed to the general weakening of Nikkyōso throughout Japan."[40] There is no question that the national level infighting, combined with the acceleration in the decline of the membership, can only have had the effect of reducing the power and influence of school-based teachers' unions even further. This will have strengthened the discretionary powers of school management and local bureaucracy.

The Prefectural Level After the Schism: Five Categories of Outcome

Rohlen's analysis of the prefectural level of the education system and how it is interconnected with the other two levels provides a useful starting point for arriving at explanations for the different prefectural outcomes of Nikkyōso's schism. We will deal with each category in turn.

Category one: Nikkyōso unchallenged. Rohlen's point about the history of the relationship between prefectural union leadership and the prefectural political establishment (governor, board of education, and prefectural legislature) is important here. The category of prefectures in which Zenkyō failed completely to set up an organization includes Kanagawa and Okinawa, prefectures that were well known before the schism for having good relations between the prefectural union leadership and the local governor. The category also includes Oita, a prefecture whose pre-schism politics will be looked at in more detail in chapter seven. In this prefecture, local LDP politicians had courted the support of teachers' unions since the 1960s and, thus, from the point of view of the unions in Oita, Nikkyōso's policy in the 1980s of compromising with the LDP nationally did not represent any kind of a betrayal.

Another feature of Oita prefecture is the lack of influence of the local Communist Party. Electorally, the JCP in Oita has always been very weak and this may have been a factor in accounting for the lack of support for Zenkyō when the schism came. If this is true for Oita, how true is it for other prefectures? Zenkyō had, from its very beginning, close connections with the JCP and with other unions associated with the JCP and the Communist national union federation Zenrōren, so it would be logical to assume a correlation between JCP strength in a given prefecture and Zenkyō strength. However, we have already seen in the case of Saitama prefecture that a given teacher's membership of Zenkyō did not necessarily mean that he or she was a JCP supporter, and so any simple theories of correlation must be approached with caution. In fact, looking at Table 3.5, we

Table 3.5 Comparison of JCP Strength and Zenkyō Strength

Prefecture	*% vote for JCP*	*JCP LH Members '96*	*% Zenkyō Membership*
Hokkaidō	7	0	10
Aomori	6	0	15
Iwate	4	0	0
Miyagi	5	0	0
Akita	7	0	10
Yamagata	6	0	0
Fukushima	4	0	5
Ibaraki	4	0	5
Tochigi	2	0	1
Gunma	4	0	11
Saitama	10	1	20
Chiba	7	1	3
Tokyo	14	5	23
Kanagawa	7	0	0
Niigata	4	0	2

continued

Table 3.5 *continued*

Prefecture	*% vote for JCP*	*JCP LH Members '96*	*% Zenkyō Membership*
Toyama	3	0	20
Ishikawa	5	0	0
Fukui	4	0	0
Yamanashi	4	0	0
Nagano	7	0	21
Gifu	5	0	8
Shizuoka	6	0	3
Aichi	7	0	6
Mie	4	0	0
Shiga	9	0	25
Kyoto	19	2	46
Osaka	17	4	28
Hyogo	7	0	11
Nara	11	0	28
Wakayama	9	0	51
Tottori	7	0	0
Shimane	9	0	13
Okayama	5	0	15
Hiroshima	4	0	6
Yamaguchi	6	0	16
Tokushima	4	0	0
Kagawa	5	0	3
Ehime	4	0	1
Kochi	14	1	21
Fukuoka	9	0	0
Saga	2	0	22
Nagasaki	3	0	12
Kumamoto	2	0	0
Oita	3	0	0
Miyazaki	2	0	0
Kagoshima	2	0	0
Okinawa	14	1	0
National Figures	**6%**	**15**	**11%**

Source: Kyōiku iinkai geppōu, June 1992, and *Kokkai Yōran,* 1996. [LH = lower house]

can see that although there are other prefectures like Oita in which a weak electoral showing of the JCP coincides with the inability of Zenkyō to form a local organization (these are all in kyūshū), there are also cases, like Okinawa, where the JCP is electorally quite strong and yet Zenkyō still was unable to get an organization off the ground. The relationship between JCP strength and Zenkyō strength is clearly of limited explanatory value in analyzing why the schism took the form that it did. It was a factor in some prefectures, but not in others. Thus, Rohlen's point about the importance of the particular relationship between local politicians and officials with local union leaders is given added weight. Therefore, to analyze why Zenkyō failed to get off the ground in a specific prefecture would require the kind of anthropological analysis of the distribution of local power that Rohlen conducted for his research. Political scientists can then examine the results of anthropological research at the local level to design better models of how power is distributed at the national level.

Category two: Nikkyōso dominant. This category covers those prefectures (twelve in number) which Nikkyōso was able to beat off the Zenkyō challenge, but Zenkyō supporters were still able to set up small, local organizations. Aichi prefecture, which we have already examined in some detail, is included in this category. The existence in that prefecture of large numbers of teachers who were highly critical of Nikkyōso's shift to the right in 1989 but nevertheless remained within organizations formally affiliated to Nikkyōso should caution us against assuming that teachers in Nikkyōso-dominant prefectures will necessarily support their national leadership.

In the case of Aichi prefecture as well as in some other instances within this category, teachers were able to break away from the established organizations without too much animosity or rancor. In other cases the schism did not pass so peacefully. In Hokkaido, where, because of the size of the prefecture, another layer of union organization exists between the prefecture and the school bunkai, a bitter conflict broke out between Nikkyōso and Zenkyō supporters. Disputes arose over which group was entitled to use existing union premises and funds. The Nikkyōso establishment accused Zenkyō supporters of breaking union rules and mounting a politically motivated campaign on behalf of the JCP.[41] In the end Nikkyōso retained the loyalty of the majority of Hokkaido's unionized teachers. One reason why there is no uniform correlation between JCP strength and Zenkyō strength may be that an active JCP presence in a prefecture or city, as well as mobilizing supporters of Zenkyō, also has the effect of encouraging enemies of the JCP to become active too. The result is, as Rohlen's theory would have predicted, a very complex interaction of forces within the prefecture, the results of which do not follow any simple, national pattern.

Category three: Evenly divided. This category includes the two key prefectures of Tokyo and Osaka, metropolitan centers where radicalism and Communism have traditionally been strong, but that are of such crucial, strategic importance that Nikkyōso could not allow them to fall into Zenkyō's hands. As we have seen, it was the leaders of Osaka and Tokyo unions who were instrumental in the formation of Zenkyō. Nikkyōso loyalists were quick to respond in setting up rival organizations. In the case of Shiga prefecture, the even split between the two sides may have been due to weak prefectural leadership prior to the schism, allowing school-based activists to take the initiative when the breakup of the union began. Indeed, it it highly likely that local leadership was a decisive factor in determining the outcome of the schism for each prefecture. Thus, research into the nature of the leadership of each prefectural organization would be required to arrive at a thorough and definite explanation of why each prefecture developed as it did. The mass unionization of Japan's teachers under Nikkyōso's leadership in the late 1940s was a genuinely national phenomenon. However, when the union so created came to fall apart forty years later, the exact details of the story varied from prefecture to prefecture and city to city.

Category four: Zenkyō dominant. This category includes Saitama, the case we have already examined in detail. Saitama is also a prefecture with a reasonably strong Communist presence (by national standards). If there is a link between JCP strength and Zenkyō strength in Saitama, to what extent is this link present in other prefectures in this category? The most positive affirmation of this connection comes from Kyoto prefecture where 46 percent of the teachers belong to Zenkyō affiliated unions and only 1 percent opted to stay with Nikkyōso. In the same prefecture in the lower house election of 1993 (a fairly typical year electorally for the JCP in the 1990s) the Communists won 19.4 percent of the vote (against a national average of 6.4 percent) and two Diet seats (out of a national total of fifteen), confirming Kyoto's place in postwar politics as a Communist stronghold. Kōchi, too, is an example of a prefecture with a strong JCP tradition (represented by the veteran Diet member Yamahara Kenjirō, elected for ten consecutive times before finally being beaten in 2000) giving rise to Zenkyō dominance. However, as can be seen from Table 3.5, the same simple equation of JCP strength with Zenkyō strength does not work so well in the other prefectures in this category. None of them have had a JCP Diet member in recent memory and in three of them

(Aomori, Gifu, and Yamaguchi) the JCP vote in 1993 was below the national average for that party.

Category five: Both decimated. This category is not directly relevant to the present discussion since the breaking of the unions concerned took place in the 1950s and early 1960s. The four prefectures in this category, Tochigi, Tokushima, Kagawa, and Ehime, were all in the front line of Nikkyōso's struggles with the government and local education authorities over the teacher efficiency rating plan discussed in chapter two. They were all cases of militant union leaderships confronting unyielding, conservative, local political establishments. What is interesting is that tiny though their memberships were by 1989, three out of the four of these prefectural unions split at the time of the schism, thus weakening their voice in the prefecture even further. It is certain that the few teachers who were still union members in these prefectures were motivated primarily by ideology. Thus, when the schism occurred, they divided along ideological lines. If the experiences of teachers in Saitama is a guide, then the main ideological division would have been support for or antipathy to the JCP. Why this failed to happen in the fourth prefecture, Tokushima, is a question that can only be answered by investigating the personal motivations of the main union leaders and activists in that prefecture.

Summary of all five categories. The events of the schism have reinforced the conclusions reached by Rohlen in his analysis of the three different levels of power and confrontation within the Japanese education system. The sheer variety of outcome from the schism underlines his point about the existence of distinct sets of organizational interests that exist at the prefectural level, separate from the school and national levels. In particular, the relationship between the prefectural union leadership and the local political leadership was of crucial importance in determining what would happen in that prefecture when the schism occurred.

The National Level After the Schism

This was where Rohlen saw the most conflict taking place, and it is here the changes of recent years have been most profound. Rohlen argued that conflict was greatest at this level because there is almost no face-to-face contact between the two sides, while the responsibility for the normal functioning of the school system lay elsewhere. Indeed, it is quite remarkable how old Nikkyōso and the MOE could conduct virtually parallel debates and research programs about all kinds of noncontroversial educational issues without any form of cooperation or sharing taking place. It now seems that some Nikkyōso members and sympathizers have come to regard this as an irrational state of affairs, and so the logic of working together to deal with problems like *ijime* (bullying) and school refusal was another motivating factor in Nikkyōso's recent willingness to compromise. This is not a new argument, but it does seem that recent changes in the nature of the debate on education have, to some extent, depoliticized the discourse. Zenkyō members and sympathizers would violently disagree with this opinion and say that education is just as much a political battlefield as ever it was in the 1950s, 1960s, or 1970s. This ideological division will be dealt with more thoroughly later and in chapter five.

A desire to cooperate in educational research alone would not have brought about Nikkyōso's recent U-turn on confrontation to the MOE. I would argue that once again membership is the key factor. This is a factor that has profound effects on union leadership at all three levels. The prefectural and national organizations are nothing without active school-based unions recruiting and maintaining sufficient members. Rohlen showed how most teachers' loyalty was mainly to their school. This means that most teachers will only join and maintain their membership if doing so makes sense for their day-to-day school life. It seems that if the majority of a given teacher's colleagues are in the union, then he or she will also stay as a member, but if the membership level falls below a critical mass, then the chances are that teacher will start to think about quitting. Rohlen said that national level leaderships in the education world don't have to live with the consequences of conflict, and that that is why they are more inclined to bring about conflict. However, that is not the case with the issue of membership, because decisions made at the national level will bring teachers at the school level into conflict with their colleagues and superiors and will therefore put pressure on their loyalty to the union (except in cases in which they can see a clear connection between union aims and their own personal aims and/or the interests of their own specific school). In other words, the decline in membership brought home to the union leadership the fact that they *did* have to live with the consequences of conflict.

The Ideology of the Schism

As we have seen, the main issue over which Nikkyōso's schism was fought was the decision to join in the labor unification movement that led to the formation of Rengō. Disagreement over this issue was, of course, only the tip of an ideological iceberg. The whole history of Nikkyōso since its formation has been dogged by disagreements over ideology, strategy, and tactics. The schism provides an excellent opportunity to examine the conflict of ideas within the union that might, in normal times, have gone on in private or coded language, but was now publicly displayed for all to see. This conflict raged at every level of the union organization and throughout the country, but it contained common themes. We will now examine the basic positions of the two sides.

Zenkyō's Position

It is significant that at their first real national conference in 1991 Zenkyō delegates voted an "Action Policy" to promote two grand campaigns. These were "for the defence of the Peace Constitution and for the establishment of a genuine democratic education."[42] Both slogans are familiar to any student of pre-schism Nikkyōso, and they represent Zenkyō's determined effort to be seen as the carriers of the true mantle of teacher unionism in Japan. We will now examine in more detail what these slogans mean before moving on to consider the specific criticisms Zenkyō was making (and continues to make) about the new direction of Nikkyōso.

Zenkyō's Pacifism

1. Zenkyō adopted as its main slogan the pacifist slogan of old Nikkyōso: "Never send our children to the battlefield again."

2. Zenkyō campaigns for the elimination of all nuclear weapons. It collects signatures and sends A-bomb materials to schools in other countries.

3. Zenkyō was very active in the anti-PKO campaign, raising funds for transportation and sending demonstrators to Tokyo fifty-four times between 1991 and 1996. There were also many demonstrations at the local level, including lunch-break demonstrations in schools.

4. Zenkyō is opposed to the "glorification" of Japanese militarism in the curriculum. For example, it opposed the introduction of stories about the achievements of Admiral Tōgo in history textbooks.[43]

Zenkyō's Campaign for "Democratic Education" Main Points

1. Opposition to the legally binding nature of the Ministry of Education's "course of study" (which used to be just a guideline until the ministry unilaterally made it compulsory). Instead the curriculum should be organized "independently and democratically in each school." This campaign includes opposition to the compulsory singing of the anthem and flying of the flag (introduced in the 1989 course of study) and opposition to the central screening of textbooks.

2. Campaign to do away with the whole high school entrance exam system. All students should automatically get into high school free of charge (This involves increasing the proportion of the national budget spent on education by cutting the military budget).

3. Proposals to hire more personnel and reduce class size. There has been a big signature campaign to achieve this—in five years they collected 100 million signatures.

4. Zenkyō convenes a four-day National Assembly for Educational Research every year. More than 15,000 teachers, researchers, parents, workers, and citizens across the country participate. (This will be discussed in more detail in chapter five). There are similar, smaller assemblies at municipal and prefectural level held throughout the year.

Zenkyō's View of Nikkyōso

The previous outline of Zenkyō's position on the issues it considers most important shows how faithful the new union remained to Nikkyōso's traditional principles. Zenkyō and its supporters believe that Nikkyōso has been diverted onto a mistaken and heretical path by a right-wing leadership that, by proposing collaboration with the old enemy, must be either foolish or traitorous or both. In fact, many of the aims and objectives of Zenkyō are shared by Nikkyōso. The significant difference lies more in the methods used to achieve these aims. Roesgaard remarks that now Nikkyōso's "reactions are tempered by the desire to be a mainstream organisation and the desire to be on good terms with the Ministry of Education in order to play a more important part in the policy making stage."[44] Zenkyō believes that this kind of attempt to gain more influence over policy-making is doomed to failure. Certainly, since the schism

Nikkyōso's leadership has watered down its adherence to strict opposition to the ministry in many areas. However, it still claims not to have abandoned its principles. We will now examine post-schism Nikkyōso's position more closely.

Nikkyōso's Post-schism Position

The right-wing group within Nikkyōso's mainstream faction believed that it was essential that Nikkyōso should fully play a part in the unification of the labor movement as it gained momentum during the 1980s. Not to do so would sideline Nikkyōso to the margins of Japanese unionism. They believed that the militancy that characterized Nikkyōso and its public sector union allies in the 1950s would be inappropriate and counterproductive for the 1990s and beyond. If the decline in Nikkyōso's membership and influence was to be addressed, a new direction would have to be embarked on. This would involve compromise with the union's traditional enemies, the LDP and the Ministry of Education. However, even to talk of compromise was to invite hostile attack from the left wing of the union. The word the right used to describe the kind of compromise they were promoting was *ayumiyori,* which literally means walking together and implies concession-making by both sides. In response, the left joked that what was really happening was *suriyori*—that is, the right sidling up to the LDP and the ministry, since all the concessions seemed to be coming from Nikkyōso's side only.[45] To fight off this criticism, right-wing leaders had to argue that they were upholding Nikkyōso's main principles while at the same time modifying their strategy and tactics in line with the changing circumstances around them.

Modernization of Nikkyōso's position has basically taken the form of removing the overtly Marxist rhetoric from their public statements. Nikkyōso had often been criticized for putting politics first and forgetting about the interests of children. The traditional left-wing response to this point has been to argue that it is precisely because the Japanese government has ignored both the spirit and the letter of the Fundamental Law of Education and the Constitution that the interests of Japanese children have suffered. Thus, addressing the problems faced by children was inevitably a political issue. The right within Nikkyōso has come to withdraw from that position and now prefers to talk directly about the needs of children and parents without a gloss of political rhetoric. Indeed, Nikkyōso now attacks Zenkyō precisely for being too political and too much under the political control of one political party, the JCP. The accusation is that Zenkyō's aims and objectives are always brought into line with what the JCP wants.[46] The right in Nikkyōso have also been critical of the way Zenkyō went about seceding from the main union. For example, in the case of Hokkaidō, Zenkyō activists were accused of illegally occupying Nikkyōso buildings and spending Nikkyōso money to publicize their case and recruit members to their cause.[47] Thus, at both the local and national levels Zenkyō supporters have been accused of using underhand methods to engineer the illegitimate political takeover of a union by a political party. In reply, JCP supporters argue that the right within Nikkyōso, especially at the executive level, has often been too much under the influence of the Japan Socialist Party. (Both sets of accusations are, of course, grist to the mill for right-wing enemies of Nikkyōso in the LDP and elsewhere who have always accused Nikkyōso of being concerned too much with politics and not enough with education.)

Both sides accuse the other of playing into the hands of the enemy. Nikkyōso is accused by Zenkyō of collaboration or surrender, while Nikkyōso, for its part, accuses Zenkyō of deliberately causing the schism to advance the particular program of the JCP. Not surprisingly, at the national level post-schism relations between the two sides are very poor.[48] However, at the local level the situation is more complicated. In the case of Saitama, prefectural representatives of the unions do not cooperate, but members of different unions in the same school often do.[49] This is not unusual because it is easy for national or prefectural leaders to avoid each other if they so choose. Teachers in the same school, however, have to work together every day.

Conclusion

Nikkyōso's schism was an event that took place in every corner of Japan and involved the decisions of tens of thousands of individual teachers. While it seems that large numbers of union members simply followed the direction of their bunkai leaders, other members chose not to, and some used the events of the schism as an opportunity to quit union membership altogether. When analyzing the motivations of such a large number of people, simple rules of cause and effect are difficult to come by. The differing ways in which the schism was played out in different prefectures confirmed the analysis of anthropologists like Rohlen and political scientists like Reed who were keen to point out how distributions of power and influence vary considerably from prefecture to prefecture. However, this does not mean that the schism was an event without pattern or order. The analysis of Saitama and Aichi prefectures contained in this chapter explains why the schism developed the way it did in those particular prefectures. Many of the particular debates and dilemmas that I came across in Saitama and Aichi would have been paralleled in other prefectures, and the similarity of union structure from prefecture to prefecture make it possible to make generalizations and theoretical propositions that can be tested by further analysis. To test these kinds of hypotheses there is no substitute for research carried out within the individual prefecture concerned.

Table 3.6 The Road to the Schism: Chronology of Events from 1986

1986, April	The "Nishioka Incident": Nikkyōso chairman, Tanaka Ichiro attends a meeting in support of LDP Diet member and Education Zoku veteran Nishioka Takeo.
1986 and 1987	Nikkyōso unable to hold national conference. This period of paralysis came to be known as the "400 day struggle."
1987, November	Tanaka and Nakakoji Kiyoo agree on a compromise to end the union's paralysis.
1988, February	National conference ratifies Tanaka and Nakakoji's compromise. Fukuda Tadayoshi becomes chairman and a policy in support of "the Sōhyō course of action toward comprehensive unification of labor" is adopted.
1988, July	National conference confirms timetable for affiliating with Rengō.
1989, January–May	A split takes place in the organization of the 1989 May Day celebration. The official organizing committee is accused of trying to exclude communist members. As a result, an alternative May Day celebration is organized.
1989, March	Left-wing members of Jichirō (the union of local government workers) form a breakaway national union and announced that they are aiming to create a "class-conscious national center."
1989, June	Preparations are made to pass a resolution at the upcoming national conference in September formalizing Nikkyōso's affiliation with Rengō.

continued

Table 3.6 *continued*

1989, July 31st	Eleven prefectural compulsory sector unions and twelve high schools unions set up a "union members' network conference." This is seen by Nikkyōso's leadership as the first meeting of a breakaway organization. Mikami Mitsuru (chairman of Tokyo teachers' union) was the chief organizer of this event.
1989, August 27	A rally is held in Tokyo to call for the formation of a teachers' union movement that will "properly carry forward the traditions of Nikkyōso" (i.e., one that will not affiliate with Rengō). The heads of 14 prefectural unions attend. Six CEC members also attend this rally and resign from the CEC.
1989, September 6	Nikkyōso national conference. Some prefectural unions choose not to send delegates or to pay subscriptions.
1989, October 27	Nikkyōso CEC decides to expel from the union the chairmen and secretaries of the 11 prefectural unions and 12 SHS unions and the federation of private schools that have stopped paying subscriptions. The CEC also expels the 6 former CEC members who attended the August rally.
1989, November 17/18	Inauguration conference of the first Zenkyō attended by 15 prefectural unions, 12 SHS unions, the federation of private school unions, and the Tokyo special schools teachers' union. Mikami Mitsuru is chosen as Zenkyō's first president. Sayama Shigeru is secretary general.
1989, November 21	The JCP backed national union federation (or "class-conscious national center") Zenrōren is established with Zenkyō as a founding member.
1989, December	Nikkyōso special conference formalizes arrangements for those prefectural unions that have withdrawn their affiliation.
1989, November, December	Prefectural unions decide which side to support. Decisions are made either at the annual conference of the union or by each union's Central Executive Committee. In many cases the losing minority breaks away and forms a new organization.

continued

Table 3.6 *continued*

1990, July	Zenkyō holds its second national conference attended by 700 delegates.
1991, March	The inaugural conference for the establishment of a new Zenkyō (the full Japanese name is slightly different from the old one). This involves the unification of Zenkyō with the SHS teachers' union, Nikkōkyō.
1991, April 1	The official day for the start of activities of the new Zenkyō. The Schism is now complete. Japan has two mass membership, national teachers" unions instead of one.

Sources: Saikōkyō (1995), Zenkyō (1997), Nikkyōso (1997), *Asahi Shimbun,* Zenkyō newsletter.

CHAPTER FOUR

TEACHERS' UNIONS AND POWER RELATIONS WITHIN THE JAPANESE EDUCATION SYSTEM

An analysis of Nikkyōso's schism must inevitably be influenced by, and have an influence on, the theoretical debate concerning power relations within the Japanese education system. This chapter begins with a survey of the different theories that seek to explain how power is distributed both within the Japanese state as a whole and within the particular arena of educational policy-making and implementation. It then discusses Schoppa's theory of educational policy-making, a theory mainly concerned with power relations at the national level. In the process of analyzing the effect of recent developments on Schoppa's theory, various theories of bureaucracy are discussed with a view to explaining the role of the Ministry of Education (MOE) in the policy-making process. An application of Katō Junko's theory of bureaucratic rationality to the case of the MOE is explored.

POLITICAL THEORY AND THE JAPANESE EDUCATION SYSTEM

Before discussing how power is distributed within the Japanese education system, it is first necessary to review the different theories that have been applied to the political system in Japan as a whole. Traditionally, the political theory debate about how Japan is governed has been conducted between elitists and pluralists.[1] The former see Japan as being run by a unified power elite consisting of bureaucracy, business, and the LDP.[2] This mutually dependent power cartel makes all the key decisions in the running of the country. Pluralists, on the other hand, argue that not only is the power elite much less cohesive than it sometimes seems, but also that the countervailing power of other actors outside this triad should not be underestimated. Because pluralism in its pure (or classical) form is a model of politics in which the interests of various groups are accommodated through negotiation or representative organs such as political parties in which no one group or fixed coalition of groups ever dominates for long, there are few people who would describe the Japanese system as being pluralist without adding some kind of qualification or modifier.[3] Inoguchi Takashi, for example, argues that even though the bureaucracy is the central force of Japanese political power, its impartiality toward various social groups and its open, meritocratic recruitment system combined with the relative autonomy of political, business, and mass media elites allows a certain amount of pluralism to exist. He calls it "bureaucracy-led, mass-inclusionary pluralism."[4] Muramatsu Michio, however, argues that Inoguchi overstates the power of the bureaucracy and understates the importance of party politics and the Diet. He prefers a model called "patterned pluralism." Writing with Ellis S. Krauss in 1987, he defined a patterned pluralist system as one that embodies the following three characteristics.

1. The government and its bureaucracy are strong, but the boundaries between state and society are blurred by the integration of social interest groups with the government and by the intermediation of political parties between social interest groups and the government. The government is not weak, but it is *penetrated* by interest groups and political parties.

2. One of the reasons for this integration between state and society is that one party is perpetually or nearly perpetually in power. This is a pragmatic, catchall party at least partially responsive to a wide variety of sometimes competing social interests.

3. There is an ideological cleavage in the system with the dominant party and its social allies in a more or less antagonistic relationship with the opposition parties and their interest group allies over im-

> portant value issues. Unlike the situation under classical pluralism, ideology plays a somewhat greater role, and, consequently, party-interest group alliances are more fixed. However the opposition has some influence on policy, even if through indirect means.[5]

Weight was added to this model by important developments in Japanese politics during the 1980s and 1990s. Various measures for liberalization and deregulation of the Japanese economy and financial system (partly forced on Japan by American pressure) have undermined the position of the bureaucracy. For example, the Ministry of International Trade and Industry (MITI), which during the 1950s and 1960s played such a crucial role in leading Japan's economic miracle, is now a much weaker force. In his classic study of MITI, Chalmers Johnson described politicians as mere safety valves for the bureaucracy who insulate it from political and interest group pressures so that it can autonomously carry out the main task of the "development state"—economic growth.[6] Whether or not this was true in the 1950s and 1960s, it was certainly not the case in the 1990s. Liberalization has caused MITI to lose its right to allocate foreign exchange and, among other things, the right to issue various business licences. Muramatsu argues that by the 1990s "MITI's strong influence over enterprises and groups [had] gone."[7] Liberalization has also brought about decline in the influence of the once mighty Ministry of Finance (MOF). Deregulation of the banking and securities business in the 1980s greatly weakened the MOF's control over both banks and securities companies.[8] This decline in the influence of the bureaucracy further undermines Inoguchi's theory that Japanese pluralism is "bureaucracy-led" as well as calling into question the present-day relevance of the more traditional bureaucracy-dominant models such as that of Chalmers Johnson. Instead, the model of patterned pluralism was more valid in explaining politics in Japan in the 1980s and 1990s.

This model is especially useful because it emphasizes two key institutional characteristics that are very important in Japanese policy-making. One is that, in most policy matters, decisions emanating from the relevant section of the bureaucracy are final. This does not mean that all or most of the power is in the hands of the bureaucrats themselves. Rather, the ministries or other bureaucratic units in which decisions are made function as arenas where outside interests can and do influence the decision-making process. Because interest groups concentrate their attention on the ministries with jurisdiction over areas that concern them directly, units of like-minded groups known as subgovernments form around each government ministry. These groups also usually form links with the corresponding division of the LDP's Policy Affairs Research Council (PARC). Thus, for example, the health and welfare subgovernment is composed of the Ministry of Health and Welfare, the PARC Health and Welfare Division, and such interest groups as the Japan Medical Association. This means that decisions are made by many actors, but within the procedures and jurisdictions of ministry arenas. The second important characteristic of Japanese policy-making is the fact that opinions of the opposition are often taken into account even when the LDP has a big enough majority in the Diet to force through legislation regardless of the opinions of opposition parties. This is due to the ability of opposition politicians and interest groups to influence (either directly or indirectly) individual LDP politicians and ministry bureaucrats. It was partly because of this factor that the loss of the LDP's majority in the upper house (lost in 1989 and still not regained) and lower house (lost in 1993 and regained in 1997) did not have the impact that might have been expected. These two essential characteristics define the Japanese political system as one of patterned pluralism. They have remained largely unchanged by recent political events. Other aspects of Muramatsu and Krauss's model, however, have been altered by the events of the 1990s. The impact of these events on the model will be discussed in chapter seven.

Schoppa's Theory of Educational Policy-Making

The previous discussion of different theories of pluralism as applied to Japan provides a useful general outline of the Japanese political system. We can now move on to a more specific discussion of the mechanics of how policy is actually produced. In an effort to avoid mere description, political scientists have developed various theoretical models to analyze more closely the processes of policy-making. Within the context of patterned pluralism, which model best suits an analysis of educational policy-making? In his book, *Education Reform in Japan*, Leonard Schoppa makes an important and practical contribution to this debate.[9] By closely analyzing the government-led education reform initiatives of the 1970s and 1980s and the reasons for their failure, he is able to build on the previous work of political scientists T. J. Pempel and John Campbell to arrive at a new model of Japanese policy-making that he names the Modified Pempel-Campbell Model.[10] Schoppa argues that this model explains the political "immobilism,"[11] or inability to implement substantive reform, of the policy-making process. The model divides conflict resolution patterns in Japanese policy-making into the following three types. Each type is followed by an historical example or examples used by Schoppa in his analysis (examples are therefore confined to the 1970s and 1980s).

Type 1. Low-conflict disputes that tend to result in incremental change or pressure group pluralism involving "contrived consensus" type decision-making.

Historical Examples: Expansion in the 1970s of kindergartens and schools for the handicapped. Agreement in the 1980s for more internationalization.

Type 2. High-conflict disputes involving *outside forces* resulting in camp conflict and either (a) forced resolution by the government or (b) opposition success in convincing at least some conservatives to back down—thereby creating a situation not unlike category three.

Historical Example (of case a): Introduction of the teacher responsibility, *shunin* system in the 1970s against the determined opposition of Nikkyōso. (The *shunin* system gave extra money to teachers with special responsibilities, e.g., those in charge of student guidance, discipline, or career advice. The union opposed it because they saw it as a method for the authorities to "divide and rule" the teacher body within each school.)

Historical Example (of case b): The *shiho* system proposed in the 1970s for the creation of a one-year probationary training program for all new teachers. In the face of opposition from Nikkyōso this period was eventually reduced to twenty days.

Type 3. High-conflict disputes involving primarily *conservative camp actors,* resulting in conflict avoidance and little change.

Historical Example: Nakasone's attempt in the 1980s to introduce six-year secondary schools. This was resisted by the Ministry of Education.[12]

It should be noted that types two and three are both predicated on the existence of two opposing camps in Japanese politics. These are the "conservative camp," which consists of the LDP, the bureaucracy, and business interests, and the "opposition camp," which consists mainly of opposition political parties or pressure groups and some public sector unions. Schoppa concludes his book by deciding that his "case study of education reform essentially reinforces the modified Pempel–Campbell model."[13] Schoppa's research was carried out before Nikkyōso's schism, and thus, within the domain of education policy, he sees Nikkyōso as the main element in the opposition camp. Furthermore he views its role in the policy-making process as being largely negative or reactive.[14] Several questions therefore arise from the change in Nikkyōso's position brought about by the schism. First, has Nikkyōso's new policy of compromise (*ayumiyori*) combined with the joining in a coalition government of the Japan Socialist Party with the LDP from 1994 to 1996 rendered the very concept of a "two camp" model redundant? Second, has the schism so weakened the stance of independent teachers' organizations that power over the future direction of education in Japan has now fallen into the hands of the Ministry of Education and its allies? (In other words, had the MOE finally emerged victorious from its long running war with Nikkyōso and the left?) The broader question of political realignment and the decline of the left will be dealt with in chapter seven. For now, we will restrict the discussion to the area of education policy. How has the schism affected our understanding of power and politics within the education system based on the two camp model and Schoppa's modified Pempel–Campbell model? We will now turn to this specific question in order to review the relevance of this model for present day education policy-making.

Nikkyōso's Schism and Schoppa's Theory of Policy-Making: Changes in Relations Between Nikkyōso and the Ministry of Education

The traditional two-camp model of Japanese politics viewed the progressive camp and the conservative camp as being at loggerheads. Furthermore, there was less communication between the two camps in the field of education than in any other area. Thurston, Duke, and Schoppa all found that Nikkyōso and the opposition's best method of influencing policy lay in putting pressure on members of the conservative camp (through threats of disruption or noncompliance in schools) in order to cause divisions within that camp (i.e., outcome 2b in Schoppa's modified Pempel–Campbell model). This tactic was successful in preventing many of the wholesale changes desired by politicians on the right, especially Nakasone, but it resulted in Nikkyōso's being tarnished with the image of an organization that always resisted change. As shown in chapter two, the Ministry of Education would often claim that its proposals (e.g., changes in the systems for assessing and training teachers), were aimed at improving education. Although Nikkyōso also had many of its own proposals in these areas and it also, independently, conducted regular teacher training and educational research programs, it could not escape the popular image that it was primarily interested in a political agenda, putting the interests of children second.[15] This partly explains moves by members of the right-wing group in the mainstream faction to start making contact with the LDP and the Ministry of Education. They were seeking a more positive role in the policy-making process. As we have seen, these moves, especially chairman Tanaka's meeting with LDP politician Nishioka, were angrily attacked by the left as a betrayal of everything Nikkyōso stood for. After the schism was over and the left had removed itself, the right was given a free hand to continue its efforts to carve out a new, more positive role. On December 16, 1994, the new Nikkyōso claimed "an historic amicable accord" when its chairman, Yokoyama Eiichi, met LDP education minister Yosano Kaoru. Three days later he also had a meeting with Mori Yoshiro, the LDP's general secretary. However, these meetings were more symbolic than anything, with little of practical importance being conceded by the LDP. For example, when Yokoyama raised the problem of his union's financial burden caused by payments to teachers who had been disciplined for strike action in the past, he was given the cold shoulder by Mori.[16] Later, the next LDP education minister, Kosugi Takashi, tried to appoint Yokoyama to the Central Council on Education (CCE), but abandoned the idea "because some former education ministers opposed it."[17] Finally, in March 1997, Kosugi succeeded in getting Yokoyama onto the CCE. Clearly, differences of opinion exist within the LDP about the degree of representation that should be given to new Nikkyōso as a reward for its more conciliatory post-schism stand. It should be noted here that some LDP politicians are keen to build bridges with new Nikkyōso purely to make deals for electoral purposes. This issue will be dealt with in more detail in chapter seven.

As far as top bureaucrats within the Ministry of Education are concerned, there is even less enthusiasm for the new teachers' union. They still maintain the ministry's traditional official line, that it is inappropriate (*tadashikunai*) for the ministry to consult directly with the union, because the ministry acts on behalf of the Minister of Education who has been properly appointed by the legitimate, democratically elected government of the day to preside over education policy. It would not be appropriate to give special consideration to Nikkyōso any more than it would be to grant it to any other group representing sectional interests (the ministry's position here is reinforced by Nikkyōso's lack of legal status as a national union). Of course, Nikkyōso has the right to make its views heard, and the ministry will listen to these views, but that is all.[18] Thus, as far as the ministry is concerned, the schism has made little difference to their attitude to Nikkyōso.

According to the logic of the ministry's position, the schism should actually make Nikkyōso even *less* eligible to consideration when policy is drawn up, since post-schism Nikkyōso represents a smaller proportion of the country's teachers than the pre-schism organization did. Thus, in the first ten years following the schism it seems that new Nikkyōso has failed to make much headway in its efforts to become a part of the main policy-making process at the national level. Nikkyōso is thus in danger of falling between two stools. It has abandoned its earlier stance of outright opposition to government policy, but it has failed to win any significant concessions from the government in return. Zenkyō have warned that this strategy represents nothing less than the handing over of control of the education system to the Ministry of Education and the LDP. To assess the justification or otherwise of this criticism it is necessary to analyze the ways in which the MOE has responded to Nikkyōso's schism and other concomitant events.

Theories of Bureaucracy and the Post-Schism Ministry of Education

The place occupied by the bureaucracy in theories of Japanese pluralism and policy-making has already been discussed. The theories of Johnson and Inoguchi were criticized for overstating the power of the bureaucracy. Schoppa, following on the work of Campbell and Pempel, showed how it is more useful to see the bureaucracy as one set of actors within the policy-making process rather than a group that is always dominant. This being the case, Schoppa went on to explain the ideological position adopted by parts of the bureaucracy with regard to education policy. The most important actor within the bureaucracy, of course, is the Ministry of Education (MOE). Schoppa found that "[t]he predominant 'attitude' of the MOE, across the whole range of policy issues, has been its desire to maintain existing practices and policies."[19] He calls this "bureaucratic conservatism" and argues that it is caused by two main factors. First, the MOE has developed an attachment to the status quo over its many years of supervising the existing education system. MOE bureaucrats have a certain amount of pride invested in what they have built. Second, Schoppa argues that MOE bureaucrats, because they deal on a daily basis with educational administrators closer to the "actual site" *(genba)* at which education is being delivered, are more inclined to resist measures that will cause disruption in schools.[20] This is similar to the argument advanced by Rohlen (discussed more fully in the previous chapter) that states that conflict is likely to be much less at the school level because of the vested interest all parties have in maintaining an orderly working environment. Schoppa is extending this argument by saying that bureaucrats throughout the system are going to be more inclined to avoid conflict than are other actors in the arena of education policy-making.

In support of his thesis about MOE bureaucrats' propensity to avoid conflict or radical change at all costs, Schoppa quotes extensively from the work of an acknowledged expert on postwar Japanese bureaucracy, Yung Park. Park sees the conservatism of the MOE as a natural result of the postwar experiences of MOE bureaucrats. "Having survived repeated confrontations over policy in the ideologically polarised environment of post war education policy making, these officials came to shy away from doing anything that might provoke unnecessary controversy."[21] This is an explanation of bureaucratic behavior based on the historical experiences of the main individuals within the bureaucracy, and one that will, by necessity, vary over time. Another approach is one that stresses the importance of the place the bureaucracy occupies in the policy-making process and then analyzes the actions of that bureaucracy from the point of view of "bureaucratic rationality" that is, an assumption that bureaucrats will follow courses of action that rationally advance their own organization's strategic interests. This is not the same as Johnson's "bureaucratic dominance" model in that it does not argue that the bureaucracy will always get its way or that it will always be in a position of detached, technocratic superiority over politicians. Instead the bureaucratic rationality model claims that bureaucrats have to become actively involved in politics and use whatever means they have, (e.g., their control of technical or "neutral" data) to win politicians over to their side. The foremost proponent of this theory is Katō Junko, who applied bureaucratic rationality to the case of the Ministry of Finance's campaign to introduce a very unpopular consumption tax during the 1970s and 1980s.[22] Bureaucrats in Japan often claim political neutrality and a devotion to serving the interests of the nation. Katō, however, argues that "a bureaucratic policy decision is closely related to organisational interests in a certain political context, and is thus in no way based on any 'objective' standard like 'effectiveness' of policies or maximisation of a simple utility function."[23] Bureaucrats propose policies that make the promotion of their organizational influence compatible with technocratic considerations. In this way, they can always claim that they are selflessly promoting the interests of the nation, while at the same time looking after their own organizational interests. During the period of the economic miracle, the general rise in living standards of the whole population meant that even if this theory of bureaucratic self-interest was true, it was not turned into a major political issue. With the slowing down of economic growth, however, this began to change, and bureaucrats have started to come under criticism. Katō's theory, not being one based mainly on historical factors, is designed to apply to the bureaucracy under any historical epoch.

It is because Katō's theory of bureaucratic rationality is not rooted in particular historical circumstances that it has wider applicability than Schoppa's interpretation of Park's theory of bureaucratic conservatism. Both Park and Schoppa assume the permanence of LDP rule and a two-camp model. Their theories, therefore, will have to be modified in the wake of the ending of both of these assumptions. Katō's theory, however, attempts to account for the actions and powers of bureaucracies in a greater range of circumstances. Both Park's claim that the MOE is basically "reactive" to LDP policy-making, and Schoppa's claim that the MOE can only get its way by recruiting allies in the education sub government, are based on the presence of a strong and fairly united education *zoku* within the LDP. Members of this *zoku* took many years to build up their knowledge and influence about education. The loss of key LDP Diet members during the period of the "New Party Boom" and lower house election of 1993, however, has successfully broken up the education *zoku*. Of nineteen lower house *zoku* members counted by Schoppa in 1989,[24] no fewer than thirteen had retired, lost their seats, or defected to other parties by 1994. This includes the two most important and high profile *zoku* members, Kaifu Toshiki and Nishioka Takeo. Of course, younger Diet members are in the process of replacing these people, but such a huge loss of experience and influence in such a short space of time is bound to take years to recover from.

What will be the likely result of this decimation of the LDP education *zoku*? Will it make significant change in the education system more or less likely than it was before? At this point it is important to remember that from the point of view of party leaders like Nakasone who wanted to bring about reform, *zoku* politicians were always a mixed blessing. Although they provided the party with expertise and experience in a particular policy area, they also "came to adopt the sectional interests of their sphere [and tended] to become attached to the established (status quo) policies of their sphere."[25] Thus, the decline of a *zoku* could hinder as much as help a ministry that wants to get its way. Turning to the theories of bureaucracy used by Schoppa and Park for help in analyzing this situation, we find that they are of limited use. These theories predict that little or no change will occur because they assume that MOE bureaucrats are sentimentally attached to institutions and procedures established by their ministry in the past, and that they are unwilling to provoke conflict or disruption at the educational *genba*. Katō's theory of bureaucracy does not deny either of these factors, but rather offers an explanation of bureaucratic behavior that goes deeper. After showing how bureaucratic institutions ensure the assimilation of individual interests with those of the organization, Katō declares that "[t]his study assumes that the bureaucratic organisation tries to increase its discretionary powers and, at the same time, to incorporate technocratic considerations into its policy making activities. . . . Bureaucrats decide on a specific policy aim through a process that makes these objectives compatible."[26] In Katō's case study, this process involved the Ministry of Finance's promotion of a consumption tax that it justified in "neutral" technocratic language, even though the ministry's prime aim was concerned with maximizing its own control over the fiscal process. We will now examine how this theory would apply to the Ministry of Education, both before and after the changes of the early 1990s.

Katō identified a two-step process by which bureaucratic organizations influence other political actors. The first step is to define the problem so that the policy proposed by the ministry will be a good solution. The second step is get recognized policy experts to support this solution.[27] Schoppa's own analysis of two periods of education reform activity supports this analysis. During the first period, the 1970s, the MOE was successful in setting the reform agenda, although it did it through the supposedly neutral Central Council on Education (CCE). Schoppa describes the situation as follows.

> From the beginning the CCE reform initiative was an MOE project. The Minister of Education (Kennoki) officially issued the crucial "request for advice" and appointed the council's

> members. The text of the *shimon* [request for advice] and other accompanying documents were drafted by bureaucrats in the MOE Planning Office and reflected the approval of all top officials in the ministry. These same officials also had a significant degree of input into the make-up of the council's membership.[28]

Here can be seen, clearly, the maneuverings of the MOE to gain control over the initiation of the policy-making process, as well as a significant amount of control over the selection of the "experts" who would be used to legitimize the process. The end result was a significant expansion of the MOE's budget in the 1970s, along with an extension of its control over private schools and universities as well as teacher training. All these courses of action were justified by CCE experts as being in the national interest. In this way, technocratic considerations were used to justify policy that helped broaden the MOE's discretionary powers.

The second period of reform studied by Schoppa, the 1980s, is more problematic because of Prime Minister Nakasone's personal intervention and the creation of *Rinkyōshin*, a body that was much more difficult for the MOE to influence than the CCE (indeed, that was the main reason why Nakasone went to the trouble of creating it). Thus, the 1980s reforms saw the MOE much more on the defensive than it had been in the 1970s, at least until Nakasone's fall from power. The MOE was able to control neither the initiation of reform nor the selection of members of the *Rinkyōshin*. It was reduced to the unusual position of having to appeal, in public, to the *Rinkyōshin* to modify its views on the liberalization of education.[29] In other words, the MOE had failed to set the terms of the education debate in such a way that they supported solutions that would benefit the MOE's institutional position. This meant that the MOE was also frustrated in its efforts to recruit "expert" opinion onto its side as it had done in the 1970s. However, the MOE was able to reassert its control during the implementation stage of the policy-making process in the 1980s. Nakasone's failure to have implementation overseen by a strong supracabinet council similar to *Rinkyōshin* meant that the MOE was left in charge of implementation.[30] The result was, not surprisingly, enactment of policies (like probationary periods for teachers) that suited the agenda of the MOE, and unenthusiastic enforcement of policies (like the setting up of more six-year secondary schools) that the MOE did not, at that time, like.[31]

Bureaucratic rationality explains the behavior of MOE bureaucrats in both the 1970s and the 1980s. Clearly, the MOE was more in control in the 1970s. This is why it suggested, with the support of the education *zoku*, that reform in the 1980s should also be initiated by the CCE.[32] When it could not get its way in the 1980s it had to resort to using its influence at the implementation stage. This was unsatisfactory because it meant that the MOE had lost control of both policy initiation and the opinions of "policy experts." Indeed, this leads us to two main areas in which Katō's theory may need to be modified. Education policy is very different from financial policy for these two reasons: In education policy implementation is much more important than it is in tax policy; and in education policy there is less trust given to technocratic experts. With these two points in mind, we will now proceed to an analysis of how the MOE adjusted to the changed circumstances of the early 1990s.

If the theory of bureaucratic rationality is correct, we would expect the MOE in the period following Nakasone's fall from power to try to reestablish control of policy initiation and the education reform agenda. We would also expect it to try to seek legitimization for those policies that suit its own institutional interests by ensuring that neutral, expert opinion is in accordance with what it proposes. If it achieves these, then it does not need to wait until the implementation stage to exert its influence. An analysis of the 1990s reveals that this is precisely what the MOE has done, through the simple device of restoring the CCE to its "rightful" place as the center of education reform deliberation and initiation. Although initial responses to Nakasone's reform proposals, including those of Schoppa and Hayao, have been to label them as mostly failures, the years following Nakasone's fall from power have caused scholars to start to revise this verdict. Distinguished Education experts Amano Ikuo and Ichikawa Shōgo have both agreed that Nakasone's period of education reform was, indeed, highly significant because it changed the way education is thought of in Japan, and started a process of piecemeal reform.[33] Schoppa himself identified divisions within the MOE between reformers and conservatives[34] but found that the immobilism inherent in the system favored the latter. This is why he came down on the side of bureaucratic conservatism. Schoppa's analysis, however, does not deny the presence of forces for change within the MOE itself, nor does it negate the actuality of incremental, consensus-based change. The question, therefore, is whether slow, incremental change can, if given enough time, amount to significant reform. The post-Nakasone era has seen the CCE continue to press for some of the reforms that *Rinkyōshin* failed to get through. (There was a continuity between many of *Rinkyōshin*'s proposals and those of previous CCEs, so their extension into the 1990s is not surprising.) One example of this is the adoption, by the CCE, of the proposal to combine junior high and senior high schools to form six-year secondary schools.[35] If the MOE really has changed its mind and this reform is widely implemented, then it will amount to much more than an incremental reform.

One problem with analysis of education reform in Japan based on an historical perspective is that it can lead the scholar to believe that any reform that does not take place at the breakneck speed of the Meiji or Occupation eras is not real reform. A more comparative perspective, however, would show that most education systems around the world change very slowly. A changeover from separate junior high and senior high schools to a single secondary school system may take twenty years or more to go from the initiation stage to the implementation stage, but that would not prevent the reform from being very significant. Chris Hood has recently written that those who wrote off Nakasone's education reforms as failures were making too hasty a judgment. The fact that success was not achieved immediately in the 1980s does not mean that the reforms did not work. Events in the 1990s have shown that many of Nakasone's ideas, far from being abandoned, are now well on the way to implementation.[36] The CCE would not propose such a radical change as combining senior and junior high schools if it did not have the approval of the MOE. Thus, the MOE is not afraid of radical change when it feels the need for it. Katō showed how the Ministry of Finance was willing to risk disruption and unpopularity to get its new consumption tax implemented. In the post oil shock world, the MOF needed the consumption tax to avoid situations in which the national budget would be either too loose or too tight.[37] The MOF rationally believed that conditions of either too much money or too little would help politicians gain more control over the budget-making process. Thus, Katō's theory of bureaucratic rationality allows ministries to press for major reform when this reform suits their institutional interests. What is true for the MOF seems to be true for the MOE too. Although it has been described as the most conservative of all the ministries[38], the MOE is also capable of change when it feels that standing still will be more dangerous to its interests than moving forward. We will now examine some of the changes the MOE is genuinely supporting to defend or increase its discretionary power.

Chapter two showed how the MOE, along with the conservative governments of the time, campaigned to win back some of the powers that had been lost by the bureaucracy during the reforms of the American Occupation. The threat to the powers of the MOE during the 1950s clearly came from the left in general and Nikkyōso in particular. The

MOE was clearly successful in regaining control over textbooks and removing the system of elections for local boards of education. In the areas of assessment for teachers and pupils, the result was more mixed, with many of the MOE proposals being reduced in effectiveness at the implementation stage. The ending of Nikkyōso as a united and militant opposition force, however, has clearly altered this situation and caused the MOE to look for potential or actual threats coming from new directions. By an analysis of secondary school reform proposals, including the previously mentioned merger of junior and senior high schools, we can arrive at some conclusions about what the MOE perceives as a threat to its interests and how it is responding to this threat.

One principle, which underlies many proposed reforms of the 1990s, is the idea that the exam and assessment system in secondary education is too rigid. This is a feature of the Japanese education system that has come under criticism for some time from observers both at home and abroad. Within the state system, parents have no choice about what junior high school to send their children to, and children have no choice about what subjects to study when they get there. Then the entrance to good academic senior high schools is rationed by extremely competitive and arduous entrance exams. This has given rise to a parallel, unregulated education system, in the form of juku, yobikō and private tutors.[39] The MOE is concerned about this phenomenon, not only for the popular reason that it causes stress and exhaustion among the children who have to use these institutions, but also because it is an area of the educational world that lies outside its sphere of control. If it is true that bureaucrats will always act in such a way as to preserve or extend their sphere of control, then it is not surprising that the MOE has tried to do something to limit the influence of the juku and yobikō industry. It has done this by introducing reforms to the entrance exam system, allowing more students to enter high school or university through the recommendation system. This has two effects. First, it allows some students to bypass the entrance exam system altogether, and because it is entrance exam preparation that is the main business of juku and yobikō, this denies them a certain number of customers. Second, it makes the whole business of entrance to high school or university much more difficult to predict. Many juku had built their reputations on being able to predict exactly which school a given pupil would be able to enter. They did this by comparing the pupil's practice test scores with a computer analysis of the scores required to get into various schools. They then could advise the pupil and his or her parents about which entrance exam to go for.[40] The introduction of a partial recommendation system, in which some pupils move forward by exams and others by recommendation, makes it much more difficult to extrapolate one year's results to the next because the ratio of recommended students to examined students is not fixed.[41] By introducing such a system, the MOE and the Boards of Education are trying to undermine the influence of juku and yobikō on children and parents.

Of course, undermining the influence of juku and yobikō is not the sole or even a major aim of current MOE policy. This example is merely one illustration of how the MOE ensures that its role as the supervisor of the nation's education system is not usurped by independent organizations. Another way to prevent the nation's parents "voting with their feet" and entrusting the education of their children to institutions outside the ministry's control (even, in some cases, by sending their children abroad for an education)[42] is to improve the present system. The task of producing positive reform proposals has been delegated to the CCE. In April 1991, it published a report containing the following three main recommendations.

1. Instead of the quantitative expansion of the past, efforts should now focus on qualitative enhancement to allow a careful response to students' individual characteristics.

2. A system should be established to enable students to choose from among a wide range of schools, courses, and subjects meeting their individual needs in order to correct the tendency to employ uniform approaches to educational content and guidance methods despite the diversity in students' abilities and aptitudes.

3. Steps must be taken to alleviate excessive competition in entrance examinations such as by diversifying entrant selection criteria. Through changes in this area, efforts should be made to liberate students from the psychological pressure of entrance examination competition and excessive reliance on standard score and strive for education based on respect for individuality and humanity.[43]

There are few in Japan who would disagree with the main thrust of these recommendations. The key point as far as the MOE is concerned, however, is to ensure that the concrete, detailed reforms that result from these recommendations are implemented according to guidelines laid down by the ministry. The MOE sees no contradiction between appeals for more diversity on the one hand, and the maintenance of strict, centralized control over the details of that diversity, on the other. The CCE, after studying the results of various pilot schemes around the country that were based on these recommendations, published three reports in 1996, 1997, and 1998. The 1996 report placed emphasis on relaxing students' lives through such measures as introducing a complete five-day school week. (The five-day week will be fully implemented by 2003.) The 1997 report called for structural reform, including the establishment of six-year consolidated secondary schools. Finally, the 1998 report called for decentralization measures that would give more power to local boards of education and school principals to decide what is taught in their schools. The report envisioned a school system with more choice and diversity than the present one.[44]

The next stage in this MOE reform process is to translate these proposals into real changes. The way this is done is by the introduction of new course of study guidelines (*gakushū shidō yōryō*). Guidelines are revised every ten years and new ones for the senior high school sector were published in March 1999 to take effect in the 2003 academic year.[45] These guidelines cut the number of credits required for high school graduation from eighty to seventy-four and allowed twenty of these credits to be designed by the school itself. These changes built on previous changes to the course of study guidelines, introduced in 1992, that had reduced the size of the core curriculum and extended the range of optional subjects.[46] Choice and diversity were thus being increased, at least on the margins. The ministry said, however, that the content taught in the majority of classes would remain unchanged.[47] Questions were immediately raised concerning how much real flexibility or diversity these new guidelines would achieve. Progress would inevitably be undermined by two factors: first, the inability of individual schools to afford to provide enough teachers to cover the extra subject choices; and, second, the enduring presence of the still dominant university entrance exam system that would force students to stick to current habits of study.[48] In other words, there was a feeling that the new guidelines did not go far enough in dealing with the ills afflicting Japan's high schools.

Whenever the study guidelines are reviewed, the MOE is keen to ensure that the results affect its discretionary power as little as possible. This process is defended by some academics, who argue that it is only right and proper that the educational problems of Japan should be discussed at a national level, and that when solutions are arrived at, they should be national solutions, with the MOE ensuring that reform programs are adhered to throughout the country and standards are maintained as well.[49] This line of argument also claims that government guidelines are not so strict as to deny boards of education and individual schools some leeway in how they are applied in practice.[50] Thus, although an individual school will often consult other schools and their local board of education when introducing a new kind of course or a review of their entrance procedures and so on, they will rely mainly on guidelines from the ministry for the broad parameters within which they must operate.[51]

The fundamental purpose of the MOE, therefore, is to put through a program of education reform designed to maintain or expand its discretionary powers, while at the same time satisfy the calls for educational change that come from many quarters. It must do this by maintaining ownership of the policy initiation process and control over the subsequent stage of policy implementation. In the 1980s, the MOE was able to prevent the introduction of a scheme to create six-year secondary schools (unified junior and senior high schools). Ten years later, the MOE-dominated CCE proposed just such a plan. The difference between the two periods is that in the former instance the MOE did not have control while in the latter it did. This proposal still remains to be implemented in full, although it is being pursued in various pilot programs around the country.[52] The other proposals outlined by the CCE that came to be included in the revised study guidelines will soon be at the implementation stage. It has already been mentioned that implementation is a different process in the education world compared to the financial world (the area in which the theory of bureaucratic rationality was developed). This is because an education policy can be completely transformed or rendered meaningless by the way it is implemented at the *genba*. The same is not true, except in exceptional instances, in the case of tax policy. Thus, the MOE has found, over the years, that if a policy does not have the support of the personnel who will implement it, then it will not be a success. This explains long-running campaigns by the MOE to break the power of Nikkyōso and win over to its side school managers and board of education bureaucrats. It also explains the MOE's desire to justify its reforms by demonstrating their technocratic superiority, that is, their suitability in answering the nation's educational needs.

This brings us to the second difference between education policy and tax policy: the role of technocratic experts. All ministries claim that the policies they propose are the best policies for the given circumstances, and to prove this they often use neutral, nonpolitical "experts" to support their claims. In Katō's study, the MOF used neutral experts to back up its claim that the introduction of a consumption tax was in Japan's national interest. Similarly, the MOE likes to claim that its policies are in the national interest too, and it uses bodies like the CCE to reinforce this position. As Schoppa and others have shown, however, the MOE always makes sure that the members of the CCE are people who will not drift wildly from its own preferred stance. Circumstances for the MOE are fundamentally different from those the MOF usually finds itself in. The debate about revenue raising for the national treasury is a highly technical one, the details of which are inaccessible to the vast majority of people (including most politicians). Of course, the majority of people will be opposed to an increase in their own tax burden, which is perceived to be unreasonable or to the introduction of a new tax that they view to be unfair, but they will have little understanding of the details of the issues. In the end, technocrats in the MOF succeeded in persuading the LDP to introduce a new tax, even though they knew it would be very unpopular in the short term. MOF bureaucrats "concentrated their efforts on obtaining approval from party leaders who have electoral bases and are more concerned with policy making than re-election."[53] Politicians, especially *zoku giin*, have a vested interest in building a strong relationship with the bureaucracy to advance their own careers. This led enough of them to put their individual long-term relationship with the bureaucracy above the short-term electoral interests of their party. The consumption tax was introduced and the LDP duly lost its majority in the upper house in the subsequent 1989 elections.

For the MOE, the problems it faces in getting its proposals accepted are different. It is not enough just to get the support of the governing party. As we have seen, lack of support among the educational workforce at the *genba* can effectively block reform too. It is also argued that, in Japan, a consensus form of decision-making is preferable where it is at all possible.[54] This is especially true of decision-making relating to education. Therefore, the MOE needs to cultivate an educational ideology that goes far beyond the corridors of power in Tokyo. It can do this because the details of the debate about education are far more accessible than the intricacies of tax reform. Thus, throughout the postwar period the MOE has been locked in an ideological struggle with its adversaries on the left every bit as significant as the brute struggle for power. The contours of this struggle have already been outlined in chapters one and two, and the efforts to move more to the center ground by Nikkyōso have been discussed in chapter three. Taking an historical perspective, Marshall has looked at this process and concluded (in 1994) that "the gap between teachers and Education Ministry may now be diminishing."[55] This will suit the Ministry of Education so long as it can retain control over the direction of reform and its guidelines set the parameters within which local actors in the policy-making process operate. Brian McVeigh has recently written about how the Ministry of Education (both prewar and postwar) has always been concerned with establishing legitimacy for its control over Japan's educational institutions. Underlying this is the belief that "the state has the prerogative to set standards, control curriculum and oversee the administration of educational matters."[56] This philosophy adds impetus to the MOE bureaucrats' desire to win any ideological war with their opponents and defend the discretionary powers of their institution. The next chapter will examine how the current debate on education is progressing, and will discuss the roles as well as the ideologies of the different political actors within that debate.

Conclusion: The Need to Modify Schoppa's Model

Because of its attempts at reaching a compromise with the Ministry of Education and the LDP, Nikkyōso has been accused by Zenkyō of *riteki kōi* or "actions that serve the interests of the enemy." This belief, that the two different camps in the education policy arena are enemies, is the kind of Cold War way of thinking that Nikkyōso's leadership was (and still is) trying to escape. So, which interpretation is the more accurate—new Nikkyōso's or Zenkyō's? If the Zenkyō analysis were accurate, then the schism would have given the conservative camp the opportunity to push its policies onto the schools without having to deal with the kind of united opposition they had to face before the schism. However, in the ten years following the schism the main concern of the MOE has been with the introduction of policies, as previously outlined, that are aimed at providing more flexibility and choice within the school system. In the area of high school education the ministry's power has continued to be confined to the setting of standards and the drawing up of study guidelines, as before. There has been no evidence of a rush to turn the clock back to prewar days. Instead, there are signs of an attempt to break away from the education ideology of the postwar period.

Schoppa's model of policy-making was predicated on the existence of two opposed, ideologically motivated camps. The efforts by the leadership of Nikkyōso to get away from this ideological battle, combined with an unwillingness of the MOE to take advantage of the situation have therefore undermined the durability of Schoppa's model. Before deciding on how to modify the model, however, other political and educational developments of the 1990s need to be explored. Continuing the theme of the changing nature of ideological conflict, the next subject to be dealt with will be the debate on education reform in Japan in the 1990s.

CHAPTER FIVE

THE CONTRIBUTION TO THE DEBATE ON EDUCATION REFORM MADE BY NIKKYŌSO AND ZENKYŌ

Chapter two outlined the chronic decline in Nikkyōso's membership and influence that was used by the right wing of the mainstream faction in the union's leadership to justify a policy of modernization and compromise. This new policy included a review of the union's position concerning education reform. Chapter three showed how the left vilified this change of direction as a betrayal of everything the movement held dear. In this chapter we will place Nikkyōso's change of direction within the context of the wider education debate under way in Japan in the 1980s and 1990s. Before looking more closely at the details of Nikkyōso's new policies, we will first carry out a general review of the debate on education in Japan at the time of Nikkyōso's schism.

The Debate on Education Reform in the 1980s

The debate on education in Japan in the 1980s was dominated by Prime Minister Nakasone and his Ad Hoc Council on Education or *Rinji Kyōiku Shingi-kai* (*Rinkyōshin* for short). The disagreement within Nikkyōso about how to respond to *Rinkyōshin's* proposals and the contribution this disagreement made to the split within the union's leadership have already been covered in chapter two. Now we will move on to a broader analysis of the importance of *Rinkyōshin*'s proposals. In his analysis, Schoppa distinguishes between two sets of educational issues that were brought to the fore by *Rinkyōshin*. First, he identifies the "old issues"—that is, those that have been a source of controversy and debate since the Occupation. They include the demands "to restore moral education to its old central position and . . . for reform of the strictly egalitarian 6–3–3–4 system." These are contrasted with "new issues" less tied to the historical experience of the main actors in the educational policy-making process. New issues include "growing criticism of the standardisation and 'qualificationism' of Japanese education."[1] These issues have arisen because of the change in Japan's economic position in the world since the 1950s. Japan's economic miracle of the 1960s and 1970s brought to an end the period of economic catch-up with the West that had been the object of much of government and business's early postwar policy. The education system, which had helped in this miracle by providing Japan with skilled and obedient assembly-line workers and fastidious bureaucrats, was now called on to provide citizens who could meet the different challenges of global economic leadership in a fast-changing commercial and industrial environment.[2] Thus, certain characteristics of the education system that had previously been regarded as strengths, such as its uniformity of educational provision and its emphasis on group harmony and cooperation, now began to be regarded as weaknesses due to their tendency to stifle individual choice, initiative, and creativity—qualities that many argue need to be nurtured if Japan is to continue to function as a successful economy and society. In light of these criticisms and demands, many specific reform proposals have been made and debated. We will now briefly consider the main ones discussed by *Rinkyōshin*, classified under the two headings: old issues and new issues.

Old Issues

Old issues are those that have been the subject of widespread disagreement and debate among those involved in education since the Occupation period. Nakasone's contribution was to make them the focus of national political discourse by making education reform, for the first time, a major plank of the LDP's political and electoral strategy. The two main issues in this category were reforming the 6–3–3 system and bringing back traditional moral education. We will deal with these in turn.

Reform of the 6-3-3 system. As pointed out in chapter one, the 6–3–3 system came under attack from the moment it was put forward as the model for Japanese schooling during the Occupation. (It was derided as a foreign imposition.) However, once it had become established, it proved very difficult to alter. Reform was hindered by, among other things, the inability of would-be reformers to agree on one alternative form of organization.[3] This did not deter Nakasone from putting his personal weight behind calls for more flexibility in the secondary school system, including the establishment of some six-year secondary schools. However, obstruction from the Ministry of Education in the 1980s prevented any change taking place.[4] The previous chapter described how the ministry altered its position on this in the 1990s, a shift that illustrates again the danger of assuming that the policy position of any actor in the education system is written in tablets of stone.

A Return to Moral Education that Emphasizes Japanese Values. This proposal had been advocated by conservatives ever since the Occupation authorities removed the Imperial Rescript on Education (see chapter one). This was one area on which Nakasone, the members of *Rinkyōshin*, the Ministry of Education, and the education *zoku* in the LDP were all broadly in agreement. They all wanted to see a return to education that cultivated patriotism and strengthened each pupil's identity as a Japanese person.[5] However, they had to face the problem that any proposals concerning moral education had to be implemented by ordinary classroom teachers, most of whom, before the schism, were members of Nikkyōso. The union had a reputation from the 1960s and 1970s of stifling government and ministry reforms at the implementation stage (outlined in chapter two). This is why *Rinkyōshin* reform measures included proposals to reform teacher training as well as the content of education for children. Teacher training and assessment would be an avenue by which right-wing reformers could create the kind of classroom teacher who would be willing to teach the kind of moral education of which they approved. This is also why the left has been traditionally opposed to any reform of teacher training or assessment that is controlled by the authorities or their appointees. The post-schism Nikkyōso has proven more flexible on these points, however, as will be shown.

New Issues

Liberalization and Flexibilization. The ending of the catch-up phase of economic development has brought about calls for deregulation in many areas of Japanese public life, from financial institutions to the restrictive personnel practices of large companies. It is only to be expected, therefore, that similar calls for deregulation should be made in the sphere of public education. In this regard the two key words that came out of *Rinkyōshin*'s deliberations were "liberalization" (*jiyūka*) and "flexibilization" (*jūnanka*). The former concept involved proposals for increasing competition in the compulsory sector of the education system (at present parents have no choice but to send their children to the school that is in their zone). The latter concept involves more student choice and more emphasis on a child's individuality. (Both concepts are also linked to proposals for reform of the entrance exam system.) Schoppa argues that these proposals were largely stymied by Ministry of Education opposition.[6] However, although it is true that Nakasone failed to get these proposals implemented during his period of office as prime minister, it is equally true that the debate about liberalization and flexibilization is far from over.

Internationalization. The concept of *kokusaika* or internationalization is very vague. No actor in the education policy-making process says they are opposed to it. More than any other concept, it seems to represent the arrival of the Japanese education system into the post catch-up world, a world in which Japan must play its part as a global economic power. On one level internationalization represents little more than efforts to increase international exchanges between Japanese students and teachers and their counterparts in other countries. It has also been used to help promote better foreign language teaching (overwhelmingly the teaching of English) in Japanese schools. In 1988, the Council of Local Authorities for International Education (CLAIR) was established jointly by the Ministry of Home Affairs, the Ministry of Education, and the Ministry of Foreign Affairs, to promote internationalization at the local level. One of CLAIR's main achievements has been the expansion of the Japan Exchange and Teaching Program (the JET program), that sends foreign nationals into Japanese secondary schools to assist with language teaching and various international exchange projects organized at the local level. There is a consensus of support for this and other, similar programs.[7] However, at the ideological level internationalization can also be a cause of conflict. For example, the right has used it as a justification for an increase in "patriotic" education, with the argument that children cannot be taught to respect the cultures of other countries before they respect their own. In this way the "new issue" of internationalization can be brought in to add weight to arguments in favor of a return to "old issue" arguments like the need for more patriotism.

The Legacy of Nakasone

For Schoppa and Hayao, Nakasone's attempts at large-scale reform of the education system ended in failure because of divisions within his own camp. For Schoppa, the modified Pempel–Campbell model (discussed in chapter four) explains how the immobilism of the system stymied most of Nakasone's ambitions. Hayao, on the other hand, points to the weakness of the office of prime minster within the Japanese political system. Both are right, of course, to note that Nakasone failed to implement the major part of his education reform program while he was prime minister. However, by putting such an emphasis on education reform and devoting so much of his political energy to this area, Nakasone, helped set an agenda for debate on education that has outlasted his premiership.[8] It could be argued that this new agenda, combining as it did traditional issues with more modern ones, was a major influence on Nikkyōso's change of direction.[9] Before looking at this change of direction in more detail, we will first examine another sector that is involved in the debate on education in Japan—business and industry.

The Contribution of Business and Industry to the Debate on Education Before and After Nakasone

The *Rinkyōshin*'s endorsement of liberalization, flexibilization, and internationalization was a direct consequence of the influence of the ideas of the business sector. In 1980, a report commissioned by MITI had called for the production of more creative, diversely talented, and internationally minded workers.[10] These demands became a standard refrain coming from all sections of business and industry during the 1980s. The business community, however, was divided about the extent to which the education system should be reformed in order to achieve these aims. Schoppa found that, while some groups within this sector were calling for radical reform, others were more cautious. The Japanese Committee for Economic Development (Keizai Dōyūkai), for example, called for extensive deregulation and a large element of privatization (especially in the national university sector), while the Federation of Economic Organisations (Keidanren) was more cautious.[11] During the 1980s, it was the caution of the more influential Keidanren that held sway. At that time there was a general reluctance to tamper too much with a system that had produced the Japanese postwar economic miracle. However, the economic problems of the 1990s have caused Keidanren to think again.

In a document published in 1996, Keidanren called for an education system that would produce "creative, talented people."[12] Such people could not be produced, the document argued, by a "one-dimensional education system." A diversity of educational organs had to be developed, and within each institution there should be choice and flexibility within the curriculum. Students should be able to transfer from one institution to another more freely than at present. In keeping with other pronouncements by Keidanren in the 1990s,[13] the document was primarily concerned with reform of university education. However, Keidanren was fully aware that any radical overhaul of the higher education sector would inevitably have consequences for the secondary and primary sectors of education as well. In particular, senior high schools are so dominated by preparation for university entrance exams that any major change in the university sector would have an immediate effect on them. One of the main conclusions of the 1996 document was that the Japanese education system as a whole had to be changed from one that resembled a single pyramid (with Tokyo University at the apex) to a system containing many separate peaks, reflecting a far richer diversity of educational provision for the nation.[14]

The above criticism, that the Japanese education system is too rigid and monolithic, is a common one. Keidanren's document, besides reflecting this general criticism, also mirrors industry's frustration with the low status given to vocational education within the system. In the secondary sector, vocational high schools are always regarded as having a lower status than academic high schools. Various measures have been put into effect to try to deal with this problem. In the 1970s, a new type of college, combining into one institution the years of technical high school and technical junior college, had been created to encourage good students to enter vocational courses. These colleges, known as Kōsen, allowed students (usually boys) to follow a vocational course up to the age of twenty and then gave them the option of transferring to the third year of a full university degree course if they wished. At present there are sixty-two of these colleges in Japan.[15] A more recent measure to overcome discrimination against vocational courses has been the development of new types of comprehensive secondary schools that encompass academic and vocational courses under the same roof. There are now twenty of these pilot projects throughout Japan.[16] These schools are designed to encourage students and parents to regard vocational secondary education courses as more than just the last refuge of those who fail to get into an academic school. But, as with Kōsen colleges, they are currently too few in number to make much of an impact on the education system as a whole.

As shown in the previous chapter, the Central Council on Education and the Ministry of Education have also displayed, in their official publications of the 1990s, a keen grasp of the rhetoric of diversity and choice and a recognition of the need for new types of secondary schools. Much of the rhetoric of the MOE and Keidanren is a shared rhetoric. However, one of the key points of divergence involves Keidanren's idea about replacing a single pyramid with a range of different peaks. One of the main concerns of MOE bureaucrats has been to maintain the ministry's discretionary powers over the education system. This is most easily done in a centralized system resembling a single pyramid. Although Keidanren is making an oversimplification in likening the Japanese system to this pyramid, the thrust of that organization's critique remains valid. To bring about a genuine, nationwide increase in diversity and choice, the present rigid system of centralized control (where, e.g., the size of students' desks from Okinawa to Hokkaido is decided by bureaucrats in Tokyo) must be overhauled. The challenge facing the MOE in the years ahead, therefore, is how to overhaul this system of central control enough to please groups such as Keidanren without, at the same time, sacrificing too many of its own discretionary powers. This is not the first time that there has been a conflict of interest between the MOE and the business sector. However, the changed ideological and political climate of the 1990s means that the potential for open conflict between actors that were previously on the same side is increased. Before discussing this phenomenon further, it is first necessary to examine the new ideological and policy differences of two of the main actors on the opposing side, that is, Nikkyōso and Zenkyō.

Nikkyōso's Post-Schism Changes

The formation of Zenkyō seriously weakened Nikkyōso as a national organization by removing about one-third of its membership. However, the departure of these members, most of whom were on the left of the union, also gave the remaining right-wing leadership more room to maneuver in its plans to modernize Nikkyōso's position on many educational issues. Chapter two showed the historical division between right and left in Nikkyōso over the basic stance that should be adopted toward the authorities. After the heated and disruptive confrontations of the 1950s, the right came to favor increased negotiation with the Ministry of Education and local Boards of Education, while the left insisted that a policy of total opposition was required over certain crucial issues like teacher training or assessment reforms. Thus, the removal of the left in 1989–1990 gave the right the opportunity to pursue its more moderate program to the full.

Two developments best illustrate post-schism Nikkyōso's program of reform and modernization. They are the commissioning of a committee to draw up and publish a far-reaching review of the union's entire structure and raison d'ētre, and the passing of a group of very significant policy U-turns at the union's 1995 national conference. We will now deal with these in turn.

The 21st Century Vision Committee

Shortly after the schism, Nikkyōso's leadership decided to set up a committee to investigate concrete ways in which the union should reform itself in order to put an end to its chronic decline and reinvent itself as an organization relevant to the new needs and challenges of the post Cold War era. National conference approved the plan, and the first meeting of the 21st Century Vision Committee duly took place on April 27, 1994. The committee consisted of twenty-three members, of whom six were university professors, two were members of other research institutes, one was the general secretary of an industrial union (Zensen), and the remainder were officials from Nikkyōso and its affiliated unions. Its aim over twelve months was to analyze the history of Nikkyōso and from this draw up a document that would set an agenda for the future, not only for Nikkyōso, but also for the Japanese education system as a whole. It claimed to be moving away from the confrontation of the postwar era while meeting the challenges that would be faced by Japan and the world in the twenty-first century. The committee chairman, Ouchi Hideaki declared that "we should say good bye to the confrontation and isolation of the Cold War era and take a bold step toward 'the century of open education.' "[17] A look at the following main recommendations of the final report published on April 12, 1995, will show us what Ouchi meant by open education.

1. To provide the extra money required to meet the educational challenges of the next century, a new national consensus has to be achieved. To do this a national "21st Century Education Conference" should be convened. This conference will also address the needs of young people in the twenty-first century. These people will need the ability to independently and creatively respond to social change, as well as the ability to live as "global citizens."

2. National and prefectural curriculum centers should be established to set minimum essential guidelines for school curricula. These guidelines should be drawn up on the basis of teachers' views.

3. The need for a uniform, centralized system has now gone, and so autonomy and decentralization should be developed. Local education councils should be set up to discuss local issues along with a local educational ombudsman system.

4. The development of lifelong learning will increase the participation of private sector institutions in education. Thus, Nikkyōso should look for ways to increase recruitment of union members in this sector.

5. Nikkyōso should also expand its membership into the pre-school education and child-care sector, and into other types of educational institution.

6. Nikkyōso should play a role in helping to build local communities through involvement in local voluntary activities, NGOs, and so on.

7. Nikkyōso should use its influence in international organizations to promote the rights of teachers' organizations around the world.[18]

It can be seen from this list that the first four recommendations are aimed at the education system as a whole, while the final three are more specifically aimed at the union itself. Item number one in particular shares many important characteristics with Nakasone's new issues previously discussed, especially the importance of developing the individuality and international awareness of the child. It should be noted also that concern to meet the needs of the individual child was the most important concept in item number two of the CCE's 1991 report quoted in the previous chapter. In some key areas, the ideas of the new issues of the Nakasone era, the proposals of the CCE, and the proposals of Nikkyōso may be converging.

At the time when it was issuing its reports, response to the 21st Century Vision Committee was mixed. When its interim report was published in November 1994, the *Asahi Shimbun* criticized it for not having the courage to deviate from the "official" union view of the past—that is, one that laid all the blame for problems in the Japanese education system at the door of the government and the Ministry of Education. The newspaper believed that a more honest appraisal of the union's past would have enabled it to come up with a more realistic program for its future.[19] Then, when the final report was published in April 1995, the *Asahi Shimbun* pointed out that some of the detailed proposals for change that involved a more flexible attitude to the teacher responsibility system and teacher training were in complete contradiction with existing union policy on those areas. The paper correctly predicted that, because of this, there would be trouble at the upcoming annual conference in September.[20] Despite vocal opposition at that conference, however, the leadership succeeded in pushing through amendments to union policy that brought that policy into line with the content of the 21st Century Vision Committee's final report. These changes represent the immediate and concrete change of direction undertaken by post-schism Nikkyōso.

Nikkyōso's Changes of Policy at the 1995 Annual Conference

Table 5.1 is a summary of the five main areas in which very significant changes were made in union policy at the September 1995 conference. National policy or "campaign policy" (*undō hōshin*) is decided on at the national conference every year. There is no doubt that 1995 will go down as one of the most historic conferences in the union's history. For Zenkyō, these changes of policy are further proof that Nikkyōso's right-wing leadership has sold out to the enemy. We will now analyze the significance of each of these changes.

Analysis of These Changes. Representatives of the education authorities broadly welcomed Nikkyōso's changes (further proof for Zenkyō that the whole exercise had been a sell-out to the enemy). Writing in the journal of school management research, Professor Kanei Hiroaki addressed the first four of these changes of policy and analyzed their significance for ongoing changes in educational administration. His conclusions are discussed next.

Table 5.1 Five Areas in Which the New Campaign Policy Represent a Change of Drection[21]

(Contrasting excerpts from the 'campaign policy' documents of 1995 and 1994)

1. The MOE Course of Study Guidelines

New position. "Based upon general principles, each school will set about implementing an education devoted to the creative faculties of children, based upon the general course of study guidelines."

Previous position. "We promote the creation of an education curriculum based on the aims of a movement of self formation (independent child-centred learning), and we oppose (external) pressure."

2. The Teachers' Meeting (Within Each School)

New position. "All the teachers, convened by the principal, take common responsibility for solving educational problems, and, using the forum of the teachers' meeting, under the responsibility of the principal, they plan the revitalisation of school education."

Previous position. "We will strengthen negotiation at the work place and strive for the democratisation of the work place, based upon the transformation of the teachers' meeting into a decision making body."

3. The Teacher Training System

New position. "We will participate in in-service training such as the training of newly qualified teachers etc. in order to effect the qualitative improvement of teaching staff. We will strive to ensure that they reflect the thoughts and intentions of teachers."

Previous position. "We will set about dismantling the newly qualified teacher training system."

4. The Teacher Responsibility System

New position. "Very great differences have arisen in the substance of the *shunin* system and the way each local union handles (the *shunin* system) at the work place. We call for an examination of ways of improving the remuneration of teachers, including the way they ought to be paid."

Previous position. "In order to prevent the establishment of a *shunin* system we will promote the donation of [the extra] pay [received by *shunin* teachers to a general fund that will be used for the benefit of all teachers]."

5. The National Flag and the National Anthem

New position. (Not mentioned at all in the 1995 'campaign policy' document)

Previous position. "1) We are opposed to the *Kimigayo* because its historical role and its words are opposed to the constitution based upon popular sovereignty. 2) We are opposed to the imposition of the *Hinomaru* on schools through the use of the general guidelines and other methods."

Course of Study Guidelines. Course of study guidelines (*Gakushū shidō yōryō*) issued by the Ministry of Education lay down basic standards of curriculum content and school organization. The ministry says they help maintain uniform standards across the nation. Nikkyōso had traditionally seen them as devices by the central government to impose its arbitrary will on the education system. Professor Kanei welcomes Nikkyōso's decision to end its opposition and calls for schools to base their teaching on these guidelines. He points out that now both the union and the ministry have come to base their guidelines on respect for the individuality of the child.[22] If both the union and the ministry are sincere about what they write in their published reports, then there should be no major ideological differences of opinion about the basic aims of education. Thus, conflict can become a thing of the past.

The Teachers' Meeting. Traditionally Nikkyōso has resisted the power of the school principal and insisted on democratic decision-making at each individual school. Ambiguities concerning the legal powers of the principal had left the door open for differing arrangements to be worked out, depending on local circumstances. As we saw in chapter four, Rohlen analyzed the way in which power relations in the teachers' room varied from school to school based on the local strength of the union and the assertiveness of its school-level leadership. Nikkyōso's change of direction in 1995 for the first time recognizes that the principal has the legitimate role of leader in the school setting. Professor Kanei points out that new challenges facing schools (e.g., their role in the new provision of lifelong learning) will require positive leadership.[23] It may be, therefore, that the more flexible relationship between union members and school principals made possible by Nikkyōso's change in direction will allow the development of a new kind of school-level management structure in the future.

The Teacher Training System. As shown in chapters two and three, Nikkyōso has always been opposed to teacher training systems administered by national or local governments. This applied to initial teacher training, probationary training, and in-service training for experienced teachers. Professor Kanei spoke for many when he welcomed the end to this opposition. Many people see the improvement of teacher training as one way to address problems like school bullying and increasing truancy.

The Teacher Responsibility (Shunin) *System.* Before 1995, the *shunin* system was a classic example of a policy that had been agreed on by the government, the Ministry of Education, and other allies in the conservative camp, but had been thwarted at the implementation stage by Nikkyōso. The system created a new class of *shunin* teachers who would have responsibility for various areas of school life—for example, career advice to pupils, staff administration, and so on. Such teachers were given a small extra payment each month to compensate them for their extra work. The union never denied that such positions of responsibility were important for the efficient running of the school. However, they believed that in a democratic organization teachers should not be paid extra for extra work, but instead should simply take turns to carry out such work. The union was afraid that the *shunin* system would help management "divide and rule" the union by creating a new administrative class of teacher. As a result of this approach, schools that were strongly under the influence of the union adopted a policy whereby teachers who were paid extra money for their extra responsibilities simply gave up this extra money to a common fund that was used to buy extra equipment or books for the school. Indeed, schools under the influence of Zenkyō still practice this policy. Professor Kanei is glad to see Nikkyōso become more flexible in its attitude to the allocation of particular responsibilities to particular teachers because this will enable *shunin* teachers to become leaders of educational subsystems within the total system of the school. And this will encourage more flexibility for school management in the future.[24]

Overall Significance of These Changes

In an editorial following the conference at which these changes were agreed on, the *Yomiuri Shimbun* argued that Nikkyōso needed to make them in order to cope with the new phase of education reforms proposed by *Rinkyōshin*.[25] The editorial made the important point that, to be meaningful, the changes must also win acceptance at the regional and school level. The presence of some very bitter opposition to reform at the conference indicates that this process will be far from smooth in certain parts of the country and in some schools. However, this line of argument contends that these changes must be fully implemented if Nikkyōso is to play a worthwhile role in the new era of education reform. This is certainly the main reason why the union leadership pushed them through. Together, these four changes, if successfully implemented, will allow significant change to take place within schools for the first time since the Occupation. This is because government-inspired changes in the structures of school management and teacher training can now take place with the cooperation of the majority of teachers rather than with their (active or passive) resistance. Thus, the true significance of these changes lies not in the measures themselves as much as in the possibilities they open up for future reform.

Has Nikkyōso reaped any benefits yet from its policy of compromise with the authorities? In the previous chapter we showed how the Ministry of Education has not changed its basic position of refusing to recognize the union as a national representative of the teaching profession. However, there are some signs of more consultations between the two former enemies over specific educational issues. In February 1996, Nikkyōso held a conference that was attended for the first time by a senior Ministry of Education official. The main topic of the conference was the prevention of bullying-related suicides, an issue of national concern at that time following a series of such suicides among junior and senior high school students. The press welcomed this newfound cooperation between union and ministry. The point was made that this new spirit of compromise allowed participating parties to be more open about their own failings, rather than putting the blame at the door of their political enemies.[26] Nikkyōso now argues that this new approach is the only way of bringing about constructive change. It accuses Zenkyō of living in the past and refusing to analyze its own mistakes and failings as well as share in the responsibility for contemporary educational ills.[27]

The National Flag and Anthem

The fifth change of direction that took place at Nikkyōso's 1995 conference concerned the very contentious issue of the flag and the anthem. This issue dominated relations between the government and unions so much in the period running from just before to immediately after the schism that it is worthy of separate and detailed consideration. To understand this issue fully, we must analyze its historical background. Legally speaking, Japan did not have a national flag or anthem until a special law was passed in 1999.[28] However, even before legalization, the universal use of the *Hinomaru* flag and the *Kimigayo* anthem at places and events at which countries normally display their national symbols gave them a de facto official status. Controversy surrounds both symbols because of their association with wartime and prewar Japanese militarism and imperialism. Unlike its Axis allies, Germany and Italy, Japan did not change or modify its national symbols after the war. Critics on the left interpreted this as a failure to signal a clear break with the past. Actually, in October 1945, as part of its program against militarism, SCAP had sent out orders forbidding the official raising of the *Hinomaru*, only to reverse this decision in 1949, hoping, rather optimistically, that from then on the unmodified flag would become a "symbol of peace."[29] This failed to happen, and both the flag and the anthem have been controversial ever since.

It was inevitable that the flag and the anthem would become a contentious issue between the Ministry of Education and Nikkyōso. In some ways, this has been the most overtly political and ideological conflict between the two sides. Ever since the Minister of Education, Amano Teiyū, announced, in 1950, that raising the flag and singing the anthem would be "desirable" (*nozomashii*), the ministry and conservative politicians have consistently tried to extend recognition of these national symbols into schools.[30] Their aim has been to instill patriotism into children. Nikkyōso, for its part, has been opposed to the reintroduction of the flag and the anthem into school life for two main reasons. First, they share the opinion, previously outlined, that the flag and the anthem are reminiscent of war and imperialism, and, second, they are opposed, in principle, to the authorities giving orders to schools about how to conduct their affairs—in this case school ceremonies.[31] The second objection arose in the mid-1980s when the Ministry of Education stepped up its efforts to increase recognition of the flag and anthem.

As already emphasized in this chapter, the debate on education in the 1980s was dominated by *Rinkyōshin*. Schoppa has shown how many of Nakasone's intended reforms were blocked by the immobilism of the policy-making system. One or two proposals were "largely implemented" however, because they had the backing of a "conservative consensus"—that is, they were agreed on by the main conservative actors in the policy-making process.[32] One of these proposals concerned the compulsory flying of the flag and singing of the anthem at school functions. The need for increased patriotism was justified by Japan's increasing internationalization. As we have already seen, it was argued that Japanese people could not properly learn to respect foreign cultures until they had learned to respect their own.[33] Nikkyōso and other opponents saw this as merely the latest justification for a long-established effort by conservative forces to turn the clock back to prewar style jingoism.

The Ministry of Education responded to *Rinkyōshin's* call for greater recognition of the flag and anthem by including in its 1989 revision of the course of study guidelines (*gakushū shidō yōryō*) a change in the wording concerning regulations about the flag and the anthem. From now on flying the flag and singing the anthem at school ceremonies were no longer merely desirable (*nozomashii*), they were something that "must be done" (*suru mono to suru*).[34] Prior to 1989, over half of elementary and senior high schools had failed to comply with ministry wishes. The figure for junior high schools was a little over 60 percent.[35] The ministry was now aiming for 100 percent compliance and was prepared to discipline principals who resisted. In every prefecture boards of education were instructed to compile lists of which schools did and did not fly the flag and sing the anthem. In 1991, 125 school principals (90 percent of whom were in Kōchi prefecture) were disciplined, the first to be so punished under the new rules.[36] In schools with strong union representation and a militant leadership, the school principals now found themselves in a difficult position. They would be punished by their superiors if they did not comply with the regulations, but they would meet with resistance and disruption if they did. In many cases the principal and vice-principal tried to find ways around this dilemma by obeying the letter of the law while appeasing opponents by enacting the regulations in meaningless or even farcical ways. There are reports of the vice-principal singing the anthem alone while playing the tune on a small cassette player,[37] and of principals running the flag up a flagpole, leaving it there for a few seconds, and then pulling it down.[38] Reports of flags being flown in inappropriate places, for example on the tops of buildings, in the corners of playing fields, or among copses of trees, are even more numerous.[39] On one occasion high school students chose to fly *koinobori* carp streamers from the flagpole in place of the *Hinomaru*.[40] Humorous examples of opposition to official policy should not detract from the intense pressure school principals were sometimes put under when they were sandwiched between orders from above and resistance from below. In February 1999, a high school principal in Hiroshima prefecture was driven to suicide by this pressure.[41] Proponents of the flag and anthem used this tragedy to call for legal recognition of the *Hinomaru* and *Kimigayo* as national symbols.[42] Opponents used the same tragedy to call for an end to government imposition of the flag and anthem at school ceremonies.[43]

Despite continued resistance and disruption, the Ministry of Education seemed to be gaining ground over its opponents.[44] In terms of the official statistics of compliance there is no doubt that it has mostly achieved its aims.[45] Thus, it seems that Nikkyōso made its 1995 decision to omit any reference to the flag and the anthem in its campaign policy document to try to bring an end to a lost battle. In 1999, when the issue of the flag and the anthem was revived by the controversy over legalization, Nikkyōso was compelled to make a stand on this issue again. However, the union was careful when it issued its statement of opposition to the legalization bill to make sure that this opposition was only incorporated into its policy on political collective action, not into its educational policy.[46] Throughout the dispute over the flag and the anthem it has been notoriously difficult to separate "political issues" from "educational issues," but Nikkyōso's national leaders were keen to be seen not to be promoting school disruption, as this would undermine the new, more respectable and moderate image they were (and are) trying to cultivate.[47] This is another area, therefore, in which Zenkyō accuses Nikkyōso of surrendering to the enemy, and it is an area where ordinary Nikkyōso members have had the most trouble following the national lead. Indeed, many Nikkyōso-affiliated prefectural and city unions continue to informally oppose use of the flag and the anthem in schools despite the formal change to national policy.[48] However, from the point of view of the national leadership, if it wanted to make a serious shift from confrontation toward compromise with the government and the MOE, such a change in policy was inevitable. As we have seen, Zenkyō has repeatedly warned of the folly of trying to compromise with the government. This does not mean, however, that Zenkyō is only concerned with resisting change and hanging on to the past. It has its own set of proposals that seek to address problems in the education system in the 1990s. It is to this program that we now turn.

Zenkyō's Post-Schism Position

Zenkyō has retained the basic position it put forward following its initial creation in 1989. The specific points of Zenkyō's pacifism and its campaign for "democratic education" were outlined in chapter three. Since then, Zenkyō has been active in support of campaigns against American bases. In this way Zenkyō has maintained old Nikkyōso's traditional links with left-wing causes. In the case of educational issues it has also retained the traditional, confrontational approach. Although new Nikkyōso has started to admit a certain amount of self-criticism—for example, on the subject of bullying—Zenkyō sticks to the line that problems like bullying are the result of poor working conditions and an authoritarian education system.[49] When a junior high school student was charged with the gruesome murder of an elementary school boy in Kobe in May 1997, Zenkyō's official position was that such crimes were the result of "the current highly controlled and discriminative education system [in which] children were denied . . . humane growth and development."[50] Zenkyō has also retained a policy of total opposition to the flying of the *Hinomaru* and the singing of the *Kimigayo* at school ceremonies. It also continues to oppose the *shunin* system on the grounds that it divides teachers and is the first step on a road of turning schools into organizations run like private companies.[51]

Zenkyō has also been working on its own, new positive policy proposals. The most important of these has been a "draft charter on essential rights of teachers and staff," the second draft of which was presented to the 1995 national conference. The preamble of this draft gives a good indication of the underlying ideology of the union. A summary of it is as follows:

> Authoritarian control over education has been tightened and, as a result, pressure upon both staff and children has increased. Teachers are unable to do what they think necessary for the children in their care. Thus teachers desire both autonomy of education and respect for their dignity as human beings. Teachers should enjoy "educational rights" in their capacity as education professionals, as well as human rights in their capacity as human beings and workers. The spirit of the Fundamental Law of Education and the Japanese Constitution should be respected. "It goes without saying that the well-to-do (*sic*) development of education based on the rights of every child is closely related with the establishment of rights of teachers and staff."[52]

The contents of the charter detail ways in which the ideals outlined in this preamble would be realized and/or safeguarded. The charter is based on an interpretation of the Constitution and the Fundamental Law of Education that sees power over educational issues resting in the hands of ordinary teachers and their organizations. There is very little that new Nikkyōso would disagree with. One demand, the demand for a five-day week, is already on the way to being achieved. Concerns over health and safety at the workplace, the prevention of overwork, and security of tenure for teachers would also win consensus support, not just among teachers' organizations but among education administrators too. Article 10, however, calls for the elimination of the "enforcement from above" of regulations relating to the course of study and textbooks. Nikkyōso's 21st Century Vision Committee was also in favor of reducing central control over these areas. However, Nikkyōso's ending of its opposition to study guidelines from the Ministry of Education shows that it is willing to support a certain amount of regulation from above while the long-term goal of decentralization is pursued. Zenkyō, on the other hand, wants a radical and immediate curtailment of the MOE's powers. Zenkyō maintains that surrendering to the MOE will only increase the ministry's powers in the long run.

The Fundamental Law on Education and the Constitution have been articles of faith for teacher union activists since the 1940s. In the 1990s, another document was added to this list of canonical texts. This was the United Nations Convention on the Rights of the Child ratified by Japan on May 22, 1994. Zenkyō argues that the provisions of this convention should be incorporated into Japanese domestic law.[53] The union's campaign for the protection of human rights—for both staff and children—can be seen as another part of its struggle to limit the discretionary powers of central government.

The Split in the National Conference on Educational Research

Another result of the schism is the splitting into two of the teachers' national conference on educational research. This was an annual meeting in which thousands of teachers and education experts from across Japan met to discuss every conceivable aspect of school education. There are now two of these meetings that take place usually in January and usually at the same time (making it very difficult for anyone to attend both meetings). In 1999, Nikkyōso held its National Conference on Education Research in Okayama prefecture from January 21 to January 24. On exactly the same four days Zenkyō held its National Assembly for Educational Research in Shiga prefecture. Both conferences are attended by thousands of teachers and are broken up into dozens of seminars and symposiums spread out over several different locations during the four days. Nikkyōso, because it is the larger union, receives more media attention. Most of this media attention is nonpolitical, reflecting the content of the seminars.

The issue that grabbed the headlines in 1999 was *gakkyū hōkai* or "collapsing classrooms," which is the shorthand term for the perceived collapse in the teachers' authority in many classrooms across Japan, particularly in elementary schools (places that were previously considered immune from this kind of thing).[54] Prominence given to this issue reflects the press's preoccupation with the issue at that time. Actually there were dozens of subjects discussed at Nikkyōso's conference and the same was true of Zenkyō's conference. Although when making public statements Zenkyō leaders tend to blame the government-imposed system for Japan's educational woes, when ordinary teachers get together to discuss problems like the teaching of specific subjects, counseling, health and safety, and so on they are every bit as practical-minded as Nikkyōso teachers or teachers anywhere.[55] One small difference between Nikkyōso and Zenkyō meetings is that the latter still sometimes have a large security presence because of threats by rightist groups against Zenkyō.[56] Such threats against Nikkyōso have diminished, but union leaders are still wary. (Security at their Tokyo Headquarters is tight after an incident when a man entered the offices brandishing a pistol.) It seems, therefore, that the effect of the schism in the area of union-sponsored educational research has been to duplicate previously existing arrangements. This could be regarded as beneficial to the teaching profession because it results in more teachers being able to discuss educational issues with colleagues from other parts of Japan. The disadvantage of the present setup, however, is that the two unions conduct their research and discussion in isolation. This results in unnecessary duplication and a lack of intellectual cross-fertilization between members of the two organizations.

Conclusion: The Effects of Nikkyōso's Change of Direction on the Debate on Education Reform in Japan

The newspaper editorials quoted in this chapter have all welcomed Nikkyōso's more moderate and conciliatory stance. They have pointed to the way in which important concerns, like those relating to bullying and truancy, have not been properly dealt with owing to political fighting between left and right within the education system. They argue that in the post-Cold War world, this kind of ideological conflict is anachronistic. They all also agree on the important role played by Nakasone and *Rinkyōshin* in starting off a new round of debate on education reform. Although Nakasone himself was disappointed by his inability to achieve significant change while he was still in office, it now looks as though the great education debate that he initiated will have a real impact. Continuing public concern about issues like truancy and bullying combined with pressure from business and industry for an education system that meets Japan's changing economic needs has created a climate that politicians and bureaucrats cannot ignore. This is why the Ministry of Education has adopted some of the rhetoric of change (e.g., calls for flexibility, diversity, and internationalization) in order to adopt these popular slogans as its own. At the time of writing the changed language of education of the 1990s has yet to be translated into real structural change within the system itself. (Admittedly there are some interesting pilot projects involving new types of comprehensive school, and there has definitely been a relaxation of entrance procedures for senior high schools and universities. Secondary and primary schools are also in the process of introducing a five-day school week to replace the old five and a half day system.) However, the likelihood of more significant change taking place is now much stronger than it was under the period of the two-camp structure of policy-making and implementation examined by Schoppa. This changed state of affairs involves the change in direction of Nikkyōso as well as the changes that have taken place in the wider world of Japan's polity and economy

By abandoning its Marxist rhetoric and adopting the language of modernization and compromise, new Nikkyōso's leadership have taken their union on a course that suits the new mood of reform. In contrast, the leaders of Zenkyō have refused to let go of their traditional certainties. The importance of Nikkyōso's change (or rather series of policy changes) is that it will allow new educational initiatives a much greater chance of implementation than was previously the case. Already, in those areas where Nikkyōso and the Ministry of Education are in broad agreement (e.g., the promotion of more flexibility and choice as well as more international education) there are signs of genuine change taking place where it really matters, the *genba*. The educational needs addressed by these and other modern policies are quite different from the educational needs of Japanese society as it emerged from the destruction of total war. The new atmosphere of cooperation between the Ministry of Education and Nikkyōso reflects this fundamental shift in the nature of the debate on education in Japan. The ending of the Cold War and the concomitant ending of the two-camp model of education policy-making have helped remove a straitjacket from Japanese educators that had prevented them from cooperating with one another in addressing the practical problems facing the education system and the children in its care.

CHAPTER SIX

THE PLACE OF TEACHERS' UNIONS WITHIN THE WIDER UNION MOVEMENT

This chapter seeks to answer the following key question: What kind of an organization is Nikkyōso and how has it changed during the events of the schism? In the process of addressing this question, we will inevitably touch on the issue of what Nikkyōso's recent experience tells us about the broader condition of unions in Japan today. In chapters one, two, and three we examined Nikkyōso's historical evolution as a union, making note of the unions' particular characteristics. This chapter will adopt a more theoretical approach, involving the use of the theoretical literature on unions in general, teachers' unions, and unions in Japan

THEORETICAL APPROACHES TO THE STUDY OF UNIONS

Unions originally came into existence to protect the workforce, and they have continued to perform this primary function regardless of what later theorists may have said. However, there are many ways in which the interests of the workforce can be protected or promoted. For Marx, unions were organs of economic struggle that arose out of the working class for the primary purpose of guaranteeing the worker the wage that amounted to the real value of his labour-power. It was out of this unequal struggle against the power of capital that workers collectively became class conscious and imbued with the will to overthrow the capitalist system.[1] This is the origin of the Marxist belief that, although unions have useful functions as defenders of the short-term interests of workers (pay and conditions, etc.), their main function lies in the long-term goal of raising the consciousness of the working class in preparation for the final revolutionary struggle against the capitalist system. Some Marxists under the influence of the revisionist Eduard Bernstein (1859–1932) have tempered this view, however, and put forward the theory that, although the interests of workers were certainly opposed to those of capital, working-class organizations could successfully use their own strength and the institutions of the state to promote their own interests without necessitating a wholesale revolution. Thus, the mere label "Marxist" when attached to a union leader, activist, or theorist does not, by itself, place that person into a neat pigeonhole, from which all their views and opinions can be deduced.

Non-Marxist theories of unions tend to be more concerned with classification and the placement of unions within the social, economic, and political contexts of the nation-state. Allen, for example, argues that unions ought to be examined in the contexts of their whole environment with the primary and secondary social and political forces isolated and assessed.[2] This approach allows for the comparison of unions in different countries. Clearly, the economic, political, and social structures within which a union operates will have a decisive influence on its organization, aims, and ideology, as well as its success or failure in attracting members and defending their interests. A non-Marxist approach to unions is also significant because it allows for the possibility that the interests of workers and capitalists need not be at odds with each other. A non-Marxist union leader, activist, or theorist can thus entertain the possibility that cooperation with capitalists and their representatives can be of benefit to union members.

Teachers' Unions

Although there has been literature about individual teachers' organizations since such organizations first came into existence in the late nineteenth century, it is only recently that the specific area of teacher unionism has been addressed by scholars seeking to arrive at general theoretical explanations that could cross national boundaries. In 1985, Martin Lawn edited a book about the politics of teacher unionism and drew together some common strands from the case studies contained therein.[3] He noticed four main similarities among the unions studied. First, there was usually a history of petty restrictions imposed on the teachers and their organizations by local or central governments. Second, there was the perennial issue of low pay. Third, there were the common attempts by teachers to free themselves from the economic, political, and cultural control exercised over their lives by state authorities. Finally, Lawn noticed that teachers' unions always make links with other unions and the wider labor movement.[4]

Lawn's book provided some very useful case studies of teachers' unions, but did not devote much space to thorough comparative analysis. It was not until 1992 that a really thorough comparison of teachers' unions in various countries was published.[5] This book consisted of case studies of fourteen countries, including the United States, England and Wales, Australia, Mexico, Israel, and China (but not Japan). The editor, Bruce S. Cooper, agrees with the validity of Lawn's main conclusions and also observes that "in the fourteen nations represented in this book, all have well-established [teachers'] unions, protected by national or regional labour laws, and they engage in collective action, much as blue-collar union organisations have long done."[6] In other words, both Lawn and Cooper have found that teachers' unions in the latter part of the twentieth century have many of the characteristics of other kinds of labor union.

In many countries the evolution of teachers' organizations into these kinds of unions was accompanied by criticism to the effect that teachers, "those paragons of civic virtue and moral responsibility,"[7] should not join or form labor unions and indulge in the kind of "industrial action" that is really the province of proletarian organizations. This view, that teaching is a significantly different type of work from that of "ordinary" workers, manifests itself in various ways. For example, the formation in England of the Professional Association of Teachers (PAT) in the 1970s was an example of the creation of an organization dedicated to avoid the tactics of labor unions (especially strike action), in favor of a campaign for the recognition of teachers as a professional group on a par with lawyers or doctors.[8] Although PAT failed to recruit teachers in large numbers, its existence illustrates a conundrum in the minds of many teachers whatever their nationality. Cooper describes it as follows.

> Teachers often wonder whether they are "professionals" with a primary concern for their students, or "workers" employed by a state-run system. Are they working on behalf of their families and communities who entrust their children to the school? Or are they working for themselves and their fellows best by joining a union, becoming active in political life, and taking concerted action to improve their lot?

Given this conundrum, what are the main motivating factors for teachers joining unions rather than professional associations like PAT? Cooper answers this question:

> In country after country, teachers find themselves cast as workers, as civil servants in a system that values regularity, regulation and control. . . . Teachers have responded by joining the trade union movement or by siding with national and regional political parties to increase their power to compete for scarce resources. As such, teachers turned to union leadership to represent them in the halls of power: national, state, provincial, and local legislatures and councils.[9]

It should also be noted, that in many cases teachers' pay levels are closer to those of other unionized workers like railwaymen and electricians, rather than "professionals" like doctors or lawyers. This factor also makes it more likely that teachers will find a natural home in a union, rather than a professional association.

Overall, the work of Lawn and Cooper underlines the general point made by Allen earlier in this chapter—that is, teachers' unions, like other kinds of trade unions, need to be examined in the contexts of their whole environments: social, political, and economic. Because my own study is mainly concerned with a political analysis of teacher unionism, it is to the political environment in particular that we now turn.

The Politics of Teacher Unionism

Teacher unionism is inevitably political in two distinct ways. First, it is political for the reasons mentioned by Cooper—it is involved in power relations with state organizations in an effort to compete for resources and defend the interests of teachers. In this respect teachers' unions have a function much like any other trade union. They try, by whatever means available, to exert influence over the relevant policy-making processes to promote their own interests. However, if the particular means available include industrial action, then teachers' organizations face certain issues that most other types of union do not have to deal with. This is because industrial action must, by definition, damage the interests of the children whose education is affected. Thus, teachers' unions, like the unions that represent providers of essential services or emergency services, can be accused of callous selfishness when they organize strikes and stoppages. Some scholars have argued that teachers' strikes, by definition, must be political.[10] In the private sector unions strike to inflict economic harm on their employers, but in the public sector the intention is to put pressure on employers and government through disruptive tactics or tactics of disobedience. This adds a political dimension to public sector strikes that private sector strikes do not have. In most countries we also find that public sector industrial relations are more heavily regulated by the government than the private sector equivalent. Strikes by emergency services, are often illegal. In the case of teachers, the legal status of strike action varies from country to country and sometimes within countries. In most states in the United States for example teachers' strikes are a crime, and the leaders of unions that indulge in strike action can be sent to jail.[11]

The second way in which teacher unionism is political, however, is more involved with the political nature of education itself. Whenever there is ideological debate or conflict about the content of education, teachers and their organizations are inevitably at the center of it. Such debate and conflict are often at their sharpest when a broader social or political change is under way.[12] In Hungary, for example, teachers' unions were an essential part in that country's move toward *perestroika* and democratization.[13] Similarly, authoritarian regimes will always try to crush or co-opt teachers' organizations as part of their efforts to control the nation's citizens. Such regimes take a particular interest in the teaching of history and moral education.

Nikkyōso as a Case Study in Teacher Unionism

The main question of this section is: How does the theoretical literature on teacher unionism help us to understand the evolution and the current status of Nikkyōso (and Zenkyō)? To answer this question, we will first examine the practical application of different theoretical perspectives by union leaders and activists and then move on to the specific debate about the status of teachers and their duties with respect to strike action. This debate is a highly controversial and sensitive one for teachers' unions in every country.

Marxists Versus Non-Marxists in Nikkyōso

Theories relating to unions often have a practical dimension as well as an academic one. This is because union leaders and activists, as well as their opposite numbers in government and management, have their own views about what the aims and tactics of unions are or should be. They can select from the various different ideas about unionism those theories that best suit their own agenda. It is highly significant, therefore, that the early leaders of the unions that eventually came together to form Nikkyōso had an overtly Marxist approach. Chapter one surveyed the success of the left-wing leadership in their struggle to build up a mass membership teachers' union. It also analyzed the complete failure of rival teachers' unions with an anti-Marxist leadership to win the support of ordinary teachers. Although successful in attracting a mass membership, the leadership of the early Nikkyōso was divided between Communists and Socialists (and there were also disagreements *within* the Socialist camp). Disagreements arose mainly over aims and tactics, and over affiliation and support for political parties and union federations. This early leadership can be described as Marxist in its general orientation, although the extent to which it adhered to a revisionist style of Marxism, rather than a pure, revolutionary Marxism is a more complex issue. Nikkyōso's rhetoric certainly portrayed the LDP (and its predecessor conservative governing parties) and the Ministry of Education as "the enemy." Whether this enemy had to be totally defeated by revolutionary action, or whether it was a more revisionist tactic of using state institutions to promote the interests of teachers and workers that was being advocated, it is more difficult to say. The existence of Marxist ideology within the leadership of the early Nikkyōso—whether hardline or revisionist—is significant, however, because it was a deciding factor in sowing the seeds of confrontation between the union and the ideologically conservative government. The unwillingness of this government to talk to any teachers' representatives, whatever their color, played into the hands of confrontationist teachers' leaders. It was that confrontation that was to define industrial relations in the education sector in Japan in the postwar years.

The most significant factor behind the strength of postwar Nikkyōso was the ability of its leadership, until the 1980s, to retain the allegiance of the majority of ordinary teachers. Most of the early national programs, with their pacifism, their demands for better pay and conditions, and their anti-conservatism were designed to appeal to a broad range of the rank-and-file. People of greatly differing political persuasions could bring themselves to support the same broad program, especially if they found themselves on the defensive. As Thurston noted in 1973, "It is necessary to keep in mind [the] distinction between opposition to the government based on Marxist ideological grounds and that based on the desire to keep education free from excessive government control if one is to understand the high degree of support [Nikkyōso] receives from its predominantly non-Marxist membership."[14] So long as there was a broad agreement over the program of the union, an uneasy alliance of Marxists, moderate socialists, and nonpolitical teachers could be maintained. However, once a fundamental review of this program was proposed, this alliance was bound to come under threat.

Struggles for control of unions between Marxists and non-Marxists are common, but they can take on a distinctive character when the union in question is a teachers' union. As we have seen, teachers' unions, as well as serving the function of protecting the interests of their members, are also of political significance because of their role in education. A strong teachers' union can have a strong influence on the content of education, or, conversely, a weak union can allow the government to have the decisive say. We have already seen how important the issue of control over education has been in postwar Japan. Both sides warned of the extreme danger of allowing the other side too much control over impressionable minds. In the early years of the postwar period each side could point to concrete examples of the other side's extremism. In 1951, a Japanese newspaper published what it claimed was a draft of "An Outline of Ethical Practice of the Japanese People", which included references to the transcendental moral character of the state and Japan's peculiar emperor-centred national polity. It claimed that the author of the article was the Minister for Education, Amano Teiyū.[15] Nikkyōso and its allies used incidents like this to warn of what would happen if the central government were allowed to regain the sort of control over education it had enjoyed before the war. In a similar way, the government and its allies used incidents like the Yamaguchi diary case of 1953 to warn about what would happen if the education of children were left in the hands of "red" teachers.[16] It should be noted that moderates within Nikkyōso resisted the influence of Marxists, not only because of their own personal ideological disagreements, but also because of the bad publicity and disruption brought on the union by incidents like the Yamaguchi diary case. In the case of Yamaguchi prefecture, the prefectural union lost a significant amount of members due to the controversy surrounding the case.[17] This experience, that moderate members will quit a union if too much disruption is caused by militants and if the consequences of that disruption are perceived to have adverse consequences for members, is not an unusual experience for teachers' unions in other parts of the world too.[18] In the case of Nikkyōso, however, the debate over teachers' industrial action did not always proceed along lines familiar to students of teachers' unions in other nations.

Strikes and the Debate Over the True Status of Teachers

We have already noted the particular problems faced by teachers' unions with regard to the use of strike action during industrial disputes. In some nations strike action by teachers is illegal. In the case of Japan, chapter one reviewed the very brief honeymoon under the Occupation during which teachers and other public sector workers enjoyed the right to strike. This period ended in 1948 when SCAP banned this kind of strike. Two years later this ban was written into the Local Public Service Law, and every teachers' strike since then has been declared illegal by the government. This has not prevented Nikkyōso from organizing strikes, sometimes in the guise of a mass taking of leave of absence.[19] However, because of the legal autonomy of prefectural teachers' unions, a universal, nationwide strike has never been achieved. Whenever Nikkyōso's central executive planned a national strike, it was always unable to win support from those prefectures that were unwilling to take action. Even at the height of Nikkyōso militancy, during the campaign against the Teachers' Efficiency Rating Plan in 1958, a national strike called for by the central leadership won only the support of seventeen prefectures.[20] Strike action was usually accompanied by severe disruption in the form of police raids on local union offices, arrests, and dismissals of participating teachers. Physical violence between strikers and police was not uncommon. (The negative effect of all this on union membership figures had already been noted.)

It is unsurprising that the above period of intense industrial action coincided with the domination of the union's Central Executive Council (CEC) by Communist Party-supporting members. Ideologically, they were the most predisposed to mistrust the government's proposed rating system and to shun any suggestions that compromise with "the enemy" should be an option. However, the hard line taken by the CEC and those prefectures that undertook strike action did not pay off. Militant prefectures like Ehime saw a drastic decline in union membership. Instead it was the moderately led Kanagawa prefecture that provided the model solution to the efficiency rating threat. This involved implementing the system, but also allowing principals to consult with teachers before grading them. In effect, all the grades given to teachers were favorable.[21] (See chapter two for more on why the original proposals in the efficiency rating system were regarded as a threat by Nikkyōso.) Tactically, the lesson was obvious—the aims of the union could still be achieved without the need for costly disruptive action. From that point on an ideologically committed Marxist would not necessarily be on the side of confrontational strike action. This helps explain the major dispute that arose between Socialists and Communists over the tactics of strike action by teachers in 1974.

In April 1974, a one-day "strike for the right to strike" took place involving Nikkyōso and other public sector unions. This strike signaled a return to the use of national strike tactics by Nikkyōso's leadership who were worried about the lack of effectiveness of other forms of action.[22] As usual, the strike option was unpopular with many within the union. What was new about the internal union dispute in 1974, however, was the way the two political wings of Nikkyōso took sides. In 1974, it was the JCP-supporting wing of the union that opposed unfettered strike action. On April 17, an editorial in the JCP newspaper, *Akahata*, declared that since teachers were members of a "sacred" profession, they should not be considered the same as ordinary laborers, and should consider other forms of action, other than strike action. If they did decide on strike action, then they should ensure that some teachers stayed behind to see that the children in their care were properly looked after.[23] The official newspaper of Nikkyōso along with JSP publications angrily denounced this view. The argument that teaching was a "sacred" profession was one that had been traditionally used by the right in its attacks on Nikkyōso, and as a justification for the law denying teachers' unions the right to strike. There followed a technical Marxist debate about the true position of teachers within the working class and the possibility of a united front between teachers and parents against the common enemy of the government and the Ministry of Education.

The main argument of the JSP and its supporters within Nikkyōso was that it is regrettable, but inevitable, that the short-term interests of children will be harmed by strikes taken by teachers. But this is a price that must be paid for the sake of the wider struggle for democratic education and the long-term interests of both teachers and the children they teach. This echoes the argument that accompanies industrial action by teachers in any country. In England and Wales in 1985–1986, the "guerrilla-style" series of short strikes undertaken by the NUT and the NAS/UWT were criticized both by the government and the right-wing press as well as by rival teachers' associations like PAT and AMMA for exactly the same reasons.[24] What is unusual about the Japanese case in 1974 is that it was the Communist left who were arguing against unfettered strike action while those to their right, politically, were arguing the contrary. This apparent contradiction can partly be explained by the unusual circumstances of the early 1970s that saw the JSP under a relatively militant leadership while the JCP courted a more populist position in the country (this will be explored in more detail in the next chapter). Tactical considerations seem to have been a motivating factor behind the union factions too. One of the prefectural unions at the center of the dispute about whether to leave some teachers in school to supervise children during strike action was the Tokyo prefecture teachers' union (for teachers in the compulsory sector of education). The leaders of this union, which affiliated with Zenkyō at the time of the schism, now argue that although they were vilified by the JSP and its supporters in 1974, "history" has proved them right, because it is the JSP-supporting wing of the union that has "sold out" to the enemy.[25] In other words, the Communist tactic of avoiding the alienation of parents by compromising with them was preferable to the JSP tactic of not compromising on strikes, but later seeking to compromise with the LDP and the MOE on more fundamental matters. It should also be noted that Zenkyō pronouncements (as distinguished from those by the JCP) on the status of teachers avoid using the phrase "sacred profession" or anything like it. It seems that the use of that language was just a short-term, opportunistic ploy by the JCP in the early 1970s to try to win votes from a wider section of the electorate. JCP supporters within the union were never happy with it. The current Zenkyō position on the status of teachers is as follows: "Teachers should enjoy 'educational rights' in their capacity as education professionals, as well as human rights in their capacity as human beings and workers."[26] This combines the claim that teachers are, at the same time, both professionals *and* workers, a common claim made by teachers' unions around the world. Thus, despite the strange interlude in the early 1970s of Socialists appearing to be more militant than Communists, the overall trends within Japanese teacher unionism are unremarkable by comparative standards.

NIKKYŌSO AS A CASE STUDY OF JAPANESE UNIONISM IN THE 1980S AND 1990S

An examination of unions from a comparative perspective showed us that many of the concerns and difficulties, aims and tactics of an individual union can be understood by reference to its external environment. In every country this environment will be different. In its own particular case, Nikkyōso had to deal with external factors the most important of which were the legal environment in which it operated, the ideological position of the governing party with which it had to contend, and the ideological disputes between the two main parties with which it was allied. These factors are not static, but change over time. It is also an artificial exercise to isolate them since they are interconnected in many ways, and influenced by many other factors, both national and international. Unions within the same national system, however, will share many external factors that are the same or similar. For example, they will operate within the same framework of industrial relations laws, they will share national labour confederations, and so on. Thus, a full understanding of an individual union cannot be arrived at without an analysis of the national system of unions within which it exists. Similarly, any analysis of Nikkyōso's schism and its aftermath would be incomplete without an account of this union's place within the broader framework of Japanese unionism. We will start this account with an overview of the theory of Japanese private sector unionism, and then move on to the controversial concept of the "privatization" of the public sector unions.

Theoretical Approaches to Private Sector Unionism in Japan

Paralleling the wider theoretical debate between and among Marxist and non-Marxist approaches to the study of unions, there has been a lively debate about unions in Japan. As with the study of other nations, Marxist and non-Marxist scholars and activists have been divided primarily over the issue of whether the interests of workers and capitalists can be reconciled. Because Marxists believe that this is not possible, they regard attempts by union leaders to cooperate and compromise with employers or managers as "collaborationist."[27] From a Marxist perspective collaborationist labor relations have been a strong characteristic of Japanese unionism since its earliest days. This derives from the long-standing tendency of Japanese unions in the private sector to be organized around the enterprise rather than a craft or industry. Defenders of this system of enterprise unionism argue that it is a natural form of organization that derives its characteristics from broader Japanese culture. Cook, for example, argues as follows:

> Japanese life in general is characterised by organisations modelled on the family and replete with attitudes of loyalty, deference to the chief or eldest or head, obligation and even stronger personal attachment to one's superiors, ... Paternalism in the Japanese factory on the part of the employer therefore generates strong feelings of subordination, obligation, loyalty and gratitude on the part of the workers.[28]

It is not only Marxists who are critical of this kind of "cultural" explanation. Journalist and critic Karel Van Wolferen, for example, notes that while Japanese industrial relations are often described as harmonious, "quite a few unions had to be busted before harmony was established."[29]

Scholars who have adopted a broader historical perspective have arrived at a more complete explanation than those who rely on cultural explanations. R. Bean, an expert in comparative industrial relations, has noted how a lack of pervasive craft history in the areas of industrial mechanization and technology meant that early Japanese unions did not make a sharp separation among job groups a basis for organization.[30] Another factor pointed to by Japanese industrial relations scholar Kawanishi Hirosuke was the practice during industrialization of individuals leaving their rural village to go and work in the new factories and mines without taking their families with them. Labor came to be supplied through labor recruiters or other connections and this led to a "vertical consciousness" rather than the creation of "horizontal" bonds within proper industrial working-class communities like those that were formed in the drift of labor from countryside to town in Western European countries.[31] Thus, the particular circumstances of Japan's "late" industrialization help explain why it developed a different system of industrial relations compared to earlier industrializing economies. Later, the vertical consciousness of workers was exploited by the Japanese state as it mobilized the country for total war. The ideology of the nation as a kind of family state with the emperor at its head was promulgated and taught in schools. Industrial employers borrowed from this rhetoric to develop the idea of their firm as a kind of large substitute family for all its employees. Much of this ideology was couched in traditional or conservative language, but the ideology itself and the purposes it served were every bit as modern as the twentieth-century assembly lines, machines, and war effort that it accompanied.

In chapter one we discussed some of the efforts of the postwar Occupation reformers to sweep away the kind of emperor worship ideology described above. It was also noted that Occupation policies of democratization included the creation of a free and independent union movement. Inevitably, a fear of communism shared by both the American and Japanese elites brought this honeymoon period to an end. MacArthur's banning of the general strike in 1947, and the Red Purge begun in 1949 harked back to the prewar suppression of independent union activity. However, these early events were exceptional, and the postwar taming of the labor movement was to be quite different from the state authoritarianism of the prewar days.

The return to compliant, nonradical unionism in the private sector was brought about by two main tactical ploys on the part of the employers and their conservative allies. Both of these tactics can best be seen in use during an early test of strength between employers and a typical example of the new style of postwar industrial union. This was the Densan dispute, which took place in 1952, and it involved labor organization in the electrical power industry.[32] The first anti-union ploy used was the plan to divide power generation in Japan into nine regional enterprises. This effectively divided the electrical workers union (Densan) into nine parts that could be dealt with under a policy of divide and rule. The second tactic was the encouragement of the growth of a competing union movement within the industry. Personnel staff encouraged workers to join the new unions (one for each of the nine new enterprises). Many did so to avoid being thought of as reds or subversives. Then, after Densan lost an industrial dispute, the drift of members to the new unions increased (another example of an industrial dispute with negative consequences causing a loss of members for the union or unions invovled).

This pattern of creating new more cooperative "second unions" within enterprises was widespread throughout the 1950s and 1960s. (From now on in this chapter these types of union will be referred to as second unions, even in situations where more than two competing unions are involved.) Workers soon realized that their promotion prospects were much greater in these new unions than they were in the old industrial unions. Furthermore, union officials of the new style unions were often given promotion within the company after they had finished their period of office in the union. This practice encouraged a cooperative atmosphere between union leaders and management and ensured that the cooperation achieved would be of the sort that suited management.[33] In a similar vain, Andrew Gordon's account of the development of postwar labor–management relations in Japan's Steel industry describes how the managerial ideology of the 1950s became the industrial hegemony of the 1960s and the decades that followed.[34] Sheldon Garon has pointed out that the practice of management encouragement of moderate tendencies within the labor movement had its precursor in the late 1920s.[35] However, the postwar model of enterprise unionism, despite some continuities with prewar days, is really an identifiably new model of unionism. Furthermore, it is a model that has won praise in the West. Ezra Vogel in *Japan as Number One*, for example, has praised the Japanese form of industrial organisation. One point he makes, writing from an American perspective, is that in a Japanese company, workers are more likely to believe that their future is best served by the success of the company.[36] This point is also made in Ronald Dore's classic study of a Japanese company and a British one.[37]

In the case of Britain, the adoption of "Japanese" industrial relations practices by British companies became a source of contention in the 1980s. Japanese companies building factories in Britain tried to reproduce some of their own practices of enterprise unionism. Not surprisingly, these practices were more popular with employers' organizations and conservative politicians than they were with the trade union movement. When the electricians' union, the EETPU signed a "no-strike," single union deal with Nissan in 1988 it was expelled from the Trades Union Congress.[38] This shows how enthusiasm for or antagonism to "Japanese-style" industrial relations usually has more to do with the domestic agenda of the Western nation concerned, rather than an objective approach to what is going on in Japan. This tendency is not just confined to industrial relations practitioners. Kawanishi remarks that "to some extent it could be said that the image of Japan's industrial relations has changed with the times and at any particular time has reflected the intellectual climate of the times more than it has the actual realities of Japan's industrial relations."[39] Thus, Japan's industrial relations, which were at one time regarded as feudalistic by the West, came to be regarded as an exemplary model by the 1970s. The evolution from one judgment to the other roughly coincides with the growth of Japan's postwar economy. Enterprise unionism has not only been seen as a successful model worthy of imitation by foreign observers, its success has also inspired imitation at home, most controversially in the application of private sector industrial relations practices to traditionally public sector domains. It is to this that we now turn our attention.

The 'Privatization' of Public Sector Unionism

Privatization as a process by which public sector industries or services are transferred to the private sector is a concept that can be clearly understood by reference to the many examples, around the world of its application. In the context of contemporary Japanese industrial relations, however, it can have further connotations. Thus, besides referring to the transfer of industries like telecommunications and railways to the private sector, it can also apply to the adoption of private sector industrial relations practices in areas, like compulsory education, that remain in the public sector.[40] In Japan this tendency has gone hand in hand with the convergence of public and private sector union federations into a single, all-embracing organisation, Rengō. For the Japanese union movement, both the issue of privatization, and the issue of the formation of Rengō have been extremely divisive in recent years. Chapters two and three showed how the issue of whether to affiliate with Rengō was a decisive factor in bringing about Nikkyōso's schism. Was this an unavoidable and typical reaction to the formation of Rengō? To answer this question we need to look at what went on in other unions faced with a similar dilemma. We also need to examine the effect of privatization on these unions and Japanese industrial relations in general.

Before examining the effects of privatization on public sector unions, we must first review the main differences between public and private sector unions in the period up to the late 1980s. Conventional wisdom has drawn a distinction between the cooperative nature of industrial relations in the private sector and confrontational industrial relations in the public sector.[41] We have already discussed how the growth of enterprise unionism in the private sector brought about the kind of cooperation and harmony that gave Japanese industrial relations the favorable reputation they enjoyed from the 1970s. Why did this model not encompass the public sector as well? Ohmi gives four reasons.

> 1. Basic workers' rights in the public sector were restricted and the government did not recognize public sector unions as legitimate representatives of the workforce.
>
> 2. Public corporations were not empowered to conclude collective labor agreements.
>
> 3. Because ultimate decisions on working conditions for public sector workers were made by the Diet or the local governments, the public sector union movement gave priority to political activities, which resulted in a movement opposed to the ruling party, the Liberal Democratic Party (LDP). This created an unfavorable reaction to the union movement by the LDP.
>
> 4. There were many left-wingers among the trade union leaders who aimed at a class struggle and whose activities were focused on ideology.[42]

An analysis of Nikkyōso's history up to 1988 (as reviewed in chapters one and two) indicates that all four factors are applicable to the case of that particular public sector union. They are also equally important in the histories of the other main national public sector unions, (i.e., those unions that represent railway workers, telecommunications workers, postal workers, and local government workers).

Common grievances, especially over the denial of basic workers' rights like the right to strike and the right to collective bargaining, brought these unions together in common cause against the government. One tactic employed was the use of appeals to the International Labour Organization (ILO), starting in the latter half of the 1950s.[43] Because of the number and seriousness of the appeals, the ILO set up a special fact-finding commission, the Dreyer Commission, that reported in 1965. It concluded that there was a "failure both by the government and the trade union organisations to distinguish between the Government as government and the Government as employer."[44] This had resulted in the government's inclination to "assert an authority which it can properly claim in its capacity as government but which is inconsistent with the establishment of harmonious labour-management relations."[45] This, in turn, resulted in the politicization of many industrial disputes and a basic lack of trust between the two sides. (Government and unions could not agree on how to go about resolving the problems outlined in the Dreyer Commission report and thus industrial relations in the public sector deteriorated even further.) We have already seen how in the educational world government programs aimed at improving the standards of both teachers and pupils were opposed by Nikkyōso on the grounds that they were a political ploy to increase government control over teachers. In the end Nikkyōso split between those who decided they had to try to build a relationship of trust between themselves and the government and those who wanted to continue the mistrust and confrontation. How was this process mirrored in other large public sector unions? We will deal with this question by starting with the case of the railway workers, and then comparing it to the case of the telecommunications union.

The Japan National Railway Corporation (JNR), a public corporation, was set up in 1949 to replace a system whereby the railways were directly run by the government. The running of the railways soon became politicized. Because only the Diet had the authority to decide the budget for the railways, the president of JNR could not decide fares or other charges. LDP politicians blatantly used their power to provide subsidized train services to constituents and channel work to favored construction firms.[46] At the same time they allowed JNR's debt to reach astronomic proportions. This environment, along with Ohmi's four factors, brought about the politicization of industrial relations in the railway industry. This can be contrasted sharply with industrial relations developments in the private sector. Workers in private companies were amenable to appeals from their employers to make certain sacrifices in return for guarantees regarding security of employment and a fair share of the fruits of the company's success. Rising demand allowed many companies to hire new workers even as they rationalized production. At the same time, status differences between managers and employees were minimized.[47] Thus, the appeal by enterprise unions that cooperation with management made sense was backed up by tangible benefits for many workers in the private sector. The same could not be said for similar appeals in the case of JNR. Before privatization the strongest union by far in the railway industry was Kokurō, the National Railway Workers' Union, which had a membership of around 240,000, and was affiliated with Sōhyo. JNR's second union (i.e., the union that wanted to cooperate more with management) was Tetsurō, which was formed in 1968, attracting a membership of about 50,000. Tetsurō was opposed to Sōhyo's political activism and so it affiliated with the more moderate national federation, Dōmei.

In an attempt to imitate the tactics successfully employed in the private sector, JNR managers in the late 1960s tried to pressure Kokurō members and members of the smaller locomotive drivers' union, Dōrō, to join the second union Tetsurō. Not only did this campaign fail to bring about the large-scale defections hoped for, it also had the effect of radicalizing workplace union branches and worsening relations between the unions, and between union and management. Humiliated, management had to call off the campaign in 1971. Tactics that had worked successfully in the private sector had failed badly in the publicly owned railway industry. Most railway workers could see little incentive in cooperating with management to improve productivity. Clearly, one solution to this impasse would be to move JNR into the private sector and the LDP began to draw up plans to do exactly that.

It is extremely difficult to judge just how important the "union-busting" motive was for those politicians and mangers who drew up the plans for the privatization of JNR. In the course of interviewing Zenkyō leaders and members, I found that they all believed that there was a "hit list" of public sector unions to be busted by the LDP. The two most important targets on this list were Kokurō, followed, chronologically, by Nikkyōso. There is no direct evidence, however, from the statements of those involved in the JNR privatization that this was a conscious object of policy.[48] There is also conflicting evidence concerning vital behind-the-scenes negotiations between management and the three different unions. These negotiations resulted in the once militant Dōrō making a dramatic

U-turn to side with Tetsurō in a conciliatory posture toward management. Kokurō, on the other hand, refused to compromise. Some say that this was because JNR authorities deliberately proposed conditions they could not possibly accept. Others blame the union itself for its recalcitrance. Because so many important negotiations went on behind closed doors it is impossible to be sure exactly what happened.[49] Whatever the exact causes, there was no question about the effect of Kokurō's failure to reach an accommodation with JNR. In three years its membership dropped from 200,000 to 34,000. This was because the privatization of JNR involved the breaking up of the company into seven separate parts. Many Kokurō members were simply not hired by these new companies. Others resigned rather than accept transfers to inferior posts. Others quit the union to avoid discrimination.[50] Whether or not it had been a deliberate intention of management, by the end of the privatization process Kokurō as a powerful, independent, and militant union had been well and truly "busted".

Post-privatization industrial relations in the railway industry resemble very closely the private sector model. The second union (renamed Tetsudōrōren after the absorption of Dōrō by Tetsurō) has overtaken the original militant union, Kokurō, in terms of membership and influence. It played a part in the formation of Rengō while Kokurō joined a militant alternative to Rengō, Zenrōkyō. Kokurō's unreformed militant stance is in sharp contrast to the stated aims of the leadership of Tetsudōrōren that include talk of participation with management and offering stock options to JR workers.[51] (JR, Japan Railways, is the generic post-privatization name for the companies that have replaced JNR.) The flourishing of a management-friendly second union, which had not been possible while the railways remained in the public sector, had been achieved by the transfer of that industry into the private sector.

The privatization of NTT (Nippon Telegraph and Telephone) was different in many respects from the privatization of JNR. In contrast to the competing railway unions, telecommunications workers, both before and after privatization have been represented by only one union—Zendentsū. Furthermore, this union had been thorough in purging itself of pro-Communist cadres in a way that Kokurō had not. This meant that Zendentsū's leadership was not subject to the same factional infighting that Kokurō had suffered from.[52] In the telecommunications industry no attempt was made by management to foster a second union. Instead the privatization process was marked by practical, nonconfrontational negotiations between management and union leadership. The result was a positive outcome for Zendentsū and its members (i.e., privatization went ahead with no dismissals).[53] A significant factor in aiding the smooth running of negotiations in the telecommunications sector, compared to the railways, was that NTT was in a considerably better financial state than JNR in the 1980s. However, in his analysis Mochizuki argues that an even more significant difference lay in the organizational differences of Zendentsū and Kokurō. The latter's leadership was faction ridden while the former's was not. This is significant if the following hypothesis is true.

> A union whose organisation is highly centralised and whose leadership enjoys considerable autonomy from the rank and file is more likely to adapt successfully to environmental change and to reach an accommodation with management and the state that promotes labour interests. Union factionalism and the lack of leadership autonomy will complicate this adaptation and the negotiation of a positive accommodation.[54]

Although for the sake of convenience we will refer to this statement as Mochizuki's hypothesis, this is not a new theory about the internal organization of unions or similar organizations. This kind of theory can trace its origins back to Robert Michels' "iron law of oligarchy" first formulated in 1911,[55] which states that socialist parties or trade unions, although proclaiming themselves democratic, are in fact inevitably going to be run along oligarchic lines once they grow to any substantial size. Michels proclaimed that this tendency was an iron law that would apply to any large political organisation. Whether such an iron law exists is a controversial question. For the purposes of the present discussion, however, it only needs to be argued that if an organization like a political party or a trade union is structured along centralized, oligarchic lines, then the organization in question will be much better equipped to deal with changes to its environment. One of the benefits that oligarchic structure bestows on an organization is the autonomy of leadership. As an example of the importance of leadership autonomy in the privatization process, Mochizuki mentions the decisive shifting of gears by Zendentsū leader Yamagishi Akira in 1982 when he successfully switched union policy to embrace privatization. By contrast, Kokurō leader Yamazaki Shunichi was unable to steer his union to the more cooperative response he considered more desirable. Mochizuki argues that further support for this hypothesis is supplied by the sudden U-turn of the once militant rail union Dōrō. If Mochizuki's hypothesis works in the case of railway and telecommunications unions, how applicable is it to the case of teachers? It is to this question that we will now turn.

There are clear similarities and differences between Nikkyōso's experiences in the 1980s and those of Kokurō and Zendentsū. Of course, Nikkyōso was not facing the threat of a literal privatization of the compulsory or secondary education sectors. However, as we have seen, it interpreted the education reform proposals of the 1980s as a threat. Like Kokurō but unlike Zendentsū, Nikkyōso was afflicted by serious factional differences within its leadership (including the presence of a Communist and a left-Socialist contingent). Unlike Kokurō, however, it was not threatened by the growth of a serious rival second union (although there were prefectural unions similar to this in Tochigi and Ehime, they were not organized on a national scale). Most teachers who left Nikkyōso (and did not defect to Zenkyō) tended not to join any rival union at all. With Nikkyōso, therefore, we find a case of a pragmatic, nonmilitant leadership trying, from the mid-1980s onward, to come to an accommodation with the authorities (i.e., attempting to lead their union in the same direction as the leaders of Zendentsū and Dōrō), but suffering from precisely those weaknesses identified by Mochizuki's hypothesis—factionalism and a lack of leadership autonomy (both compounded by the decentralized, prefectural basis of Nikkyōso's organization). In the end, this resulted in Nikkyōso's moderate leadership failing to achieve the kind of influence with management that Zendentsū's leadership had. On the other hand, the lack of a national second union threat meant that the consequences of this failure (in terms of a decline in membership numbers) were not as serious as they were for Kokurō. The next question to address is whether new Nikkyōso has learned any organizational lessons from this experience. Is it applying or considering any reforms that will increase the autonomy of the leadership or reduce the union's propensity for factional infighting?

The best guide to Nikkyōso's current thinking about its own organizational reform can be found in its 21st Century Vision Committee Report (already referred to in chapter five). There is very little in this report that addresses the problems highlighted by Mochizuki's hypothesis. Under a section entitled "Strengthening the function of the union's head office" it is stated that the head office "must urgently strengthen its abilities to do research, and to *formulate and implement policy*"[56] (emphasis added). However, there is no practical program for how to bring this about. The reality is, of course, that Nikkyōso's central leadership is as much plagued by the problem of a decentralized, prefecture-based structure now as it was when it was first formed. Without any strong, legal status, there is little Nikkyōso can do to bring about a greater autonomy of leadership like that enjoyed by Zendentsū. Throughout its existence there have been numerous cases of prefectural unions flouting the authority of the center, and there has been very little that the center could do about it. Instead Nikkyōso continues to press, in its recent 21st Century Vision report and elsewhere, for a greater decentralization of the education system. If the locus of power in the education system were shifted from Tokyo to the prefectures, this would increase the influence of each prefectural branch of Nikkyōso, and the struggle for influence at the national level would be less crucial.

There is nothing in the 21st Century Vision Committee report about the second problem identified by Mochizuki as a cause of weakness in unions, namely, factionalism. Although the anti-Communists in Nikkyōso benefited from the Red Purge carried out by the American authorities under the Occupation, they have never, unlike Zendentsū, carried out a purge of their own. Thus, factional infighting has never been far below the surface within Nikkyōso's CEC and at national conference, and it grew to such a height in the 1980s that it paralyzed the national union organization. This is exactly the danger of factionalism that Mochizuki's hypothesis warns about. It could now be argued, however, that with the breakaway of Zenkyō, the Communists and left-Socialists within Nikkyōso have carried out a self-purge, leaving the right-wing Socialists and moderates in command of the union. Thus, the post-schism Nikkyōso, although it has lost a significant proportion of its membership, should be better placed to meet the changing demands of the future.

What conclusions, therefore, can be drawn about the privatization of public sector unionism in the 1980s? The railway industry has seen the most drastic changes and the clearest introduction of private sector union practices. Telecommunications has changed the least, although that might be different if the NTT is broken up into smaller companies the way JNR was (indeed, the LDP sometimes use the threat of a breakup of NTT as a means of putting pressure on Zendentsū's leadership)[57]. In the case of education, there has been no literal selling off of schools into the private sector. Nor has there been the creation of a national second union. However, the changes that Nikkyōso had undergone around the period of its schism have led to its abandonment of some of the main tenets of traditional public sector unionism in Japan and its adoption of aims and objectives that are more in keeping with a typical private sector union. This is why Nikkyōso has been accused of collaborationism by Zenkyō, and why Karel Van Wolferen has referred to "the demise of Nikkyōso as a genuine teachers' union."[58] These critics see Nikkyōso as having transformed itself into a classic example of a collaborationist second union. In other words, there was no need for the government or education authorities to foster the growth of a separate second union, because Nikkyōso would provide them with one on a plate. Is this a fair criticism of new Nikkyōso? Before addressing this question, it is first necessary to take a closer look at the wider context within which Nikkyōso changed its policies and its philosophies—that is, the transformation of the national union confederations in Japan that took place at this time.

Nikkyōso and the Formation of Rengō

The formation of a single all-embracing national confederation of labor had long been a goal of trade unionists in Japan. In the 1970s, particularly after the 1973 oil crisis, this campaign assumed a particular form. Thurston aptly summarizes what happened:

> After the oil crisis private labour unions representing the export sector of Japanese industry came to realise that they had to be concerned not merely with wage hikes but also with such matters as governmental pricing policy, the tax system, and social welfare policy, since these areas greatly influenced workers' real wages and jobs. This wing of labour came to understand more clearly that it had to participate in policymaking in order to protect the interests of workers.[59]

It is highly significant that the impetus for this unification campaign came from private sector, enterprise unions, and that one of their main aims was to achieve more involvement in policy-making. Many within the public sector Sōhyō unions were afraid that this would result in a collaborationist sell-out to government and big business. However, despite this opposition, reformers within Sōhyō succeeded in 1982 in joining the setting up of the Japanese Private Sector Trade Union Council (Zenmin Rōkyō), which was to act as a preparatory committee for the unification of the labor movement. By 1989, the process was complete. Dōmei and Sōhyō had both disbanded themselves and their constituent members had joined Rengō making it the largest union confederation ever formed in Japan.[60]

In the case of the railway and telecommunications industries the campaign for the formation of Rengō ran side by side with the campaign for privatization. In the education system, the campaign for the formation of Rengō accompanied the deliberations and reports of *Rinkyōshin* and its various committees. In all three cases, traditional, mass membership public sector unions faced challenges that were pulling them in the direction of becoming more like private sector, enterprise unions. Zendentsū's leadership decided, as it were, to swim with the tide, and, as a result, succeeded in surviving the transition with little loss. Kokurō on the other hand, put up a fight and paid the consequences. Nikkyōso's national leadership moved in the same direction as Zendentsū but, in the process, lost a third of its membership. The overall result was the triumph of the enterprise union model. Some have even argued that Rengō itself is really an enlarged version of an enterprise union.[61] For those, in both Japan and abroad, who regard enterprise unionism as a successful model of modern industrial relations, this statement is a compliment. For those defenders of traditional Japanese public sector unionism, however, it represents a complete betrayal of the main principles of trade unionism.

Conclusion: What Kind of Union Is Nikkyōso?

This chapter has analyzed Nikkyōso from two main theoretical perspectives: comparative teacher unionism; and Japanese unionism. From the perspective of comparative teacher unionism, Nikkyōso is a union that has suffered the dilemmas and conflicts common to many teachers' organizations in the developed world. It has had to contend with the particular problems teachers always have to face when they use strike action or other kinds of industrial action that harm the short-term interests of the children in their care. This has been connected with the more general debate about the true status of teachers. Are they ordinary workers, special professionals, or a combination? Furthermore, the union has had to deal with the issue of teacher politics interconnected as that is with the status of teachers as government employees. Finally, the issue of control over education has also been a source of conflict between union and government. None of these debates is unusual when put in the context of comparative studies of teacher unionism. Where Nikkyōso does seem to stand out is in the intensity and duration of its confrontation with the government in the 1950s, 1960s and 1970s. Even this, however, has been exaggerated, as Rohlen's study of conflict on three levels of the education system showed. It was only at the top level—the national level—where the conflict was really sustained, and this tended to be mostly a war of words. (Rohlen's argument was reviewed and updated in chapter four.) Even this conflict, however, seems to have come to an end as Nikkyōso adopted a policy of compromise and cooperation toward its previous enemies—the MOE and the LDP. This move toward compromise, which was one of the main causes of the schism, can best be understood not from the perspective of teacher unionism, but instead from another viewpoint—that of the broader arena of trade unionism in Japan.

From the perspective of Japanese unionism we can locate Nikkyōso's recent policy and attitude changes within a broader national trend. Since the late 1980s, moves toward the adoption by public sector unions of private sector aims and tactics have coincided with other national changes like the privatization of public industries and the move for root and branch reform of the nation's education system. Nikkyōso could not help being influenced by the growth of a movement for national labor unification, and as the experience of those in other industries showed, resistance to this movement would have been more costly than cooperation. So far the creation of Rengō has resulted in more contact between unions and government.[62] There have also been symbolic gestures like Prime Minister Hashimoto's attendance at union-sponsored May Day celebrations in 1996.[63] However, it is too early to say whether all this has resulted in a significant qualitative improvement in labor's influence over government policy-making. If, in the long run, it turns out that Rengō and Nikkyōso fail to achieve a significant input into policy-making, and the MOE and government refuse to relinquish any of their power, then critics like Zenkyō and Van Wolferen will feel justified in their accusations that Nikkyōso has "sold out." As we have seen, however, the judgment of Nikkyōso's moderate leadership—that a policy of confrontation was getting it nowhere—meant that, from their point of view, the union had no choice but to try to aim for an increase in contact and cooperation with the government. Thus, the change of Nikkyōso, from a teachers' union based on confrontation to a teachers' union based on conciliation was a product of the times. The 1980s in Japan were a period of intense change for public sector unions. The changes Nikkyōso underwent were just one part of this process—the process of the "privatization" of public sector unionism.

CHAPTER SEVEN

CHANGING TEACHERS' UNIONS AND POLITICAL REALIGNMENT

Chapter four dealt with the effect of Nikkyōso's schism on power relations within the Japanese education system. In doing so it analyzed Schoppa's theory of policy-making. The discussion was confined to the particular arena of educational policy-making, although more general theories of pluralism and bureaucratic behavior were also addressed. It is now time to broaden the discussion and consider the relationship between Nikkyōso's schism and political change in general in Japan. The 1990s are now regarded as a period of political realignment in Japan, with the two most important events being the LDP's loss of control of the House of Representatives in the 1993 general election, and the subsequent adoption of a new election system. At the same time a "New Party Boom" redrew the map of Japanese party politics. All this occurred against a background of important economic changes (centered on the bursting of Japan's bubble economy), international developments (the end of the Cold War), and a realignment of the trade union movement (the subject of the previous chapter). Because of such complexity the issue of Japanese political realignment has become a controversial one. The intention of this chapter is to use Nikkyōso's experience to shed light on the process of realignment. More particularly, Nikkyōso as an important component part of the progressive camp is certainly a subject worthy of serious analysis. A discussion of Nikkyōso's experiences around the time of its schism will shed light on the decline of the left in Japan, and this in turn will help us to understand more about changes taking place across the political spectrum. When this has been done we will be able to consider the modifications needed to update Schoppa's model of policy-making to take account of these changes. This process will also entail modifying Muramatsu and Krauss's model of patterned pluralism. Before looking at recent changes, however, we will first briefly discuss what the established postwar political system was like before the 1990s.

Nikkyōso's Place in the Postwar Political System

Chapter two contained a section that examined Nikkyōso's part in the formation of the "1955 system," the system by which Japan's postwar politics became divided between a progressive and a conservative camp, with the latter controlling most of the levers of actual power at the national level. Now we will take a closer look at the ties that kept members of a given camp mutually dependent. Specifically, we will be looking at the complex set of relationships between political parties, factions within those parties, and unions. We will take Nikkyōso as the focal point for this analysis.

Nikkyōso's Relations with the Japan Socialist Party

Throughout the duration of the 1955 system, the relationship between Nikkyōso and the JSP provided one of the foundation stones of the progressive camp. However, one of the most important characteristics of the JSP as a political party was its overdependence on trade unions. It relied on unions to provide not only financial support, but also organizational support at the local level (especially during election campaigns), and supply candidates for local and national elections.[1] Furthermore, most of this support came from unions affiliated with Sōhyō. As we have already observed, Nikkyōso was one of the main component parts of Sōhyō and Nikkyōso's role as a linchpin between the JSP and that union federation was therefore highly significant. One of the main problems facing any analyst of the relationship between party and union, however, is the circumspect and informal nature of this relationship. This characteristic can be traced back to the 1950 Local Public Service Law that banned local public service personnel from becoming officers in a political party or from election campaigning in support of a party. Another restrictive law was the 1952 Law Regulating Political Funds that prevented organizations like labor unions from directly contributing to political parties. To circumvent this obstacle, Nikkyōso set up a separate organization, Nihon Minshu Kyōiku Seiji Renmei (Japan Political League for Democratic Education), or Nisseiren for short, to take care of political funds for the JSP. This legislation of the early 1950s created an environment that made direct, overt connections between Nikkyōso and the JSP (or other political parties) very difficult to establish. Instead channels of communication were maintained by front organizations, informal contact, the use of retired teachers, and so on. The situation was further complicated by the decentralized nature of *both* organizations, meaning that the arrangements made between union and party in one prefecture might be quite different from those in another.

This complex relationship between Nikkyōso and the JSP could best be observed at election time. As previously noted, the law clearly prevents the participation of teachers at election time. However, as Thurston pointed out, writing in 1973, "prefectural unions circumvent the spirit of the law by one means or another."[2] As an example Thurston describes a typical front organization set up in Iwate prefecture that enabled teachers to campaign on behalf of JSP candidates.

The JSP's reliance on local union organizations to run the campaigns of their candidates, while at the same time neglecting to cultivate a strong party organization at the local level, was an unreliable strategy to follow. There was the ever-present danger of a local union deciding to throw its weight behind a candidate other than the JSP candidate. Usually the JSP and its supporters were concerned that this might happen as the result of the activities of Communist activists. This scenario will be investigated in a moment. Other scenarios were also possible, however, as Gerald Curtis found in his investigation of an election campaign in Oita prefecture. Curtis made a detailed analysis of the 1967 House or Representatives election campaign in that prefecture and discovered that the high school teachers' union there was in an ambiguous position. Nationally, a small high school teachers' union had broken away from Nikkyōso in 1950. Three years later this movement had grown substantially, feeding off the dissatisfaction of high school teachers who believed their interests were not being properly addressed by a Nikkyōso dominated by teachers in the compulsory education sector. In 1956, this union adopted the name Nihon Kōtogakkō Kyōshokuin Kumiai (Nikkōkyō for short). This union was split into two factions, right and left wing. In 1967, 98 percent of Oita prefecture's high school teachers were members of a union (Kōkyōso) that was affiliated with Nikkōkyō's right-wing faction.[3] They found themselves in a highly ambiguous position during the election campaign, a position that illustrates many of the complexities and paradoxes of relations between parties, unions, and individual candidates in Japan.

In 1967, the national headquarters of Nikkōkyō decided not to endorse a slate of candidates in the general election. Instead they left the decision about which candidates to recommend up to individual prefectural unions. In Oita number two constituency (the one studied by Curtis), the prefectural high school teachers' union, Kōkyōso, officially gave its support to the socialist candidate, Komatsu Kan. However, it was well known locally that the majority of the leaders of the prefectural union were opposed to this candidate and preferred one of the LDP candidates, Sato Bunsei. This state of affairs arose from the way in which Kōkyōso was formed in the mid-1950s. At the time of the split between high school teachers and compulsory sector teachers Komatsu was an officer in the prefectural teachers' union, Kenkyōso. The nature of the struggle between the two sides led to a lasting animosity between Komatsu and some of the high school teachers. Thus, when Komatsu came to stand as a JSP candidate in 1967 he found that those high school teachers who were over forty-five years of age (which included the high school union leadership of course) were privately opposed to him. They could not make this opposition public however, because of their union's affiliation to a prefectural association of labor unions called Kenrōhyō. This association consisted mainly of workers in the public sector, and it was affiliated with Sōhyō at the national level. Thus, Kenrōhyō endorsed the JSP candidate Komatsu in the Oita number two constituency. Although Nikkōkyō at the national level was *not* affiliated with Sōhyō (and therefore was not obliged to draw up a national list of candidates or parties to support), Nikkōkyō's prefectural level affiliate in Oita *was* affiliated with Sōhyō's prefectural level affiliate and therefore had to go along, officially, with the candidates that that association endorsed. Curtis summarized the result as follows.

> Though the top-level leadership of the [Oita prefecture] High School Teachers' Union is opposed to [JSP candidate] Komatsu, the need to maintain their position in Kenrōhyō and to avoid a serious split among the membership of their own union led the leaders to acquiesce in the Kenrōhyō endorsement and covertly campaign for [LDP candidate] Sato.[4]

This prevented an effective, coordinated campaign by the union on behalf of the JSP candidate from taking place, and is a good example of the dangers of the JSP's reliance on union organizations to do their campaigning for them. It shows how union activists and leaders may have different agendas from those of the party and personal rivalries or antagonisms may come into play. It is also an example that should caution the student of Japanese politics from taking at face value the official endorsement by an organization of a particular candidate or party. Yet lack of official endorsement cannot be taken to mean actual lack of support, as a study of Nikkyōso's relationship with the Japan Communist Party will demonstrate. Before embarking on this study, we must first consider another main link between the JSP and unions under the 1955 system—that is, the provision of candidates for local and national elections.

Writing in 1973, Thurston could safely conclude that Nikkyōso consistently had had a larger number of its leaders elected to both the House of Councillors and the House of Representatives than any other single union in Japan.[5] In the 1950s and 1960s, this worked out as an average of twenty-seven Diet members at any given time. They were all in the moderate or center-right factions of the JSP. Because of the legal restrictions previously discussed, they all had to resign from Nikkyōso before standing for election. The same restrictions prevented the union from officially endorsing anybody. To get around this, local front organizations were set up, as well as a national organisation, Nisseiren (the aforementioned Japan Political League for Democratic Education). Nisseiren also collected and distributed money for campaign purposes and issued recommendations for sympathetic, non-Nikkyōso candidates. These recommendations would always go to JSP candidates or JSP-endorsed independent candidates. In return for such an important role in providing money and personnel, Nikkyōso was given effective total control over the JSP's education policy-making apparatus.[6] Thus, under the 1955 system, Nikkyōso functioned in some ways as a component part of the JSP, but in others as a detached supporting organization. A decline in the fortunes of one would have an immediate impact on the other.

Nikkyōso's Relations with the Japan Communist Party

Chapters one and two outlined the main struggles between Communists and Socialists during Nikkyōso's formative years. By 1961, the mainstream JSP-supporting faction was firmly in control of the union's national leadership. The JCP-supporting anti-mainstream faction had to content itself with voicing dissent from the sidelines whenever the leadership seemed to be straying from the correct ideological path. Communist supporters also had the consolation of having the upper hand in certain prefectures and cities. Nikkyōso's pre-schism relationship with the JCP was therefore more fractured and complex than its very close relationship with the JSP. For its part, the JCP was always less dependent on money, personnel, and support from the unions than the JSP was (since it could provide all these from within its own party organization). Of what significance therefore were relations between the JCP and Nikkyōso?

If the JCP is less dependent on Nikkyōso for practical support at election time, then its interest in the teachers' union is more likely to be an ideological one. During the period when the 1955 system was in operation the JCP's main goal can be described as the building of a united front (under its leadership) of "progressive and democratic forces."[7] It wanted to further the cause of pacifism and socialism against the reactionary forces of militarism and nationalism. Postwar education policy proved a natural battleground for this kind of ideological conflict. We have already seen some of the examples of the struggles that raged between teachers' unions and the Ministry of Education over control of the hearts and minds of Japan's children. Within this struggle the JCP usually found itself allied with the JSP and their supporters in Nikkyōso. The conservative camp provided a common enemy against whom the Left could unite.

Nikkyōso and the End of the 1955 System

The ending of the 1955 system came with the fall from power of the LDP at the 1993 House of Representatives election. Defeat was brought about not by a successful challenge for power from a party or parties in the progressive camp, but by the defection of LDP Diet members who formed two new parties with which to fight the election. The election was also fought by the popular Japan New Party under the leadership of ex-LDP House of Councillors member and governor of Kumamoto prefecture, Hosokawa Morihiro. There was certainly a popular reaction against the governing LDP, tainted as it was by a series of particularly bad corruption scandals, but this resentment was exploited, not by the left, but by a new generation of right-wing or center-right politicians who promised to be cleaner and more dynamic than the tired old masters of the LDP machine. They campaigned on the slogan of political reform and promised a revitalization of Japanese politics. Both the LDP and the JSP, representatives of the "old" politics, were duly punished by the electorate at the polls in 1993. Because Nikkyōso's attachments are with the progressive camp, we will focus on this area in our analysis of the ending of the

1955 system, starting with an examination of the political impact of union reorganization.

The Political Impact of the Formation of Rengō

The first development in the undermining of the 1955 system concerned the reorganization of the union movement. The JSP's total dependence on the support of public sector unions affiliated with Sōhyō meant that any major change in public sector unionism would have a direct impact on that party. Traditionally, private sector unions affiliated to the union federation, Dōmei, had supported the rival Democratic Socialist Party (DSP). The coming together of Sōhyō and Dōmei into the new federation, Rengō, therefore brought about a period of uncertainty. This was compounded by Rengō's decision to form its own, independent parliamentary party. Twelve Rengō candidates ran in the 1989 House of Councillors elections, in the prefectural districts, and eleven of them were elected. At the same time some Rengō strategists were trying to engineer either the reunification of the JSP and DSP (the DSP had originally been formed by the breakaway Nishio group from the right wing of the JSP in 1959) or a coalition centered on these two parties.[8] At this crucial time an issue arose in the Diet that brought to a head some of the defining ideological differences between the two parties. This was the debate over the Peace Keeping Operations (PKO) Bill, conducted against the backdrop of the Gulf War. The DSP supported the bill while the JSP organized an infamous filibuster within the Diet based on the "ox-walk" tactic (i.e., each member of the party walking to the speaker's chair to cast their vote at an infinitesimally slow speed). In this atmosphere coordination and cooperation on the left proved impossible. At the subsequent 1992 House of Councillors election all but one of the Rengō-sponsored candidates were defeated and none of the opposition parties made major gains. The chance for unification of the center left had been lost. It has been argued, for example by Toru Shinoda, that the 1992 defeat caused individual unions to look elsewhere for their political links. "This defeat led the major affiliated unions to abandon the idea of a reconciliation between the JSP and DSP focusing instead on a commitment to a more drastic party alignment."[9] Stephen Johnson, in his analysis of events leading up to the 1992 defeat, argues that reconciliation between the JSP and the DSP was extremely unlikely to happen because of long-term factors. "For the JSP and the DSP, which have relied on organised labour for their electoral machines, historical and economic factors ensured that unions worked as separate and discrete groups undermining their ability to cooperate."[10] The formation of Rengō was an event that, on paper, had unified most Japanese unions. However, the underlying reality of competition, disunity, and lack of trust between many unions at the prefectural level meant that this could not be translated into anything like the political machine that was required to deliver an effective, unified, center-left challenge to the parties of the right and center-right at election time. The stage was set for a more drastic political realignment, involving the breaking of traditional links between ex-Sōhyō unions and the JSP.

Teacher Union Politics and the Fortunes of the JSP and JCP in the 1990s

Nikkyōso in the 1990s can be taken as a case study of an ex-Sōhyō union undergoing significant transformations both internally and in its external relations. As we have seen, Nikkyōso's schism has resulted, nationally, in one larger union that is affiliated with Rengō and supportive of the JSP, and one smaller union that is affiliated to Zenrōren and supportive of the JCP. What was the effect of this development on union–party relations? We will deal with them in turn.

The JSP. Since the schism new Nikkyōso has embarked on various modernization exercises concerning both its policies and its organisation that are discussed elsewhere in this book. At first, it tried to remain loyal to the JSP, and its new policy of compromise and consultation with the MOE and government ministers had been decided on at a time when the JSP itself started to abandon some of its main policy positions that previously had put it at loggerheads with the LDP. The question arises whether this is a coincidence or if there are links between Nikkyōso's U-turns and the JSP's U-turns. We have already seen how Nikkyōso's review of its position was inspired by fears over a declining membership combined with a recognition that the political situation in Japan had changed significantly since Nikkyōso's heyday in the late 1940s and 1950s. If a key statistical index of a union's strength is membership, then the equivalent for a party is number of votes. By this standard the JSP's decline under the 1955 system had been more complex than Nikkyōso's. At the 1989 House of Councillors election in particular it had profited from the LDP's unpopularity and enjoyed something of an electoral revival. This, however, proved short-lived, and in the 1993 House of Representatives election the JSP suffered a crushing defeat, losing almost half its seats. This defeat resulted in a similar debate within the JSP to the one that had occurred in Nikkyōso during the debate about whether to affiliate with Rengō. Left and right attacked each other, each insisting that if their course of action were not followed, the result would be disaster for the party and the cause. Let us now examine this debate with a view to exploring the similarities and differences between it and the debate that had pulled Nikkyōso apart only a few years earlier.

The debate between left and right in the JSP in the 1990s was similar in many ways to one that had rumbled on within the party since the two halves had been brought back together in the reunification of 1955. The platform of that year had, by necessity been one of compromise, and thus, as Hrebenar argues, it has proved extremely difficult to revise in subsequent years.[11] Having said this (and leaving aside for one moment the issue of the formation of Rengō), it is important to note two very important factors, external to the JSP, that have made political life in the 1990s qualitatively different from the way it was during the years of the 1955 system. These factors are the collapse of the Soviet bloc (bringing with it the end of the Cold War) and the debate over, and subsequent introduction of, a completely new election system for the House of Representatives. How precisely have these factors influenced the JSP?

The global discrediting of state socialism and Marxist ideology that accompanied the collapse of the Soviet Union and its satellite East European states in the period 1989–1991 provided a golden opportunity for the moderate social democratic tradition within the JSP to assert itself. However, we have already seen how the first major international crisis of the post-Cold War era (i.e., the Gulf War), brought to the fore the particularly Japanese brand of pacifism that had characterized the Japanese left since the end of World War II. This ideology made the "peace clause" in the Constitution (article nine) into an article of faith that could not be criticized publicly by anybody on the left. Even thought other aspects of the JSP's platform could be altered (e.g., the specific repudiation of the Soviet and Chinese models made in the New Declaration of 1986), the devotion to the Peace Constitution went unquestioned. Not only did rigid devotion to defending the Constitution prevent the JSP from responding productively to the challenges presented by the Gulf War, it also diverted the party's attention from coming up with its own substantive, positive policies with which to challenge the LDP and the other political parties. A political scientist specializing in the study of the JSP, Yamaguchi Jiro, has made the point that because the mechanics involved in amending the Japanese Constitution are so complex, it was quite possible for the JSP to remain as a minority within the Diet, while still being able to prevent the Constitution from being changed. Thus, throughout the years of the existence of the 1955 system, the JSP was quite content to stay in Opposition.[12] This is why the JSP was unable to capitalize on its sudden recovery in the polls in 1989, and why many politicians within the party, frustrated by the JSP's inability to adapt to changing times, started to look outside for a hope of change.

The second factor that marks the 1990s as being qualitatively different from the years of the 1955 system is reform of the electoral system. It had long been argued that the system for electing Japan's lower house, the House of Representatives, whereby between two and five members are elected in each constituency by a nontransferable vote,[13] should be reformed. It was argued that this system, by forcing members of the same party to compete with each other in the same constituency encouraged factionalism within parties, especially the LDP, and with this factionalism came money politics and other forms of corruption. As the LDP reeled from a series of particularly damaging corruption scandals, most notably the Recruit Scandal and the Sagawa Kyūbin Scandal, the pressure for reform, within the LDP as well as within the public at large, grew. It was partly as a result of Prime Minister Miyazawa's postponement of electoral reform in 1993 that Ozawa Ichiro, Hata Tsutomu, and Takemura Masayoshi defected from the LDP to form breakaway parties. These same politicians as part of Hosokawa's new non-LDP government then proceeded to help put into effect plans for electoral reform. Although disagreements existed about the exact form the new system should take, there was a general consensus that the multimember constituencies should be abolished and replaced in part by a single seat constituency system. Such a system would make alliances and electoral pacts between non-LDP candidates inevitable if they were to avoid splitting the non-LDP vote. Thus, when a single seat constituency system (combined with regional proportional representation constituencies) was actually introduced in 1994, JSP lower house Diet members were faced with the reality that they would now have to do deals with their political rivals whether they liked it or not. Such a reality was easier to stomach for those on the right of the party. Forty of these politicians had already formed a group within the JSP called "the democrats." The leaders of this group were Akamatsu Hirotaka, Kubo Wataru, and Tanabe Makoto. Their group was formed with an eye to forging a new political alliance with the DSP and two of the new parties, the Japan New Party (JNP) and the New Party Sakigake.[14] This attitude fitted in with the mood of the times, which saw a large amount of alliance making and breaking, culminating first in the collapse of Hosokawa's government and then the breakdown of its successor, the minority government of Hata. This government was then replaced by the unlikeliest coalition of all, a government created by the LDP and the JSP (plus the small New Party Sakigake) with JSP chairman Murayama Tomiichi as prime minister. This development was to prove to be another nail in the coffin of the JSP.

The formation of the Murayama government was greeted with great surprise by most Japanese people. The question on everyone's mind was what possessed the JSP to go into government with its arch-enemy, the LDP? Fukatsu Masumi, an editorial writer for the Asahi Shimbun, has pointed to two factors motivating the JSP leadership. First, they were trying to avoid internal breakup, and second they decided that joining with the LDP was the lesser of two evils when the alternative was an alliance with Shinseitō and Kōmeitō (the new president of the LDP, Kōno Yōhei being closer to the JSP in many policy areas than the Shinseitō or Kōmeitō leadership).[15] Once in office, however, Murayama as head of government found it expedient in the space of a few days (at the end of July 1994) to pronounce complete reversals of JSP policy concerning previously sacrosanct articles of faith regarding the SDF, the Japan-U.S. security treaty, the sending of Japanese security forces beyond the shores of Japan, and the flying of the national flag and singing of the national anthem. Furthermore, it was difficult for JSP members and supporters to see what they were getting in return for these policy U-turns. As a final addition of insult to injury, the hope expressed by Murayama's supporters that the coalition with the LDP would prevent the disintegration of the JSP also turned out to have been unfounded. By the end of 1994, a breakaway group on the right of the party led by former JSP chairman Yamahana Sadao, announced their plan to leave the JSP in the new year. This plan was postponed by the great Hanshin earthquake of January 17, 1995 (exactly the day the breakaway was planned for). Instead, Yamahana went ahead with his plan four months later, taking with him four lower house and two upper house JSP members.[16] For the rest of 1995 and 1996, the JSP was described by the newspapers as suffering from a serious identity crisis as it struggled, unsuccessfully to find a new role for itself and to prevent further defections.[17] By the time of the October 1996 House of Representatives election the situation had deteriorated to such an extent that the JSP only managed to win fifteen seats.

What were the similarities, differences, and connections between the fate of the JSP and Nikkyōso in these years? The most obvious similarities lie at the level of ideology. Both organizations had, since their foundation contained hard left and moderate elements. The divisions within Nikkyōso's mainstream faction tended to mirror very closely ideological divisions within the JSP of the 1960s, 1970s, and 1980s.[18] Furthermore the ideological challenges posed by the end of the Cold War affected both organizations in a similar way. Pacifism, enshrined in a devotion to the Peace Constitution, was something the leaderships of both organizations had in common, but it was an ideology that cried out for critical renewal in the changing international situation that followed the coming down of the Berlin wall. Yamaguchi Jiro has likened the JSP's devotion to Article Nine of the Constitution to the British Labour Party's devotion to Clause Four of its own party constitution (the clause that called for the "common ownership of the means of production, distribution and exchange"). Labour's (internally democratic) replacement of this clause by a much more moderate one preceded its return to power in the 1997 general election in Britain. The JSP's failure to modify its devotion to Article Nine right up until Prime Minister Murayama's decision to completely and singlehandedly reverse his party's pacifist policies preceded its destruction by the combined forces of the ballot box and defection. In other words, the JSP had failed to amend out-of-date, ideologically inspired policies until it was too late. How did Nikkyōso fare in this respect?

Nikkyōso, as a representative organization of teachers, has fewer problems maintaining a pacifist ideology than a political party suddenly and dramatically thrust into a position of executive power does. Murayama's position as the new head of government forced him, in July 1994, to quickly clarify exactly what his position was in relation to the Japan–U.S. security treaty and Japan's PKO commitments. If he had refused to endorse established government policy, the international consequences for Japan would have been severe. Clearly, no leader of Nikkyōso would ever be placed in a remotely similar position. Nikkyōso's problems, as we have seen, were more long term and chronic. The immediate similarity one can recognize between Nikkyōso and the JSP was the former's amendment of its position on the flag and anthem (covered in chapter five). This represented a retreat for the union, but not as drastic a reversal of policy as that forced on the hapless Murayama. In contrast to the JSP, Nikkyōso has been able to conduct a thorough and considered review of its policy, and so shows more sign of surviving the present political changes than its erstwhile political ally. To continue the comparison with Britain's Labour party, it has been possible for the present leadership of both Nikkyōso and Labour to argue that, as well as being democratically arrived at, the policy reviews their organisations have recently carried out are also consistent with the basic principles the movements were founded on. In both cases there has been dissent from the left, but not enough to prevent the review process proceeding with the endorsement of a majority from each organization. In contrast, the JSP leadership has failed to please either the left or the right of its organization, or to arrive at a credible, modernizing vision. In the 1996 election it paid the price for this failure.

As far as the connections between the JSP and Nikkyōso are concerned, they too have inevitably undergone significant change in the political turmoil of the early 1990s. In fact, some analysts see the breakdown of the traditional relationship between the JSP and the Sōhyō unions as the main cause of the collapse of the JSP.[19] We have already noted in the above analysis of the traditional, pre-1989 relationship between unions and the JSP and how dependent the latter was on the former, especially at election time. The link between public sector unions and the JSP that had previously been so solid came under severe strain in the 1993 general election and then snapped altogether in 1996. The previous chapter examined the privatization of the public sector unions that took place in the 1980s. This created an environment in which traditional alliances between union and party came under closer scrutiny than previously. Thus, when the New Party Boom that preceded the 1993 election came along, some traditionally Socialist-supporting unions found themselves shopping around for candidates other than those of the JSP. One newspaper found forty-two cases in which JSP candidates lost the backing of unions that had previously supported them. In most cases the unions switched their support to candidates from the new parties.[20]

Nikkyōso was not one of the unions that deserted the JSP in 1993, nor did any of its affiliated prefectural unions (Zenkyō is a different story that will be dealt with later). However, as the next general election came nearer, the first one to be carried out with single seat constituencies, even this situation began to change. The major policy overhauls instituted by Nikkyōso at its September 1995 conference (discussed in detail in chapter five) were followed by a series of overtures made by the LDP toward the union. Hashimoto became the first LDP Prime Minister ever to show open support to the union when he sent a congratulatory message to Nikkyōso's Education Research Meeting in February 1996. (This particular meeting drew press attention for its discussion of the topical problem of school bullying.)[21] This approach was accompanied by parallel overtures from the Ministry of Education. JSP Diet members were suspicious that the LDP's motives were purely concerned with enlisting the cooperation of Nikkyōso at election time. These fears seemed justified in June of that year when the *Yomiuri Shimbun* ran a story saying that Nikkyōso had decided to endorse some LDP candidates at the next election.[22] The article explained that since the JSP was only fielding eighty candidates in 300 single-seat constituencies, it meant that Nikkyōso would have the option of endorsing candidates from other parties in the remaining 220 constituencies. Since, at that time, the JSP was in a coalition government with the LDP and Sakigake, then it was a fairly logical step for the union to support candidates from these parties. Another factor to be considered by Nikkyōso leaders and members was that the main opposition to the governing coalition was now the new catch-all party Shinshintō, a party dominated by Ozawa Ichiro, an ex-LDP politician who was particularly unpopular with the left in general and had published ideas about education that made him even more unpopular with teachers in particular.[23] The present leader of the LDP, on the other hand, showed signs of a more moderate and flexible approach.

When asked to confirm that Nikkyōso would indeed be supporting LDP candidates at the next election, Nishizawa Kiyoshi, the vice-president of Nikkyōso, replied that the *Yomiuri Shimbun* was deliberately giving a false impression of what was happening. It was not true that Nikkyōso as a national organization was supporting the LDP. However, at the prefectural level each organisation has the right to decide what to do in response to local circumstances. Ordinary union members want to involve themselves in local campaigns to further the political causes they believe in. Therefore, if there is no JSP candidate in their local constituency, they will have to examine the other candidates to see if there is anyone who is advocating policies compatible with the goals of the union.[24] The effect of the introduction of the new electoral system, therefore, is to reduce even further the central control Nikkyōso's national headquarters has over the prefectures. Nikkyōso's policy since 1961 of only giving endorsement to JSP candidates only made sense as a national policy if the JSP were running candidates in every constituency. With the introduction of the new system this policy now only applies to the regional PR constituencies, not to the more numerous single seat constituencies. Similarly, the mathematical logic of the new system, which dictates that for a candidate to win, he or she needs a much larger percentage of the constituency votes than required in the previous system, has forced LDP candidates to expand their appeal beyond traditional LDP voters. As LDP secretary general Kato Koichi said in the summer of 1996, "Unless we manage to stretch out our wings beyond the conservative voters, it will be impossible for LDP to win an election under the single seat constituency system, which requires more than 51% of the vote for victory."[25] This explains the LDP's newfound friendliness to Nikkyōso and other unions that were previously thought of as being in the enemy camp.[26] Cooperation between unions and the LDP is also made easier by the more moderate and business-friendly stance of Rengō. If recent changes in political circumstances have made Nikkyōso more flexible in its approach to political endorsements, then how have these same changes affected Zenkyō's relations with the JCP?

The JCP. Of all Japan's political parties, the JCP seems to have been the least affected by the dramatic changes of the early 1990s. This seems to be rather ironic, given that the biggest international development of the early 1990s was the death of Marxism-Leninism as a serious force. Indeed the JCP in recent years has managed to increase its share of the votes in national and local elections.[27] It appears to have attracted some JSP supporters disenchanted by Murayama's abandonment of so many Socialist policies. Zenkyō and Zenkyō-affiliated prefectural unions do not officially endorse the JCP or JCP candidates.[28] The national federation to which Zenkyō is affiliated, Zenrōren, also does not officially endorse the JCP. However, most observers of Japanese unionism can see that the alignment between party and unions is strong. Williamson, for example, comments as follows. "Although it claims to observe 'the principle of independence from political parties' Zenrōren is aligned firmly with the JCP."[29] Exactly the same comments have been made about Zenkyō and its affiliated unions.[30] It was not surprising, therefore, that when Mikami Mitsuru, a former president of both Zenkyō and Zenrōren, stood as a candidate for governor of Tokyo at the gubernatorial election of April 1999 that the JCP adopted him as their recommended candidate.[31] As mentioned earlier, although the JCP welcomes any electoral support it can get, it is at least as interested in ideological support and influence, especially with teachers' organizations. Therefore, at the same time that Nikkyōso has become more concerned with professional and educational issues stripped of their political content, Zenkyō has continued Nikkyōso's pre-schism tradition of involving itself in national campaigns—for example, against American military bases in Okinawa.[32] In these populist campaigns Zenkyō joins hands with the JCP and is just as keen as the JCP to present a "clean" image unsullied by contact with politicians or organisations of the right.

Nikkyōso's Changed Political Role in Japan's New Politics

Chapter four discussed the effect of Nikkyōso's schism on its position in the policy-making process. Schoppa's theoretical model of educational policy-making, which he labeled the Modified Pempel–Campbell Model, was based on the assumption that Japan's main political actors were divided clearly into two camps, the progressive camp and the conservative camp. Between 1955 and 1993, this model sufficed as a useful tool for the analysis of Japanese politics. Since 1993, however, the Japanese political system has entered a period of realignment. It is still too early to say what the final result of this realignment will be. However, there are already clear signs regarding Nikkyōso's ideological adaptation to the new political reality. Chapter five examined Nikkyōso's revised program with regard to the debate on education. Here we will examine the political implications of Nikkyōso's post-schism ideology.

Nikkyōso's New Political Ideology

The best guide to post-schism Nikkyōso's new program for renewal of itself and the education system is provided by the final report of the 21st Century Vision Committee published in April 1995. This report recognizes that the 1990s represent a period of significant change for Japan. In keeping with all commentators on Modern Japan, it points out that the 1990s represent the culmination of international developments (the end of the Cold War), economic developments (the end of the catch-up phase of Japan's economic development), and domestic political changes (the fall from power of the LDP).[33] The report then went on to argue that, because of these changes, the rigid, top-down structure of Japanese political, social and economic organisations was now out-of-date.

> The company system based on lifetime employment and family support is expected to change. In order to secure sustainable social development in this context, the conventional (so-called vertical) system which involves excessive dependence on companies and families for the education of children and care for the aged should be replaced by a horizontal social system in which citizens support each other, fulfil social responsibilities and coexist on the principle of respect for individuals.[34]

This idea of replacing "vertical" relations with a "horizontal social system" underpins the report's subsequent proposals regarding lifelong learning, education for the individual, and decentralization of the education system. It argues that the time has come for a shift from quantitative expansion of the education system to a qualitative improvement of education. So education should no longer be seen as primarily fulfilling the function of providing industry with the workers it needs. Instead the emphasis should be shifted to seeing children as individuals with rights, whose contribution to Japan's economy will be a creative and flexible one, rather than a passive one. This philosophy, Nikkyōso believes, is both a humane and a practical one to adopt as Japan enters the twenty-first century.

A Comparison of Nikkyōso's Ideology and New Party Ideology

The basic ideas contained in the 21st Century Vision Committee's report had a great deal in common with the rhetoric of the Japan New Party (JNP). The JNP's leader Hosokawa Morihiro partly based his critique of the LDP and Japan's central bureaucracy on the frustrations he endured as governor of Kumamoto. He proposed wide-ranging deregulation and decentralization for many aspects of Japan's administration, including education. He believed that Japan's regions could be revitalized if they were allowed more latitude and freedom in running local education.[35] This view was shared by JNP's members, many of whom also had a background in local government. Imai Hiroshi, for example, JNP Diet member and ex-mayor of Soka city in Saitama, argued that the power of local politicians was constantly undermined by the "vertical" nature of power in Japan. Taking education as an example, he pointed out that the head of the Soka city board of education could only be appointed with the approval of the prefectural board of education. In turn, the head of the prefectural board of education could only be appointed with the approval of the Ministry of Education. Experiences of this kind of "vertical flow" of power led Imai to stand as a candidate for the JNP on a platform of decentralization.[36]

During his short period as prime minister Hosokawa was unable to make any progress in implementing the JNP's program of decentralization. Since then the recapture of the reins of power by the LDP has reduced the likelihood of implementation even further. However, this does not mean that the logic of the argument has been undermined, and it may well be that the ideology of deregulation, decentralization, and individualism becomes the progressive ideology of the post-1955 system replacing that mix of Marxism and Social Democracy that characterized the previous "progressive camp." Sōhyō has gone forever, the unions that once made it up have now been "privatized," and the JSP (now known as the SDP) is on its knees. At present a new party system is still in the making. The mid-1990s bore witness to a bewildering series of party splits, defections, amalgamations, and failed attempts at amalgamation involving every party except the JCP. Previously held ideological positions seemed to count for little as Socialists, social democrats, conservatives, and members of the Buddhist sect Sōka Gakkai (i.e., Kōmeitō politicians) jumped in and out of bed with one another as a drama of unprecedented political fluidity unfolded.[37] The 1996 general election served the purpose of clearing up the mess somewhat. If the new party chaos was like a game of musical chairs, then the October 1996 election was the moment when the music stopped. The LDP was the overall winner, gaining nearly enough seats to get back into power by itself (something it succeeded in doing the following year). The largest of the new parties, Shinshintō, led by Hata and Ozawa won 155 seats, slightly less than its pre-election total. Meanwhile, Minshutō (the Democratic Party) formed earlier that year by a mixture of politicians from new parties and the JSP won an impressive fifty-two seats. The big loser was the JSP (renamed the Social Democratic Party—Shakai minshutō—in January 1996), which was reduced to a rump of fifteen seats. The JCP probably profited from JSP failure and was able to win twenty-six seats—almost double its previous total. Following the 1996 election and Hosokawa's retirement from politics, Kan Naoto, the leader of Minshutō, became the new hero of the anti-LDP camp. As Minister for Health and Welfare in the first Hashimoto government (1995–1996) Kan had made a name for himself by vigorously uncovering the bureaucratic corruption and incompetence that had led to the infecting of thousands of haemophiliacs with HIV contaminated blood. Many voters now looked to Kan as a politician who would do something about the ingrained corruption at the heart of Japanese politics and administration. Kan's status as a potential future non-LDP prime minister was further boosted by the fragmentation of Shinshintō (New Year's Eve 1997) and the relaunching of his own party as new Minshutō in April 1998. Thanks to the arrival of defectors from other parties, Minshutō at that time had ninety-three members in the lower house. It also had thirty-eight members in the upper house, a total that was boosted to forty-seven in the subsequent July election. At the same election the LDP suffered an embarrassing setback, losing fifteen seats when it was hoping to gain some. Hashimoto took the blame for the defeat and resigned as prime minister. Under its new leader, Obuchi Keizō, the LDP stayed in power and formed a new coalition, this time with Ozawa's latest political creation, the small Jiyūtō (liberal Party).[38]

What is new Nikkyōso's place in this still fluid political system? Now that the JSP has been reduced to a parliamentary rump, Nikkyōso has started to build bridges with Minshutō at the national level. Despite its recent successes, it is still too early to say whether or not Minshutō will become the major opposition that the party aspires to be (i.e., the second half of the new two-party system that the new lower house election system was designed to bring about). So Nikkyōso will continue to work with individual politicians whom it believes share the union's main aims and objectives. The union will be especially able to work with politicians who have experienced the frustrations of local government and who can sympathize with Nikkyōso's resentment against the heavy-handedness of the center. At present there is distrust between traditional Nikkyōso activists and politicians who are usually given the label "conservative." However, members of the union are now coming to realize that the choice is to either remain completely politically uninvolved, to build bridges with politicians in the new parties or LDP, or to take the road of Zenkyō members and put their trust in the JCP. The lasting choices to be made by many Nikkyōso members and local leaders still remain to be seen.

In June 1997, Nikkyōso celebrated its fiftieth anniversary. Its annual convention in the same month was described as having a "quiet atmosphere."[39] The following year's convention included a visit by the education minister. The interesting thing about this event was how unremarkable it now seemed.[40] Now that Nikkyōso has ended its political confrontation with the MOE and the LDP, it seems to be groping for a political role. As pointed out in the previous chapter, there are many in Japan and abroad who argue that it is not the place for a teachers' organization to have a political role at all. It is unlikely that Nikkyōso will eschew politics altogether in the years ahead, but whatever politics they are they will be completely different from the union's first fifty years. Zenkyō and its allies, on the other hand, will act as a kind of living museum, continuing with the old style of politics into the future.

Implications for Theoretical Models of Japanese Politics

Chapter four included a review of the political theory debate that was relevant to Japanese politics under the 1955 system. One of the reasons why Nikkyōso's schism is of such interest politically is that it coincides with what is widely seen as either the ending of this system or its radical transformation into something new.[41] Many assumptions on which the older theoretical models relied are now no longer valid. In chapter four it was concluded that the model of political pluralism that best suited Japanese politics in the 1980s was that devised by Muramatsu Michio and Ellis Krauss that they termed "patterned pluralism."[42] This was a modification of classical pluralism designed to suit the Japanese case. However, two of the main assumptions underlying their theory (viz., that Japan was a one-party dominant system and that an ideological cleavage existed between government and opposition), have come to be seriously challenged by events since 1989. Although the LDP regained a small majority within the lower house of the Diet in 1997, it lost it again in the 2000 general election, making it dependent on its coalition partners just to form a government. It has also been unable to regain the control of the upper house that it lost in 1989.[43] The political turmoil of the mid-1990s has shaken previous assumptions that the LDP would control the reins of Japanese government in perpetuity. Similarly, the formation of the moderate Rengō followed by the collapse of the JSP has considerably diluted the importance of ideology in 1990s politics. Pempel summarizes the consequences of this as follows.

> The [LDP's] defeat in 1993 was less a defeat for 'conservatives' and more a defeat for the party. By the mid-1990s the once vibrant political left had, in fact, surrendered to conservatives on most of the issues that once divided the two camps, and conservatism as a broad philosophy had undeniably triumphed over socialism in a way that was unlikely to be reversed.[44]

It is interesting that Pempel uses the word "surrendered" here to describe the collapse of the non-Communist left. This is the same term used by the JCP for the same process. For its part, the JCP and its allied union federation Zenrōren continue to fight an ideological battle, but they occupy the margins of Japanese politics. The choice faced by ordinary unionized teachers in 1989 was whether to go with Nikkyōso into a non-ideological, more pragmatic future or align with Zenkyō into a continuation of the old ideological struggle. In a very real sense this was the same choice faced by the Japanese left as a whole at that time. By the end of the 1990s, it has become clear that the majority of those concerned took the former course, not only within the teaching profession but within unionism in general and also with respect to party political allegiance. This movement has clearly had important consequences for theoretical models of Japanese politics.

While making note of the changes of the 1990s, it is also important to be aware of what has stayed the same in Japanese politics. From the point of view of the model of patterned pluralism, two particular characteristics remain unchanged. These are, first, the strength of the bureaucracy,[45] and, second, the blurred boundaries between state and society. Both these characteristics of Japanese politics and policy-making mark Japan as a polity in which unmodified, classical pluralist theory clearly does not apply. The main consequence of these characteristics has also survived the ending of the 1955 system—namely, that if an interest group wants to influence policy-making, it must get access to central government bureaucrats either directly or via politicians belonging to the governing party who can act on its behalf.

Bearing in mind the changes and continuities since Muramatsu and Krauss came up with their theory of patterned pluralism in the 1980s, I now propose to update it with a *modified theory of patterned pluralism.* This model defines Japan as a system that embodies the following characteristics.

1. The government and its bureaucracy are strong, but the boundaries between state and society are blurred by the integration of social interest groups with the government and by the intermediation of political parties between social interest groups and the government. The government is not weak, but is penetrated by interest groups and political parties. [This section is unchanged from the original model.]

2. One of the reasons for this integration between state and society is that one party is nearly perpetually in power either alone or in coalition with a smaller ally or allies. The main party is a pragmatic, catchall party at least partially responsive to a wide variety of sometimes competing social interests.

3. Ideology does not play a significant role in deciding alliances or allegiances. Thus, most opposition parties are potential members of a coalition government, and most interest groups have flexible and

pragmatic political allegiances. Only a few, smaller party-interest group alliances are fixed mainly by ideological considerations.

Because the model of patterned pluralism was closely related to Schoppa's model of education policy-making, a modification of one must imply a modification of the other. We saw in chapter four how Nikkyōso's new policy of avoiding ideologically based opposition undermined Schoppa's theory. In this chapter and chapter six we have charted the decline of the rest of the progressive camp. Schoppa's model will have to be modified to take account of this withering away of the two camp cleavage in policy-making. Bearing this in mind, I propose the following *modified Schoppa model.*

Conflict resolution patterns in Japan's education system can be divided into the following two types.

1. Low-conflict disputes that tend to result in incremental change. This incremental change has, over time, the potential to develop into substantive change to the education system.

2. High-conflict disputes involving actors in any part of the education system (whether they previously belonged to the progressive or conservative camp is of little relevance). As in Schoppa's original model, high conflict disputes will continue to result in little policy change.

We will now examine some examples of these two types of conflict resolution pattern.

1. Examples include the introduction of the five-day school week, along with the proposal to merge junior high schools and senior high schools into single six-year secondary schools that has now been accepted by the MOE. Implementation, however, will take some time

2. There has not been an example of a new high conflict dispute since the schism. However, the imposition of the observance of the national flag and anthem at school ceremonies is an example of a policy that was started before the schism and carried over into the new post-schism period.

The issue of the flag and anthem is probably the last example of the old type of policy resolution forced on the schools by the MOE and LDP. It is also significant that as this dispute entered the late 1990s the role of teachers' unions became less important and the role of students' associations working with parents' groups and lawyers gained a higher profile.[46] It follows that when similar high conflict disputes arise in the future it will be much less likely that the actors involved will be formed into neat alliances based on ideology (or at least the old established ideological cleavages of the 1955 system). We must wait for the first big, controversial policy initiative of the new system before this part of the modified model can be tested properly. By then, of course, the model may need modifying again due to important changes in the political environment within which policy-making takes place. The mere contemplation of such a modification (of a model already modified twice before!) must surely give rise to doubts about the usefulness of this kind of policy-making model for explaining any kind of political reality beyond that confined within very narrow parameters. We will return to the limitations of this kind of model in the concluding chapter.

Conclusion

Under the 1955 system, Nikkyōso's role was to provide a pillar of support for Sōhyō and the JSP. The coming to an end of the 1955 system has borne witness to the "privatization" of Sōhyō's public sector unions and the collapse of the JSP. The progressive camp that formed part of the basis of Schoppa's (and many other people's) political model has been changed beyond recognition. Furthermore, it is still unclear what political system will replace the 1955 system. For example, the question of whether the new electoral system will give rise to a two-party system is the subject of much debate both within Japan and among Japan-watchers abroad.

If it is too early to be sure about what will replace the 1955 system, it is not too early to arrive at some conclusions as to the way in which it came to an end. An analysis of the experiences of Nikkyōso helps us to understand why the traditional center-left in Japan was unable to capitalize on either the unpopularity of the LDP or the changing political environment of the late 1980s and early 1990s. For almost forty years Nikkyōso had been stuck in a position of opposition to the government and the right. As was the case with other public sector unions and their political ally the JSP, the fundamental ideological position of Nikkyōso had been determined early on in that period. This position entailed a defense of the Occupation-era reforms and, compared to democratic Socialist traditions in other comparable countries, quite an extreme form of pacifism and neutralism.

As time went by, the relevance of this position for ordinary union members and ordinary Japanese voters faded, and it was up to the unions and the JSP to adapt their ideological position and practical programs of action in accordance with these changes. Efforts to do this were made at various times, but always came under attack from die-hard traditionalists. In the case of Nikkyōso the chronic decline in its membership, combined with the opportunity provided by the formation of Rengō finally forced the right-wing led half of the mainstream faction to push for radical modernization and change. The resulting clash with the left brought about the union's schism. In the case of the JSP, at the same time that Nikkyōso was splitting in two, that party was enjoying something of an electoral revival at the 1989 House of Councillors' election. With hindsight we can now see that this was a false dawn for the JSP. The LDP was so unpopular in 1989 that rigid opposition and a rigid devotion to principle, combined with a popular leader, brought great success for the JSP. This success allowed them to avoid grasping the nettle of reform so painfully felt by Nikkyōso during the same period. Therefore, when the Japanese electorate were presented in 1993 with an alternative choice to either the (still unpopular) LDP or the unreformed JSP, they opted for that alternative (i.e., the new parties) in large enough numbers to deal a severe body blow to the JSP. Following this result, the JSP did indeed change, but the changes of policy (especially Prime Minister Murayama's drastic U-turns) seemed to many of the JSP's supporters to be cynical and opportunistic. They were regarded by the left as a betrayal, and in subsequent elections this was reflected by an upsurge in the JCP's vote. This was the JSP's equivalent of the formation of Zenkyō. Although no top personnel or Diet members defected to the JCP from the JSP, many ordinary voters did when it came to polling time. As for the right, many left the JSP during the hectic party formation and reformation that took place in the middle 1990s. They hoped that a new party image would save their political skins. They could also see that many unions that had traditionally supported JSP candidates were now shopping around among the new parties to see what deals could be made in return for political endorsement. Nikkyōso and its affiliates were not initially among this group of unions. However, the decline in stature of the JSP combined with the electoral arithmetic of the new election system forced them to look to new political alliances.

In the 1980s and 1990s the progressive camp in Japan found itself faced with drastic changes in the international, economic, and political environment to which it had become accustomed. Elements within the progressive camp responded to this in various ways. The story of Nikkyōso's transformation during these years is the story of how one section of the camp coped. Other unions coped in different ways; Zendentsū was very conciliatory and, as a result survived largely intact, and Kokurō took the opposite militant stance and suffered the consequences. Changes for these unions were bound to have a knock-on effect on the JSP, a party entirely dependent on union support at election time. However, the JSP failed to either face the consequences of the changes that had taken place among the unions or to learn the lessons about adaptation to external changes that the unions had so painfully learned themselves. The result was the destruction of the JSP in the 1990s. Nikkyōso was loyal until the end, but in the final analysis it was up to the JSP to save itself. This it was unable to do.

CONCLUSION

In focusing on Nikkyōso's schism, the purpose of this book was to do more than just tell the story of a particular organization going through a particular, traumatic stage in its history. Examining the Japan teachers' union as it pulled itself apart gave us the opportunity to arrive at a fuller understanding of both the organization itself and the political environment within which it existed. Indeed, throughout this study we have seen an interplay between the internal and external forces that made Nikkyōso the organization it was, and which eventually caused it to break into two. Because of the close connection between internal and external factors, it must inevitably follow that a contribution to our knowledge of Nikkyōso must also involve an understanding about the wider world of Japanese politics, education, and unionism.

This book has built on the foundations laid by the two most important scholars of Nikkyōso, Donald Thurston and Benjamin Duke. However, its approach to the subject has been different from that of these two experts. Instead of focusing on a detailed examination of Nikkyōso's internal structure and development, it has broadened its scope of inquiry to include the application of recent developments in political science to an analysis of Nikkyōso and its environment. Different tools of analysis, in the form of social scientific models, have been applied, depending on the aspect of Nikkyōso under consideration at any given time. One purpose has been to use Nikkyōso's schism as an opportunity to view the inner workings of an important organization, and, in so doing, to throw light on broader developments taking place in the arenas within which that organization functions. A parallel purpose has been to test the applicability of these models in a changed political environment. Various modifications to these models have been found to be necessary. The conclusions that have been made can be divided into five categories:

1. Teacher unionism in Japan

2. Power and policy-making in the contemporary Japanese education system

3. The current state of unionism in Japan

4. The realignment of Japanese politics

5. The use of theoretical models in analyzing political organizations and policy

We will now deal with these categories in turn.

TEACHER UNIONISM IN JAPAN

Previous writers on Nikkyōso had not considered the union from a comparative perspective—that is, how it compared to teachers' unions in other countries. This study, and in particular the discussion in chapter six, has tried to view Nikkyōso not as a unique case, but as an organization with particular goals and features that are identifiably part and parcel of the main function it undertakes (i.e., representing the interests of schoolteachers in Japan). It is important never to lose sight of the fact that Nikkyōso owed its strength and importance in postwar Japan primarily to the fact that tens of thousands of individual teachers chose to belong to it. Furthermore, it was the lessening of this support that caused a major rethinking within Nikkyōso's leadership about the direction of their movement.

Edited collections by Lawn[1] and Cooper[2] have shown how the problems and dilemmas of Nikkyōso are, at root, the same as those faced by any teachers' union in a modern, industrialized democracy. All teachers' representative organizations have to face up to the dual nature of teachers as both salaried workers employed by the state and skilled professionals undertaking a job that involves the entrusting of children into their care. Nikkyōso frequently came under attack from the right for allegedly neglecting the interests of children in order to further the interests of teachers as "educational laborers." The cases collected by Lawn and Cooper show that it is not an uncommon problem for teachers' unions to be attacked in this manner. The main aims and objectives of Nikkyōso are also not remarkable when compared to those of other teachers' unions. All these organizations are concerned with the salaries and conditions of work of their members, as well as the issue of control over education, especially if the government is viewed as threatening the independence of teachers in the classroom. What was different about Nikkyōso's position was that it faced for so long a government that was consistently hostile to everything it stood for. Unions in other countries usually had a more ambiguous relationship with government, varying between periods of hostility and cooperation. In Japan, under the 1955 system, the situation was one of unmitigated hostility at the national level. However, the research of Rohlen,[3] reinforced by research carried out for this study, has shown that at the level of prefecture and school the situation in Japan is much closer to that of industrial relations in the education systems of other countries. Indeed, this was how Japan for the entire postwar period was able to maintain the paradoxical situation of permanent conflict at the national level of education, alongside the extremely successful provision of education to the population at the school level. Principals cooperated with the leaders of school *bunkai* to ensure the smooth running of the school, just as they do in schools in other countries. With the splitting of Nikkyōso, it now looks as if the larger of the resultant organizations will now try to operate a policy of cooperation at the national level, as well as the prefectural and school levels, thus making new Nikkyōso even more like a typical teachers' organization.

Nikkyōso's schism has also allowed us a deeper look into the inner workings of that union than would normally have been the case, throwing open inner squabbles for public scrutiny. Of particular interest here was the importance of ideology to many union members. In its attachment to ideology not directly related to the profession of school teaching (the main example being pacifism) pre-schism Nikkyōso exhibited the characteristic that most set it apart from teachers' unions in other countries. The unusual circumstances of Nikkyōso's formation—its creation during a period of foreign occupation and drastic overhaul of all of Japan's institutions—left it very firmly wedded to a particular political ideology. It is not unusual for teachers' organizations to have connections with political parties and other pressure groups, but it is unusual for such a union to have its very identity so closely bound up in a particular radical ideology. Thus, Nikkyōso's slogan of "Never send our children to the battlefield again," which seems, by comparative standards, to be an unusual slogan for a teachers' organization, was regarded as being entirely appropriate in the circumstances of a country emerging from the wreckage of a disastrous war. However, as memories of that war faded, the necessity arose for Nikkyōso to rethink its radical, pacifist ideology. From the late 1960s onward, new teachers entering the profession had no memory of the war, and for most of them their requirements of a representative organization were more similar to the requirements of teachers in any country. Nikkyōso was faced with the challenge of adapting itself to meet the needs of this new generation. The struggle within Nikkyōso's leadership became one between modernizers trying to meet this challenge and traditionalists defending the union's founding ideology. The resulting schism has brought about the creation of a reformed Nikkyōso that eschews a lot of the ideological baggage of the postwar era. As a result, new Nikkyōso is a teachers' union more similar to those in other countries, while Zenkyō represents those ideologically inspired elements of the old organization that are more out of keeping with the character of typical teachers' unions. For these reasons new Nikkyōso may be able to halt the decline in its influence and membership whereas Zenkyō is probably destined to shrink further until it becomes a hard core of mostly ideologically motivated teachers. It is significant here to note that it is Zenkyō that has retained the old Nikkyōso slogan of "Never send our children to the battlefield again." This slogan is displayed prominently at all union conferences and on most union publications. It is a public display of Zenkyō's commitment not to let go of the past.

Power and Policy-Making Within the Contemporary Japanese Education System

With respect to education policy-making in Japan, the main theoretical model that has been discussed in this book is the Modified Pempel-Campbell Model devised by Schoppa. This model divides conflict resolution patterns in Japanese policy-making into three types and was used by Schoppa to explain the failure of education reform initiatives of the 1970s and 1980s. In chapter four it was pointed out that one of the main foundations of this model (i.e., the presence of two opposed camps in Japanese politics) had been seriously weakened by the political realignment of the 1990s. For Schoppa it was always vitally important to identify an actor in the policy-making process as being either in the conservative or the progressive camp. Recent political developments, however, have now blurred what was once a very clear distinction. Furthermore, Schoppa's model of bureaucratic conservatism was criticized from the standpoint of Katō's theory of bureaucratic rationality. Finally, Schoppa's conclusion that the education system is immobilist and can only accommodate incremental change was called into question by reference to education reforms (proposed and actual) of the 1990s, and by changes in the debate on education. The fact that Schoppa's model was created to describe events in the 1970s and 1980s meant that its usefulness for an analysis of other decades was always limited. (The historically contingent nature of this kind of model will be discussed more fully later.) The fact that the pace of educational change now is slower than it was in the Meiji period or during the Occupation era does not mean that change is not taking place. Important changes that were initiated in the 1980s did not bear fruit until the 1990s.[4]

Having made the above reservations, however, it is important to note that much of what Schoppa wrote about education policy-making still remains valid. For example, he made the point that most of the people in the education bureaucracy (local and national) are usually concerned with avoiding disruption to education if at all possible. This point still remains valid, and continues to act as a break on politicians who have radical plans for the education system. It is a feature of the system that continues to allow those who are excluded from the formal policy-making channels a chance to influence policy, at least in a negative way. Under Schoppa's model, members of the progressive camp had to rely on this indirect influence because they were always excluded, at the national level, from these formal policy-making channels. Since the schism new Nikkyōso has tried to gain access to these channels, with, to date, only minimal success. On the other hand, there is also no evidence to date that the Ministry of Education has taken the opportunity of the union's schism to seek to impose a right-wing set of reforms onto Japan's schools, something that the left in Japan were very much afraid of in the aftermath of the Occupation. Instead, the evidence now makes it seem that the MOE's main enemies are from the right and center, not the left. Proposals, dating from Nakasone's *Rinkyōshin* and backed by Keidanren, for increased flexibilization and deregulation of the education system, combined with calls from the some of the new parties for decentralization, are very serious threats to the centralized control of education that the MOE currently enjoys. The MOE also employs some of this rhetoric in its official announcements (except the idea of decentralization), but is now involved in a struggle to make sure that when change does take place it does not lose too many of its discretionary powers. Paradoxically, the weakening of radical teacher unionism in Japan may result in a serious undermining of the strength and dominance of the MOE. So long as Nikkyōso was strong, united, and in the hands of left-wing militants the MOE could portray itself as the defender of Japan's education from Marxist takeover. The removal of this convenient enemy now leaves the MOE open to attack by those who used to be its allies (i.e., the business community and conservative politicians).

Schoppa's model incorporated an element of infighting within the conservative camp and allowed for a lack of unity within the progressive camp. However, the splitting of Nikkyōso into a conciliatory half and an unreformed militant half, combined with the demise of the JSP and Sōhyō, mean that now the whole concept of a progressive camp has ceased to have any real meaning. This, combined with increased friction within the conservative camp, means that the two-camp model of Japanese policy-making can now be superseded. Schoppa had already been criticized for dividing people and organizations too neatly into "camps."[5] Now the whole concept of 'camp' can be done away with. This means that Schoppa's three-part model of policy-making (described in chapter four) can now be replaced with a simpler two-part model (outlined in chapter seven).

The other model related to education policy that has had to be modified is Rohlen's model of conflict resolution at the three different levels of the education system. Again, much of what Rohlen said about educational politics in the 1980s still applies for the 1990s. However, some modifications have had to be made to take account of the existence of two national unions instead of one, and the new conciliatory stance taken by the larger of these unions. Chapter three contains a full list of the modifications necessary for Rohlen's model. The main contribution of this model to the study of Nikkyōso's schism is the insights it gives to the differing political balances of power that are present at the prefectural level. This helps provide a theoretical starting point for explaining the wide variety of outcomes of the schism across the country.

The Current State of Unions in Japan

As well as analyzing Nikkyōso as a teachers' union, this study has also examined it in its capacity as a public sector Japanese union sharing many of the characteristics of other such unions. Nikkyōso was always the largest or second largest public sector union in Japan, and its close connection with public sector unionism was dramatically illustrated by the coincidence of its schism with the dissolution of the public sector union federation Sōhyō and its incorporation with private sector unions into the new federation Rengō. Chapter six argued that this reorganization of Japanese trade unionism represented the "privatization" of public sector unionism. Critics on the left regarded this process as the surrendering of the traditional principles of trade unionism by those leaders who went along with the formation of Rengō.

The experience of Nikkyōso as it went through its schism was compared to the experiences of two other large public sector unions, Kokurō and Zendentsū. The former union resisted the process of privatization and was almost destroyed as a result, while the latter cooperated with government and management and was able to survive intact. The case of Nikkyōso comes somewhere between these two examples. Moderates within the leadership were able to steer the union in the direction of affiliation with Rengō, but at the cost of losing a large section of the membership who left the union under the leadership of Communists and left-Socialists. In order to analyse the role of union leadership in this process a hypothesis devised by Mike Mochizuki (and referred to as Mochizuki's Hypothesis) was used. This stated that, to adapt to a changing external environment, a union leadership must have a centralized organization as well as considerable autonomy form the rank-and-file. Nikkyōso's lack of legal status as a national organization meant that each prefectural union could decide for itself whether to follow the national lead into Rengō. This lack of a centralised organization (which, being a product of its legal environment, was beyond the control of the union itself) exacerbated the schism once it began. From the point of view of modernizers and moderates, however, the schism had the function of removing most (not all!) of the militant opposition to the new policy of compromise with the government and education authorities. In this sense the schism can be compared with the earlier purge carried out by Zendentsū's leadership against Communist cadres within its ranks. The removal of this influence allowed the leadership to steer a path of compromise and cooperation with the authorities when privatization of NTT took place. The alternative course of action for Nikkyōso would have been to follow the militant, uncompromising stance of Kokurō. If this had happened, Nikkyōso might have shared Kokurō's fate. The schism, although very harmful for Nikkyōso, was not therefore as bad an outcome as that which would probably have resulted from a policy of resisting change completely. Furthermore, the trauma of Nikkyōso's schism was illustrative of the kind of internal conflict that was unavoidable and that affected other public sector unions in the late 1980s to greater or lesser degrees. The traditional ideals of public sector unionism had to be compromised to allow the movement to be modernized. Letting go of these ideals was a painful process for many union members, and it is still too early to tell whether this sacrifice has been worthwhile.

The Realignment of Japanese Politics

The breakdown of the division of Japan's political actors into two camps, discussed earlier, was one part of the ending of the 1955 system of Japanese politics. Chapter seven analyzed the place of Nikkyōso in this political transformation, concentrating on its relationship with the JSP and the JCP. In this respect post-schism Nikkyōso's policy of endorsing candidates from parties other than the JSP reflects two factors. First, it displays the new flexibility of Nikkyōso's leadership unfettered by previous ideological constraints, and, second, it reflects the decline of the JSP and its inability to put up a candidate in every constituency under the reformed electoral system. In contrast, the relationship between Zenkyō and the JCP represents a continuation of the old-style of politics, carried out under old-style slogans. The JCP continues to represent an outlet for those disenchanted with mainstream Japanese politics, and has enjoyed a small electoral revival during the 1990s. The JSP, on the other hand, has shrunk to a shadow of its former self. What can Nikkyōso, a previous bulwark of support for the JSP, tell us about that party's decline? At the same time as Nikkyōso was going through the painful but necessary process of adapting to changing circumstances around it, the JSP was enjoying electoral success under the leadership of the popular Doi Takako, who led them to victory at the 1989 House of Councillors election. With hindsight, however, it can be seen that this was a false dawn for the JSP. Their success was more due to the extreme unpopularity of the LDP caught in the depths of the Recruit scandal than to any intrinsic attractiveness of the JSP's policies. Thus, the JSP continued to avoid a proper policy review until it was forced to do so by the sudden and unexpected catapulting of party leader Murayama into the premiership in 1994. The resultant U-turns that he carried out were widely regarded as cynical and opportunistic, and the JSP suffered the consequences at the 1996 general election winning only fifteen seats. A comparison of the fortunes of the JSP and Nikkyōso during this period, therefore, would seem to indicate the need for the kind of modernization and adaptation conducted by Nikkyōso's leadership for organizations previously identified as belonging to the progressive camp (i.e., public sector unions and parties of the left). A failure to carry out properly this kind of review has resulted in disaster for organizations like the JSP and Kokurō. Although the form in which the new Japanese political system will manifest itself is not yet clear, it is clear that there will be no major part played in it by the JSP or Kokurō. The JCP and allies like Zenkyō will still be fixtures of the political scene, but they will be just as marginalized as the JCP always has been in postwar Japanese politics.

The Use of Theoretical Models in Analyzing Political Organizations and Policy

The starting point for this present study was not a theoretical issue but an historical event, a key development in the life of a particular organization, the Japan Teachers' Union or Nikkyōso. The purpose of the study was not to test a particular hypothesis, but to arrive at a more thorough understanding about what actually happened during Nikkyōso's schism. The theoretical models that have been used, therefore, have been employed as tools to help in understanding and explaining what happened. When a theoretical tool is applied to a new situation, its usefulness will inevitably be reassessed. The problem with many political models is that they are historically contingent—that is, they describe an institution or a process existing at a particular time. They can, therefore, provide snapshots of reality that must be immediately modified when events move on, as they inevitably must. In this study I have used Schoppa's model of education policy-making (itself a modified version of previous models) as well as Rohlen's model of conflict within the education system. I have also used Muramatsu and Krauss's model of patterned pluralism. All these models were devised for a particular historical epoch—that is, the 1955 system in Japanese politics. The fundamental changes that have taken place in this system during the early 1990s inevitably meant that all these models needed to be modified. It is with no great enthusiasm that I offer modifications for all these models within the body of this study because I realize that it is only a matter of time before they will need to be modified again. It would be more useful to regard these models more as heuristic devices that help social scientists to analyze a particular system or institution and compare it to others. The model of patterned pluralism, for example, helps us to compare Japanese pluralism with that of other nation states. It also helps us to hold up the Japanese version of democracy with more ideal, theoretical models.

Two other theoretical tools used in this study are of a different character to the three models discussed above. These are Kato's theory of bureaucratic rationality and Mochizuki's hypothesis of union leadership (the latter derived from Michels' Iron Law of Oligarchy). These theories are less historically contingent than the three models because they are about the fundamental logic that underlies large, modern organizations. Kato's theory is about the ways in which a modern ministry will try to preserve its discretionary powers, and the theories of Mochizuki and Michels are concerned with how modern parties and unions need to have oligarchic leadership in order to adapt to changing times. These theories also need to be adapted according to changing historical epochs, but it is fair to say that they are applicable in a wider set of circumstances than the other three theoretical models.

One thing that all these models and theories have in common is that they all have been useful analytical tools in the analysis of Nikkyōso's schism. The whole point in having political and social theories is that they help us to understand political and social reality. A simple historical description of events in the life of Nikkyōso in the 1980s and 1990s would not have been so helpful in revealing the true significance of the schism for the union itself and the other organizations with which it had close connections. Theory and models are necessary, therefore, but they must never be allowed to prevent the researcher from remembering that no two human organizations are exactly alike, and that no organization remains unchanged for long by the passage of time. Nikkyōso is a large, complex organization consisting of dozens of prefectural and city organizations and thousands of school-based branches spread throughout the country. The story of how it broke into two is not a simple one, and the present study has used various theories and models to identify the main causes of the split and the most significant consequences for the union and other organizations. After all this has been said, however, Nikkyōso and Zenkyō remain the property of their members and continue to promote and defend the interests of their members as best they can. They should never be labeled or categorized in an oversimplistic way to serve the interests of a particular political theory or a particular political ideology.

NOTES

NOTES TO INTRODUCTION

1. The Japan Teachers' Union is usually abbreviated JTU in English. The Japanese name, Nihon Kyōshokuin Kumiai, is usually abbreviated Nikkyōso. In this study the Japanese abbreviated name will normally be used.

2. Thurston (1973).

3. Duke (1973).

4. Ichikawa (1984), p. 246.

5. Thurston (1973), p. 265.

6. Yoshimitsu Takei, Review of *Teachers and Politics in Japan* by Donald Thurston. *Comparative Education Review* (June 1975): 315–319.

7. Thurston (1989).

8. Duke (1973), p. xiii.

9. Duke (1973), p. 195.

10. Duke (1973), p. 202.

11. For an example of a short history of the national union written before the schism see Nikkyōso (1987). For two alternative full-length national histories written after the schism see Nikkyōso (1997) and Zenkyō (1997). For an example of the history of a prefectural union see Saikōkyō (1995), which is the detailed history of Saitama High School Teachers' union, or Aikōkyō (1997), which is the detailed history of Aichi High School Teachers' union.

12. For example, see Nikkyōso (1982).

13. Nikkyōso (1995). This report will be dealt with in more detail in chapter five.

14. Yokobori (1988).

15. Mochizuki (1987).

16. Takihara (1981).

17. Ishikawa (1985).

18. In some areas of Japan, bomb threats by ultra-right-wing groups against Nikkyōso meetings are almost routine. In addition, while union meetings are taking place it is a common practice for the "sound trucks" of these groups to cause disruption by their use of very high-volume speeches or martial music.

19. Sagara (1986).

20. Williams (1996).

21. Schoppa (1991a) and Van Wolferen (1993).

22. Van Wolferen (1993), p. 582.

23. Chapter six will cover the theoretical issues raised by this assumption in more detail.

24. Maurice Kogan, a British scholar of educational politics, has made the point that changes within a nation's education system cannot be properly understood without a wider study of the whole political and administrative system—see Kogan (1978), p. 20.

25. Because of a lack of research in other areas of Japan, conclusions related to this part of the book must be tentative. It is hoped, however, that they will provide a starting point for further research in other prefectures and individual schools within those prefectures.

26. Fitz and Halpin (1994), p. 8.

27. Turner (1995), pp. 248–252.

Notes to Chapter One

1. Trainor (1983), p. ix.

2. Smethurst (1978), p. 156.

3. Kobayashi (1978), p. 189.

4. Kobayashi (1978), p. 188.

5. Rohlen (1983), p. 65. Also see Yamazumi (1986), pp. 148–150 for examples of *suminuri* textbooks (i.e. books that were allowed to be used after they had had "militaristic" sentences painted out with black ink). Dower (1999) recounts the highly symbolic and traumatic experience of young students being told to blacken out pages of their own treasured textbooks (p. 247).

6. Trainor (1983), chapter six.

7. Kyōiku no Sengoshi Henshū Iinkai (1986, Vol. I), p. 52.

8. Rohlen (1984), p. 66.

9. Schoppa (1991a), p. 32.

10. Mayo (1980), p. 35.

11. It would be wrong to describe all American policy-makers involved in the Occupation as optimistic about the chances of democratizing Japan. Harry Wray has recently written about the very conservative views held by many Washington-based bureaucrats, diplomats, and professors involved in planning the Occupation. He concludes that the far-reaching and fundamental nature of the education reforms that were actually carried out can be largely attributed to the idealism of the staff of SCAP's Education Division working on the ground in Japan. At least for the first two and a half years of the Occupation they received only very general guidelines from Washington. See Wray (1996).

12. U.S. Department of State, *Report of the United States Education Mission to Japan,* p. 1, quoted in Marshall (1994), p. 144.

13. Tsuchimochi (1993), p. 5.

14. Tsuchimochi (1993), p. 6. The 6–3–3 system was regarded as more egalitarian than the 6–5 system because it postponed selection and specialization from the age of twelve to the age of fifteen.

15. Tsuchimochi (1993), pp. 129–137.

16. Such a plan had actually been put forward in Japan for the first time in 1936.

17. Schoppa (1991a), p. 38.

18. Marshall (1994), p. 165.

19. Duke (1973), p. 84.

20. Marshall (1994), p. 150.

21. Marshall (1994), p. 149.

22. Duke (1973), p. 83. Nikkyōso also claimed that individual candidates were pressured by the Americans to stand down—see Zenkyō (1997), pp. 71–72.

23. quoted in Kobayashi (1978), p. 190.

24. Tsuchimochi (1993), p. 210.

25. Tsuchimochi (1993), p. 214.

26. Lincicome (1995).

27. Lincicome (1995), pp. 246–247.

28. Marshall (1994), p. 156.

29. Horio (1988), p. 114.

30. Lincicome (1995), p. 247.

31. Marshall (1994), p. 152.

32. Duke (1973), p. 33.

33. Thurston (1973), pp. 52–53. The other three members were Kitamura Magomori, Inagaki Masanobu, and Masubuchi Yuzuru. Hani subsequently fell out of favor with the JCP. This may account for the fact that in the contemporary Zenkyō's official version of the events of the formation of its 1945 namesake, Hani's name is omitted from the list of names of those involved—see Zenkyō (1997), p. 50.

34. Smethurst (1967), p. 127.

35. Smethurst (1967), p. 127.

36. Smethurst (1967), p. 119.

37. See Dower (1999), chapter three, for a very good account of the exhaustion (both physical and mental) and poverty endured by millions of Japanese people after the ending of the war.

38. Thurston (1973), p. 50, and Smethurst (1967), p. 120.

39. See Zenkyō (1997), p. 69, and Smethurst (1967), p. 121.

40. Duke (1973), p. 38.

41. Thurston (1973), p. 48.

42. Thurston (1973), p. 48. Dower also emphasizes the guilt many teachers felt at the end of the war when they had to confront the fact that they had encouraged many of the boys in their charge to go and fight and die for a lost cause—Dower (1999), p. 250.

43. Duke (1973), p. 37.

44. Smethurst (1967), p. 127. Zenkyō claimed that Nikkyō did not properly address the severe economic conditions teachers found themselves in—Zenkyō (1997), p. 51.

45. Nikkyōso (1987), p. 11.

46. Smethurst (1967), p. 131. Zenkyō's official history made the point that Tokyōkyō's activities were often praised by the Ministry of Education—Zenkyō (1997) p. 54.

47. Smethurst (1967), p. 122.

48. Duke (1973), p. 31.

49. Duke (1973), p. 55.

50. Kobayashi (1978), p. 195.

51. Kyōiku no Sengoshi Henshū Iinkai (1986, Vol. I), p. 169.

52. Zenkyō (1997), pp. 66–67. The official history claimed that the law "drastically violated the rights of public sector workers" (p. 66).

53. Smethurst (1967), p. 124.

54. Duke (1973), p. 81.

55. Nishi (1982), p. 251.

56. See Nikkyōso (1987), pp. 45–48, and Zenkyō (1997), p. 77, for regional details about the number of school teachers who were purged.

57. Smethurst (1967), p. 144.

58. The Red Purge was not confined to sackings. The Occupation authorities' extensive powers to censor radio, newsreel, and cinema was also used to prevent the perceived spread of Communist ideas—Hirano (1992), chapter seven.

59. Duke (1973), p. 89. Ordinary members also had pressure put on them to quit the union—Zenkyō (1997), pp. 76–77.

60. Duke (1973), p. 59.

61. Duke (1973), p. 88.

62. The Communist side, for their part, accused the Socialists in Nikkyōso of making a turn to the right as early as 1948. Socialist leaders were accused of weakness in the face of government and Occupation force pressure—Zenkyō (1997), pp. 84–86.

63. Duke (1973), p. 93.

64. Communist supporters saw the formation of Sohyō as one part of an American plan to create an international anti-Communist trade union movement—Zenkyō (1997), p. 82.

65. *Ampo Japan Asia Quarterly Review,* Vol. 20, No. 4, and Vol. 21, No. 1, p. 62.

NOTES TO CHAPTER TWO

1. Smethurst (1967), p. 148.

2. Nakano (1989), p. 45.

3. For a recent example of a book that argues the case against the government's moral education policy see Khan (1997).

4. Duke (1973), p. 133.

5. Smethurst (1967), p. 151.

6. Marshall (1994), title of chapter seven. Rohlen also uses the same phrase and makes an analogy with a World War I type of stalemate in Rohlen (1984), p. 137.

7. Schoppa (1991a), p. 59.

8. Quoted in Duke (1973), p. 141.

9. Thurston (1973), p. 207.

10. Zenkyō (1997), p. 177.

11. For example, there are specific accounts of violent confrontations in Nikkyōso (1987), p. 110, and Duke (1973), p. 151.

12. Yamazaki (1986), pp. 91–92.

13. Zenkyō's official history, reflecting the views of the pro-Communist faction of the day, says that Nikkyōso's leadership should not have backed down but instead continued the struggle—Zenkyō (1997), p. 150.

14. Nikkyōso (1987), p. 112.

15. Thurston (1973), p. 208.

16. Yamazumi (1986), p. 215.

17. Rohlen (1983), p. 55.

18. Council on Innovation in Education and learning special report, 1936, quoted in Marshall (1994), p. 133.

19. Duke (1973), p. 195.

20. Duke (1973), pp. 195–202. But Halliday (1975) believes that Duke's analysis is "disappointing and inadequate" (footnote 50 to p. 250) and calls for a more thorough study of how left-wing militancy came to be such a powerful force among teachers and other groups within Japan at this time.

21. Shimahara and Sakai (1995), p. 231.

22. Shimahara and Sakai (1995), p. 230, and the present author's own experience as a student teacher in a teacher training college in England (viz., Kingston Polytechnic) 1984–1985.

23. This was a common theme in my interviews with union members, activists, and leaders. Also see Douglas Lummis's interview with a teacher trainee in *Ampo Japan Asia Quarterly Review,* Vol. 19, No. 1, pp. 36–38.

24. Thurston (1989), p. 202

25. Schoppa (1991a), pp. 151–152.

26. See Kyōiku no Sengoshi Henshū Iinkai (1986, vol. III), chapter 3, for details of the tests.

27. Duke (1973), pp. 160–161

28. Thurston (1973), p. 212.

29. Thurston (1973), pp. 124–125.

30. *Kyōiku iinkai geppō* (Board of Education Monthly Reports).

31. Okano and Tsuchiya emphasize these points in their discussion of Nikkyōso's membership decline. See Okano and Tsuchiya (1999), p. 168.

32. Thurston (1989), pp. 200–201.

33. Schoppa (1991a), pp. 198–203.

34. Stevenson and Stigler (1992), p. 162.

35. Thurston (1989), p. 200.

36. Interview with an ex-union member at a high school, Saitama, July 19, 1996.

37. Thurston (1989), p. 201.

38. Thurston (1989), p. 201.

39. Thurston (1989), p. 201.

40. Okano and Tsuchiya emphasize the efforts the government put into portraying Nikkyōso as a left ideologue union, and the effect that this propaganda undoubtedly had on young teachers—Okano and Tsuchiya (1999), p. 168.

41. Duke (1973), pp. 145–148, and Thurston (1973), pp. 139–140.

42. Thurston (1973), p. 143.

43. Thurston (1989), p. 188.

44. *Kikan Kyōikuhō*, May 1987, pp. 98–102.

45. Thurston (1989), p. 189.

46. Interview with Nishizawa Kiyoshi, vice chairman of Nikkyōso, July 23, 1996.

47. The background to the formation of Rengō will be discussed in more detail in chapter six.

48. Kawanishi (1992) gives an account of this process.

49. Quoted in Schoppa (1991a), p. 212.

50. For a statment of the detailed reasons for Nikkyōso's opposition to the "reactionary nature" (*handōteki honshitsu*) of *Rinkyōshin*'s proposals, see Yokobori (1988), chapter one.

51. Critic of Nikkyōso, Ishikawa Sachiko, complained that Nikkyōso treated the *Rinkyōshin* proposals like "waste paper" (Ishikawa , 1989, pp. 225–226).

52. Thurston (1989), p. 199.

Notes to Chapter Three

1. See, for example, Roesgaard (1994), pp. 114–117.

2. Thurston (1989), p. 193.

3. Thurston (1989), p. 195.

4. Quoted in Thurston (1989), p. 195.

5. Nikkyōso (1997), pp. 55–58.

6. Zenkyō (1997), pp. 624–625.

7. Zenkyō Newsletter, No. 1, September 1991.

8. Saitamakyōso News, February 1992.

9. Interview with Hatayama Hidetaka, member of Zenkyō national executive, June 16, 1993.

10. *Kyōiku iinkai gepō*, June 1992, puts the figures as 408,000 for Nikkyōso and 128,000 for Zenkyō out of a total number of teachers of 1,166,000.

11. There are currently twelve "designated cities" (*seirei shitei toshi*) in Japan. They have similar administrative functions to prefectures. The cities are Sapporo, Sendai, Chiba city, Kawasaki, Yokohama, Nagoya, Kyoto city, Osaka city, Kobe, Hiroshima city, Kitakyushu, and Fukuoka city.

12. Saikōkyō (1995), pp. 45–52 Also, a short history of the union is contained in pocket diaries issued to Saikōkyō members.

13. Saikōkyō (1995), pp. 431–435.

14. Interview with two Saikōkyō members at a Commercial High School July 18, 1996

15. *Kyōiku iinkai geppō* (Board of Education Monthly Reports).

16. Saikōkyō (1995), p. 444.

17. Interview with a Commercial High School teacher member of Saitama Kōkyōso, July 18, 1996.

18. Yoneyama (1999), pp. 105–109, and Aikōkyō (1999), Vol. II, pp. 40–41. An example of Aichi's conservatism given by both these sources is Tōgō High School, a school with strict regimentation and discipline. This school became a model school of the 1970s. Prefectural authorities regarded it as a countermeasure against the threat of student indiscipline and unrest—a phenomenon of the universities of the 1960s and early 1970s that had spread to some high schools.

19. The abbreviation of Nagoya City High School Teachers' Union is "Meikōkyō" because the first Chinese character of the name "Nagoya" can be read as either "na" or "mei."

20. For the Aikōkyō account of its decision to join Zenkyō, see Aikōkyō (1999), Vol. II, pp. 225–226.

21. Interview with Takahashi Sanaru, Chairman Aikōkyō, January 17, 1999.

22. Interview with Mori Jun, Chairman, Meikōkyō, January 7, 1999.

23. Interview with Mori Jun, Chairman, Meikōkyō, January 7, 1999.

24. Source: *Kyōiku iinkai geppō* (Board of Education Monthly Reports).

25. See Rohlen (1984), Reed (1986), Jain (1989), and Muramatsu (1997).

26. Reed (1986), pp. 126–127.

27. Rohlen (1984), p. 145.

28. Rohlen (1984), p. 157.

29. Rohlen (1984), p. 158.

30. Rohlen (1984), p. 165.

31. Rohlen (1984), p. 169.

32. Rohlen (1984), p. 170.

33. Rohlen (1984), p. 170.

34. Interview with a teacher at a Nagoya City high school, September 27, 1998.

35. Interview with the principal of a junior high school, Koshigaya city, Saitama.

36. Interviews with three teachers at a commercial high school, Saitama, September 20, 1995.

37. Interviews with three teachers at a commercial high school, Saitama July 18, 1996.

38. Rohlen (1984), pp. 150–154.

39. Interview with an ex-union teacher at an academic high school, Saitama. July 19, 1996, and interview with a non-union teacher at the same high school, August 13, 1996.

40. Thurston (1989), p. 199.

41. *Kyōiku Hyōron*, March 1991, pp. 14–15.

42. Zenkyō Newsletter No. 1, September 1991.

43. Roesgaard (1994), p. 118.

44. Roesgaard (1994), p. 120.

45. Interview with Yoneura Tadashi, Secretary of Saikōkyō, March 22, 1996.

46. Saitama kyōso News, February 1992.

47. *Kyōiku hyōron* March 1991, pp. 14–15.

48. Interview with Nishizawa Kiyoshi, vice chairman of Nikkyōso, July 23, 1996

49. Interview with Yoneura Tadashi, Secretary of Saikōkyō, March 22, 1996.

Notes to Chapter Four

1. Here "elitist theory" and "pluralist theory" are interpreted very broadly. Each category includes more sophisticated subcategories and models, some of which may not use the words "elitist" or "pluralist." They include, for example, the two contrasting models used by Bradley Richardson in his book *Japanese Democracy* that he calls "vertical-integrative" (clearly an elitist model) and "horizontal-fragmented" (clearly a pluralist model) [see Richardson (1997), pp. 2–4].

2. See Yanaga (1968) for a fairly straightforward version of this theory.

3. For a classic exposition of pluralist democratic theory as applied to local government in the United States see Dahl (1961).

4. See Inoguchi (1982).

5. Muramatsu and Krauss (1987), pp. 537–538.

6. Johnson (1982), pp. 315–316.

7. Muramatsu (1993), p. 66.

8. Muramatsu (1993), p. 65.

9. Schoppa (1991a).

10. See Schoppa (1991a), chapter one, for this discussion, which is based on Pempel (1978) and Campbell (1984).

11. The word "immobilism" to describe this kind of policy inertia was first coined by J.A.A. Stockwin. See Stockwin et al. (1988).

12. Schoppa (1991a). See p. 20 for the model and p. 259 for a summary of historical examples.

13. Schoppa (1991a) p. 258.

14. Schoppa (1991a), p. 163.

15. Authors like Takihara (1981) and Ishikawa (1985) helped to promote this kind of criticism of Nikkyōso. In reply, defenders of Nikkyōso complained that the union's efforts to improve education through research and in-service training for teachers were often overlooked by their political enemies and the media.

16. *Asahi Shimbun,* December 25, 1994.

17. *Mainichi Daily News,* March 25, 1997.

18. Interview with Oyama Shinnosuke, Planning Director, Elementary and Secondary Education Bureau, Ministry of Education, May 30, 1996.

19. Schoppa (1991a), p. 93.

20. Schoppa (1991a), p. 94.

21. This is Schoppa's summary of Park's position (Schoppa, 1991a, pp. 97–98). For Park's position, see, e.g., Park (1975) and Park (1986).

22. Katō (1994).

23. Katō (1994), p. 8.

24. Schoppa (1991a), p. 84.

25. Schoppa (1991b), p. 105.

26. Katō (1994), p. 36.

27. Katō (1994), p. 38.

28. Schoppa (1991a), p. 172.

29. Schoppa (1991a), p. 226.

30. Schoppa (1991a), p. 243.

31. See Schoppa (1991a), pp. 243–247, and Hayao (1993), pp. 62–65.

32. Schoppa (1991a), pp. 212–214.

33. Interview with Professors Amano Ikuo and Ichikawa Shōgo, June 5, 1996. See also Ichikawa's review of Schoppa's book in *Japan Quarterly*, (July–September 1991): pp. 350–354.

34. Schoppa (1991a), pp. 208–209.

35. *Mainichi Daily News*, April 7 and 9, 1997.

36. Hood (1998).

37. Katō (1994), pp. 56–69.

38. See, for example, Woronoff (1997), p. 69.

39. See Blumenthal (1992) for a useful survey of the industry that has grown up in Japan to provide these exam preparation services.

40. Interview with a juku owner, August 2, 1996.

41. Interview with Udagawa Tsutomo, senior teacher consultant, Saitama Board of Education, September 3, 1995.

42. Roger Goodman has shown how an overseas education, which at one time had been widely regarded in Japan as a handicap to a future career, can now be used as a passport to an elite career track in contemporary Japan. See Goodman (1990). One reason for the increasing employability of *kikoku shijo* (Japanese children educated abroad who then return to Japan) is their fluency in foreign languages, a skill area much in demand as Japan's economy becomes more and more involved in global competition.

43. Ministry of Education (1995), p. 40.

44. *Japan Times* September 22, 1998.

45. See any Japanese national or regional newspaper published on March 2, 1999, for comprehensive details.

46. Okano and Tsuchiya (1999), pp. 215–218.

47. *Japan Times*, March 3, 1999.

48. The *Yomiuri Shimbun* editorial of the March 2, 1999, made this point. Anyone who has ever taught at an academic senior high school can testify to the dominance of impending university entrance exams. Rohlen wrote in 1983 that "the social environment of postwar Japanese secondary education has been dominated by university entrance examinations" (Rohlen, 1983, p. 107). Little has changed substantively since then.

49. Interview with Ogawa Masahito, Associate Professor, Department of Education, Tokyo University, August 12, 1996.

50. Interview with Niisato Masao, Senior Curriculum Specialist, Ministry of Education, October 24, 1995.

51. Interview with the principal of a senior high school, Saitama, February 21, 1996.

52. Each prefecture has at least two or three pilot unified schools at present and the MOE hopes to see the creation of about 500 nationwide in the near future. See Ministry of Education (2000), pp. 122–125.

53. Katō (1994), p. 42.

54. See, for example, Schoppa's analysis of Campbell in Schoppa (1991a), pp. 18–19.

55. Marshall (1994), p. 256.

56. McVeigh (1998), p. 128.

Notes to Chapter Five

1. Schoppa (1991a), p. 52. "Qualificationism" is a phrase coined by Ronald Dore to describe the tendency of late developing states like Japan to put a great emphasis on formal qualifications as the sign of an individual's worth and employability. Furthermore: "the more jobs depend on qualifications, the more schooling depends on exam taking." Dore (1975), chapter 6.

2. At this time debates about the strengths and weaknesses of the Japanese education system were not confined to the domestic arena. Mainly because of its economic success, Japan had begun to attract more attention from foreign journalists and scholars. Following Ezra Vogel's lead (Vogel, 1979), some American academics believed that American schools could learn from the Japanese model—see, for example, Duke (1986) and White (1987). Other American academics countered this optimistic view by drawing attention to the "dark side" of the Japanese education system—see especially Woronoff (1980) and Schoolland (1990). The overseas press began to take more of an interest in Japanese education reform too—for example, see *The Economist,* April 21, 1990, for a good summary of the main issues of the debate.

3. See Schoppa (1991a), pp. 179–180, for an account of this in the 1970s. The integration of secondary schools has also been criticized for pushing back competition for places in elite schools to an even earlier age—twelve instead of fifteen. See Fujita (1997), pp 77–91, for a contemprary, detailed critique of this reform.

4. Hayao (1993), p. 64.

5. Nakano (1989), p. 59, and Khan (1997) both stress that including a specifically "moral" component in education has been a preoccupation for Japanese educational reformers since the Meiji period. Lanham (1986) compares Japan with the United States and argues that in the latter, by comparison, little attention has been given to the subjects of ethics and morality in the school curriculum.

6. Schoppa (1991a), p. 247.

7. In 1987, the year of its inauguration, 848 foreign nationals participated on the JET program. By 1999, this number had risen to 5,241. There have been

criticisms, however, that for the amount of money spent on the program, there have not been proportional improvements in the foreign language ability of Japanese students. For the best analysis of the JET program see McConnell (2000); for an overview of the JET program see CLAIR (1996) or Chandler and Maclean (1999); for a scholarly analysis of some of the problems encountered by JET participants see Komisarof (1998); and for a personal memoir of the JET experience see Feiler (1991).

8. Hood (1998) argues that Nakasone's program of education initiatives should, on the whole, be regarded as a success rather than a failure because of its influence on the long-term direction of education reform in Japan.

9. The *Yomiuri Shimbun* argued precisely this point in an editorial of September 5, 1995.

10. Roesgaard (1994), p. 141.

11. Schoppa (1991a), pp. 122–131.

12. Keidanren (1996).

13. See also Shiki (1993).

14. Keidanren (1996), p. 106. For a foreign critique of the dominance of Tokyo University over the whole of the Japanese education system see Cutts (1997).

15. Dore and Sako (1989), p. 45.

16. Interview with the principal of a senior high school, Saitama, February 21, 1996.

17. Nikkyōso (1995), p. i.

18. Nikkyōso (1995), pp. 9–27.

19. *Asahi Shimbun,* November 17, 1994.

20. *Asahi Shimbun,* April 13, 1995.

21. *Yomiuri Shimbun,* September 4, 1995.

22. *Gakkō un'ei kenkyū,* February 1996, p. 11.

23. *Gakkō un'ei kenkyū,* February 1996, p. 11.

24. *Gakkō un'ei kenkyū,* February 1996, p. 12.

25. *Yomiuri Shimbun*, September 5, 1995.

26. *Mainichi Daily News,* Editorial, February 8, 1996. *Asahi Shimbun,* February 3, 1996.

27. Interview with Nishizawa Kiyoshi, vice president Nikkyōso, July 23, 1996.

28. In March 1999, the LDP government briefly proposed making the *Hinomaru* and *Kimigayo* the legal symbols of the Japanese state. Strong opinions were voiced in the press in favor (see, e.g., the editorial of the *Yomiuri Shimbun,* March 4) and against (see, e.g., editorials in the *Asahi Shimbun,* March 3 and March 30). In the

end the LDP dropped these proposals through lack of parliamentary time. In the following session of the Diet, however, after negotiating support from the New Komeito, the government made enough time to pass an act that legalized the flag and anthem. Thus, in August 1999, the *Hinomaru* and *Kimigayo* became the legally recognized symbols of the Japanese state.

29. Cripps (1996), p. 81. See also Nakasone (1999), p. 77, for a personal account by the future prime minister of how, as a young political activist, he defied U.S. military police by insisting on flying the *Hinomaru* during the time it was banned. Right-wing activists like him used the *Hinomaru* as a nationalist symbol to rally support against the perceived threat of the Communists marching behind their own symbol—the red flag. It is interesting to speculate whether these youthful experiences made Nakasone more determined to promote the wider acceptance and use of the *Hinomaru* when he became a more mature, and powerful, politician.

30. Cripps (1996), p. 82.

31. Interview with Yoneura Tadashi, secretary of Saikōkyō, March 22, 1996.

32. Schoppa (1991a), p. 248.

33. *Gakkō Un'ei Kenkyū* [Journal of School Management Research], March 1995. Special edition on the *Hinomaru* and *Kimigayo.*

34. Cripps (1996), p. 83.

35. Cripps (1996), p. 84.

36. *Asahi Shimbun,* July 25, 1991. The principals concerened were reprimanded or warned.

37. Cripps (1996), p. 86.

38. Interview with union members at a commercial high school, Saitama, September 20, 1995.

39. Cripps (1996), p. 90, and the author's own experience at high schools in Saitama, 1989–1992.

40. 1990 graduation ceremony, Kumagaya High School, Saitama.

41. *Asahi Shimbun,* March 1, 1999.

42. *Yomiuri Shimbun* editorial, March 5, 1999.

43. *Asahi Shimbun* editorial, March 30, 1999.

44. In the late 1990s, there were some examples of the leadership of opposition to the flag and anthem shifting from teachers' unions to student organizations. The most famous example was the student council of Tokorozawa High School in Saitama, which in 1998 organized its own alternative graduation and entrance ceremonies in defiance of the school principal's instructions. The student-organized ceremonies, which did not contain the flag or anthem, were better attended than the official ceremonies. See Takenaga (1998), Yamazaki (1998), and Aspinall and Cave (2001) for more details about this incident. However,

incidents like the one at Tokorozawa were notable for their rarity. They may be a sign of times to come, but, at the time of writing, students in the vast majority of Japanese schools were not actively opposed to the flag or anthem.

45. In September 1999, the government issued figures that showed that between 80 and 89 percent of schools were singing the *Kimigayo* at school ceremonies (figures differ according to type of school and type of ceremony) and between 98 and 99 percent of schools were raising the *Hinomaru*. Incidentally, the fact that the Ministry of Education puts so much time and effort into compiling statistics like these each year is used by opponents to show the importance the ministry places on this issue relative to more conventional "educational" issues. Some argue that the fuss made about the flag and anthem is a distraction from the real, serious problems facing Japanese schools.

46. *The Daily Yomiuri*, June 15, 1999. Information can also be found on Nikkyōso's home page: http://www.jtu-net.or.jp.

47. The legalization of the *Hinomaru* and *Kimigayo* as the official national symbols of Japan, a legislative process that was carried out during the summer of 1999, gave rise to a fierce debate between opponents and proponents. The decision to submit this bill to the Diet made the issue an overtly political issue. It was no longer centered on what went on in schools, because now, as well as going over old ground, new constitutional and legal issues were added to the argument. For opposition arguments based on constitutional considerations, see Yoshikawa (1999) and Sumino (1999).

48. For example, the Nagoya City High School teachers' union, Meikōkyō, still opposes the use of the flag and anthem in school ceremonies (interview with Mori Jun, chairman of Meikōkyō, January 7, 1999). *The Daily Yomiuri* of June 15, 1999 also commented that the union rank-and-file may not take the same conciliatory line as the national leadership.

49. *Zenkyō Newsletter*, March 1995.

50. *Zenkyō Newsletter* October 1997.

51. Interview with Yoneru Tadashi, secretary of Saikōkyō (Saitama SHS union), March 22, 1996.

52. *Zenkyō Newsletter*, July 1995.

53. In this respect Zenkyō echoes the demands of *Nichibenren*, the Japan Federation of Bar Associations, which is campaigning for new legislation to bring Japanese domestic law in line with the provisions of the UN convention. So far the government has insisted that no new legislation is necessary. See Goodman (1996), p. 109.

54. See, for example, *Daily Yomiuri*, February 1, 1999, and *Japan Times*, January 22, 1999.

55. Observation by the author of several Zenkyō seminars at the annual educational research conference, January 21–24, 1999, Shiga prefecture.

56. *Kyōtō Shimbun,* January 22, 1999, contained a photograph of riot police standing by at the opening ceremony of Zenkyō's conference in Shiga.

NOTES TO CHAPTER SIX

1. For a recent analysis of Marxist theory as it applies to trade unions, see Moses (1990).

2. Allen (1975).

3. Lawn (1985).

4. Lawn (1985), pp. 4–5.

5. Cooper (1992). In the introduction the editor describes the study as "venturing into uncharted waters" (p. 4).

6. Cooper (1992), p. 6.

7. Cooper (1992), p. 6.

8. Lawn and Whitty (1992), p. 84, and Ironside and Seifert (1995), p. 110.

9. Cooper (1992), p. 304 Other authors have called on teacher unions to self-conciously adopt a stance of "Professional Unionism" in order to combine elements of both professional association and industrial union. See Kerchner and Mitchell (1988).

10. Hosmanek (1975), p. 2. For an international perspective on teachers' unions and the right to strike see Cooper (2000), pp. 262–264.

11. Cooper (1992), pp. 309–310. In contrast to the Japanese case, teachers' unions in America have recently increased their membership base. For a recent positive appraisal of U.S. teachers' unions see Peterson and Charney (1999), and for a critical point of view see Lieberman (1997).

12. Kogan reminds us that education, more than virtually any other social activity, is concerned with what *ought* to be rather than what *is*. Therefore, any ideological movement concerned with social and political change will try to use educational institutions and systems to further its own agenda. Kogan (1978), p. 15.

13. Cooper (1992), p. 6.

14. Thurston (1973), p. 87.

15. Marshall (1994), pp. 175–176.

16. Smethurst (1967), pp. 149–150. In the summer of 1953, elementary and junior high school students in Yamaguchi prefecture were given diaries published by the cultural department of the prefectural teachers' union for use over the long holiday. The diaries contained statements to the effect that the Soviet Union was a much better place to live in than capitalist America or Japan, and that South Korea, with the help of America, started the Korean War.

17. Thurston (1973), pp. 123–125.

18. The National Union of Teachers (NUT) in England and Wales benefited from a period of sustained national militancy in the 1960s because this campaign was perceived as bringing positive results for ordinary teachers (e.g., through pay increases). A similar campaign in the 1980s, however, resulted in a decline in membership figures when positive results were not so forthcoming. See Ironside and Seifert (1995), p. 86, and Barber (1992), pp. 69–70.

19. See, for example, Ota (1993), p. 252.

20. Duke (1973), p. 150.

21. Ota (1993), p. 252.

22. *Japan Quarterly,* Vol. 21, No. 4 (October–December 1974), pp. 329–332.

23. *Japan Socialist Review,* September 15, 1974.

24. For example, Lawn and Whitty (1992), p. 84, and the author's own experience as a member of the NUT, 1985–1989. Also see Ironside and Seifert (1995), chapter three, for a detailed account of interunion rivalries at this time.

25. Interview with Numata Yoshitaka, secretary of *Tokyōso* (Tokyo Prefecture Teachers' Union), May 31, 1996.

26. From the preamble to the draft *Charter on the Rights of Teachers and Staff* in Zenkyō Newsletter, July 1995.

27. See, for example, Halliday and McCormack (1973), p. 186.

28. Cook (1996), p. 4.

29. Van Wolferen (1993), p. 67.

30. Bean (1985), p. 33.

31. Kawanishi (1992) p. 23.

32. See Kawanishi (1992), chapter 6, for an account of this process.

33. It should be noted that it would an oversimplification to conclude from this that workers organized in enterprise unions were always simply the "losers" and management always the "winners." See Kume (1998, chapter eight) for a useful discussion of the literature devoted to the issue of the "weak labor" and "strong labor" hypotheses. Kume himself points to the achievements unions have made through cooperation with management.

34. Gordon (1998), p. 202.

35. Garon (1987), p. 237.

36. Vogel (1979), p. 157.

37. Dore (1973).

38. Pimlott and Cook (1991), p. 282.

39. Kawanishi (1992), pp. 7–8.

40. The phrase "privatization of public sector unions" was first coined by Professor John Crump in a paper presented at the fourth annual Colloquium of

the Japan Politics Group, University of Stirling, September 1996, entitled "Class and Class Consciousness in Japan."

41. See, for example, Carlile (1994).

42. Ohmi (1997), p. 215.

43. See Harari (1973).

44. Quoted in Ohmi (1997), p. 216.

45. Quoted in Ohmi (1997), p. 216.

46. Weathers (1994), p. 622.

47. Weathers (1994), p. 622.

48. This is the conclusion of James Doherty given as part of a presentation entitled "The Privatization of the Japanese National Railways: A Matter of Principal (sic)?" at the Nissan Institute, Oxford, December 6, 1996.

49. Mochizuki (1993), p. 188.

50. Williamson (1994), p. 157.

51. Mochizuki (1993), p. 190.

52. Mochizuki (1993), p. 191.

53. Ohmi (1997), p. 226.

54. Mochizuki (1993), p. 198.

55. Michels (1965). Michels summarized his "iron law of oligarchy" in the following famous words. "It is Organisation which gives birth to the domination of the elected over the electors, of the mandataries over the mandators, of the delegates over the delegators. Who says organisation says oligarchy."

56. Nikkyōso (1995), p. 8.

57. The LDP used this influence over Zendentsū during the period when it was in a coalition government with the SDPJ. See *Asahi Shimbun,* December 25, 1994.

58. Van Wolferen (1993), p. 582.

59. Thurston (1989), pp. 198–190.

60. In 1993 it had 7.85 million members, making it the largest single labor federation in the world. *Source:* Williamson (1994), p. 59.

61. Tsujinaka (1993), p. 203.

62. See, for example, Tsujinaka (1993).

63. Pempel (1998), p. 163.

Notes to Chapter Seven

1. Stockwin (1992), p. 107, and Hrebenar (2000), p. 247.

2. Thurston (1973), p. 223.

3. Curtis (1971), pp. 200–201 In the original text Curtis incorrectly lists the national union's abbreviated name as Nikkōso. The official abbreviated name is Nikkōkyō.

4. Curtis (1971), p. 203.

5. Thurston (1973), p. 222. See p. 225 for detailed figures.

6. Thurston (1973), pp. 248–249.

7. Langer (1972), p. 95.

8. See Carlile (1994), p. 615, and Hrebenar (1992), p. 200.

9. Shinoda (1997), p. 206.

10. Johnson (2000), p. 170.

11. Hrebenar (2000), p. 247.

12. Yamaguchi Jiro. "Why No Blair Revolution in Japan?" Paper given at the Nissan Institute for Japanese Studies, June 6, 1997.

13. Up until 1993, there was also one solitary single-seat constituency, for Amami Oshima. This was incorporated into Kagoshima number one constituency before the 1993 election.

14. Ishikawa (1994), pp. 144–145.

15. Fukatsu (1995), p. 82. For its part the LDP was motivated to form a coalition with the JSP for the simple reason that this provided the quickest possible avenue for a return to government. The LDP found that being in opposition was a very traumatic experience. In particular it missed the constant supply of information and advice that was provided by the bureaucracy for governing parties but not for opposition parties—see Yamaguchi (1997), p. 86, and Curtis (1999), p. 171.

16. *Mainichi Daily News,* May 20, 1995.

17. For example, see editorials in the *Nikkei Weekly,* January 29, 1996, *Yomiuri Shimbun,* January 17, 1996, and *Asahi Shimbun,* January 17, 1996.

18. Thurston (1989), p. 188.

19. See, for example, Fukatsu (1995) and S. Johnson (1997).

20. *The Japan Times,* July 16, 1993.

21. *Yomiuri Shimbun,* February 6, 1996.

22. *Yomiuri Shimbun,* June 17, 1996.

23. See, for example, his ideas on teaching in Ozawa (1994), pp. 207–208, which include denying teachers the rights accorded to other laborers.

24. Interview with Nishizawa Kiyoshi, vice-president of Nikkyōso, July 23, 1996.

25. *Asahi Shimbun,* July 3, 1996. Kato here is clearly talking about a hypothetical scenario involving only two candidates contesting one of the new single-seat constituencies.

26. Other unions approached by the LDP included the Telecommunications Workers' Union and the Postal Workers' Union. The LDP was always careful to ask for support only in constituencies where a JSP candidate was not standing. *Asahi Shimbun,* July 3, 1996.

27. See an editorial in the *Mainichi Shimbun,* July 25, 1997, for an overview of the JCP's successes since 1995.

28. Interview with Yoneura Tadashi, secretary of Saikōkyō, March 22, 1996, and interview with Takahashi Sanaru, chairman of the executive committee of Aikōkyō, January 17, 1999. (Both unions are affiliated with Zenkyō.)

29. Williamson (1994), p. 86.

30. Nishizawa Kiyoshi, vice-president of Nikkyōso, made this point in the interview he gave on July 23, 1996.

31. Zenkyō Newsletter, March 1999.

32. Popular outrage about the rape of a twelve-year old-schoolgirl by three American servicemen in Okinawa in September 1995 propelled the anti-base campaign to the forefront of popular discourse for several months. Zenkyō's national headquarters sent a delegation to Okinawa to join the campaign there, and it called on affiliated prefectural unions to do the same (Zenkyō Newsletter, March 1996).

33. Nikkyōso (1995), p. 1.

34. Nikkyōso (1995), p. 2.

35. Hosokawa (1993), p. 18.

36. Interview with Imai Hiroshi, November 5, 1995. When the JNP dissolved, Imai joined Shinshintō. When that party dissolved, he spent some time as an independent and then joined the LDP. He lost his seat (Saitama number three constituency) to the DPJ in the 2000 election.

37. See Stockwin (1999), chapter six, for a clear and comprehensive summary of this bewildering period of Japanese political history.

38. In October 1999, New Komeito was added to this coalition, but the LDP remained—by far—the most dominant partner in the government.

39. *Mainichi Shimbun* editorial, June 15, 1997.

40. Curtis (1999), p. 50.

41. See Pempel (1998) for one account of the fundamental changes talking place in Japanese political and economic institutions in the 1990s.

42. Muramatsu and Krauss (1987), pp. 537-538.

43. In fact, the loss of fifteen more seats in the 1998 upper house election makes the LDP's recovery of its majority in that chamber an even more distant prospect than it had previously been. (It now has 103 seats in the upper house and needs at least 127 for a simple majority. However, it is still by far the largest

single party there, and with the support of the Liberal Party and New Komeito can pass legislation with ease.)

44. Pempel (1998), p. 157.

45. This is not to say that the bureaucracy has been completely unchanged by events in the 1990s. Public confidence in the bureaucracy has been shaken by a series of corruption scandals, making future deregulation more likely. Also, as Pempel points out (1998, p. 159), Japan's national bureaucracy no longer stands together behind a hegemonic project the way it once united behind rapid economic growth.

46. The most famous case of this kind of dispute is Tokorozawa High School in Saitama. See Aspinall and Cave (2001) for more details of this case.

Notes to Conclusion

1. Lawn (1985).

2. Cooper (1992).

3. Rohlen (1984).

4. Hood (1998) argues that Schoppa's judgment that Nakasone's educational reform program was a failure was premature. Research in the 1990s shows that many of Nakasone's ideas have been incorporated into the educational policy-making process.

5. See Ichikawa Shōgo's comments about Schoppa's book in *Japan Quarterly* (July–September 1991): 350–354.

BIBLIOGRAPHY

Aikōkyō [Aichi Prefecture High School Teachers' Union]. 1997 and 1999. *Aikōkyō Gojūnenshi* [A Fifty Years History of Aichi Prefecture High School Teachers' Union] (Published in two volumes by Aikōkyō, Nagoya).

Allen, V. L. 1975. "Trade Unionism, an Analytical Framework" in Brian Barrett, Ed Rhodes, and John Beishon (eds.), *Industrial Relations and the Wider Society, Aspects of Interaction* (London: Collier MacMillan).

Allinson, Gary D. and Sone, Yasunori. 1993. *Political Dynamics in Contemporary Japan* (Ithaca, NY: Cornell University Press).

Amano, Ikuo. 1983. *Education and Examination in Modern Japan* (Tokyo: University of Tokyo Press).

———. 1986. "Educational Crisis in Japan" in W.K. Cummings et al. (eds.), *Educational Policies in Crisis* (New York: Praeger).

———. 1993. "The Dilemma of Japanese Education Today" in James J. Shields (ed.), *Japanese Schooling: Patterns of Socialisation, Equality and Control* (Philadelphia: The Pennsylvania University Press).

Aspinall, Robert and Cave, Peter, 2001. "Lowering the Flag: Democracy, Authority, and Rights at Tokorozawa High School" in *Social Science Japan Journal*, Vol. 4, No. 1, April 2001.

August, Robert L. 1992. "*Yobiko*: Prep Schools for College Entrance in Japan" in Robert Leestma and Herbert J. Walberg (eds.), *Japanese Educational Productivity* (Ann Arbor: University of Michigan).

Baerwald, Hans. 1986. *Party Politics in Japan* (Boston and London: Allen and Unwin).

Barber, Michael. 1992. *Education and the Teacher Unions* (London: Cassell).

Bean, R. 1985. *Comparative Industrial Relations* (London: Routledge).

Beauchamp, Edward R. 1978. *Learning to be Japanese* (Hamden, CT: Linnet Books).

Beauchamp, Edward R. and Vardaman, James M. Jr. (eds.). 1994. *Japanese Education since 1945: A Documentary Study* (Armonk, NY and London: East Gate).

Benjamin, Gail R. 1997. *Japanese Lessons: A Year in a Japanese School Through the Eyes of an American Anthropologist and Her Children* (New York and London: New York University Press).

Blumenthal, Tuvia. 1992. "Japan's *Juken* Industry" in *Asian Survey,* Vol. XXXII, No. 5, May 1992.

Calder, Kent E. 1988. *Crisis and Compensation: Public Policy and Political Stability in Japan,* (Princeton, NJ: Princeton University Press).

Campbell, John C. (ed.). 1981. *Parties, Candidates and Voters in Japan* (Ann Arbor: University of Michigan).

———. 1984. "Policy Conflict and its Resolution Within the Government System" in Krauss et al. (eds.), *Conflict in Japan* (Honolulu: University of Hawaii Press).

Carlile, Lonny E. 1994. "Party Politics and the Japanese Labour Movement" in *Asian Survey,* Vol. XXXIV, No. 7 July 1994 (Berkeley: University of California Press).

Carlson, Dennis. 1987. "Teachers as Political Actors: From Reproductive Theory to the Crisis of Schooling" in *Harvard Educational Review,* Vol. 57, No. 3, August 1987.

Chandler, David and Kootnikoff, David (eds.). 1999. *The JET Programme: Getting Both Feet Wet* (Published by David Chandler).

Cook, Alice. 1966. *An Introduction to Japanese Trade Unionism* (Ithaca: Cornell University Press).

Cooper, Bruce S. 1992. *Labour Relations in Education, An International Perspective* (Westport, CT: Greenwood Press).

———. 2000. "International Perspectives on Teachers' Unions" in Tom Loveless (ed.). *Conflicting Missions? Teachers Unions and Educational Reform* (Washington D.C.: Brookings Institution Press).

Council of Local Authorities for International Relations (Clair). 1995. *An Outline of Local Government in Japan* (Clair Fact Sheet No. 1, Published by Clair, Tokyo).

———. 1995b. *Education* (Clair Fact Sheet No. 6, Published by Clair, Tokyo).

———. 1996. *Council of Local Authorities for International Relations* (Brochure, Published by Clair, Tokyo).

Cripps, Denise. 1996. "Flags and Fanfares: The *Hinomaru* Flag and *Kimigayo* Anthem in Japan " in Roger Goodman and Ian Neary (eds.), *Case Studies on Human Rights in Japan* (Richmond, Surrey: Japan Library).

Cummings, William K. 1980. *Education and Equality in Japan* (Princeton, NJ: Princeton University Press).

———. et al. (eds.). 1986. *Educational Policies in Crisis* (New York: Praeger).

Curtis, Gerald. 1971. *Election Campaigning Japanese Style* (New York: Columbia University Press).

———. 1988. *The Japanese Way of Politics* (New York: Columbia University Press).

———. 1999. *The Logic of Japanese Politics* (New York: Columbia University Press).

Cutts, Robert L. 1997. *An Empire of Schools: Japan's Universities and the Molding of a National Power Elite* (Armonk, NY and London: East Gate).

Dahl, Robert A. 1961. *Who Governs? Democracy and Power in an American City* (New Haven: Yale University Press).

Dore, Ronald P. 1958 (reissued with a new introduction in 1999). *City Life in Japan: A Study of a Tokyo Ward* (Richmond, Surrey: Japan Library).

———. 1973. *British Factory, Japanese Factory: The Origins of National Diversity in Industrial Relations* (Berkeley: University of California Press).

———. 1975. *The Diploma Disease: Education, Qualification and Development* (Berkeley and Los Angeles: University of California Press).

———. 1987. *Taking Japan Seriously: A Confucian Perspective on Leading Economic Issues* (London: Athlone Press).

Dore, Ronald P. and Sako, Mari. 1989. *How the Japanese Learn to Work* (London: Routledge).

Dower, John. 1999. *Embracing Defeat: Japan in the Wake of World War II* (New York: Norton).

Duke, Benjamin C. 1973. *Japan's Militant Teachers* (Honolulu: University Press of Hawaii).

———. 1986. *The Japanese School: Lessons for Industrial America* (New York: Praeger).

Eccleston, Bernard. 1989. *State and Society in Post-War Japan* (Cambridge: Polity Press).

Edwards, Marie Alice. 1956. *Political Activities of Japanese Postwar Labor Unions* (Unpublished PhD Thesis, Northwestern University).

Feiler, Bruce S. 1991. *Learning to Bow* (New York: Ticknor and Fields).

Fitz, John and Halpin, David. 1994. "Ministers and Mandarins: Educational Research in Elite Settings" in Geoffrey Walford (ed.), *Researching the Powerful in Education* (London: University College).

Foreign Press Center. 1995. *Education in Japan* (Tokyo: Foreign Press Center).

———. 1997. *Japan: Eyes on the Country, Views of the 47 Prefectures* (Tokyo: Urban Connections Inc.).

Fujii, Shozo. 1986. "Labor Movement at the Crossroads" in *Japan Quarterly,* Vol. XXXIII, No. 3, July–September 1986.

Fujimara, Hiroyuki. 1997. "New Unionism, Beyond Enterprise Unionism?" in M. Sako and H. Sato (eds.), *Japanese Labour and Management in Transition* (London: Routledge).

Fujita, Hidenori. 1993. "A Crisis of Legitimacy in Japanese Education: Meritocracy and Cohesiveness" in James J. Shields (ed.), *Japanese Schooling: Patterns of Socialisation, Equality and Political Control* (University Park: The Pennsylvania State University Press).

———. 1997. *Kyōiku Kaikaku* [Education Reform] (Iwanami Shinsho, Tokyo).

Fukatsu, Masumi. 1995. "The SDPJ's Astronomical Shift in Politics" in *Japan Quarterly,* Vol. XLII, No. 1, January–March 1995.

Garon, Sheldon. 1987. *The State and Labour in Modern Japan* (Berkeley: University of California Press).

———. 1997. *Molding Japanese Minds: The State in Everyday Life* (Princeton, NJ: Princeton University Press).

Goodman, Roger. 1990. *Japan's 'International Youth': The Emergence of a New Class of Schoolchildren* (Oxford: Clarendon Press).

———. 1992. "Japan—Pupil Turned Teacher?" in David Phillips (ed.), *Lessons of Cross-National Comparison in Education, Oxford Studies in Comparative Education Volume 1* (London: Triangle Books).

———1996. "On Introducing the UN Convention on the Rights of the Child into Japan" in R. Goodman and I. Neary (eds.), *Case Studies on Human Rights in Japan* (Richmond, Surrey: Japan Library).

Gordon, Andrew. 1993. "Contests for the Workplace" in A. Gordon (ed.), *Postwar Japan as History* (Berkeley and Los Angeles: University of California Press).

———. 1998. *The Wages of Affluence: Labor and Management in Postwar Japan* (Cambridge: Harvard University Press).

Halliday, Jon. 1975. *A Political History of Japanese Capitalism* (New York: Monthly Review Press).

Halliday, Jon and McCormack, Gavan. 1973. *Japanese Imperialism Today* (New York: Penguin Books).

Harari, Ehud. 1973. *The Politics of Labour Relations in Japan, National–International Interaction* (Berkeley: University of California Press).

Hayao, Kenji. 1993. *The Japanese Prime Minister and Public Policy* (Pittsburgh: University of Pittsburgh Press).

Hendry, Joy. 1986. *Becoming Japanese: The World of the Pre-school Child* (Manchester: Manchester University Press).

Hirano, Kyoko. 1992. *Mr Smith Goes to Tokyo: Japanese Cinema Under the American Occupation, 1945–1952* (Washington and London: Smithsonian Institution Press).

Hood, Christopher. 1998. *Nakasone Yasuhiro and Japanese Education Reform: A Revisionist View* (Unpublished PhD thesis, University of Sheffield).

Horio, Teruhisa. 1988. *Educational Thought and Ideology in Modern Japan: State Authority and Intellectual Freedom*, edited and translated by Steven Platzer (Tokyo: University of Tokyo Press).

———. 1992. *Gendai Kyōiku no Shisō to Kōzō* [The Ideology and Structure of Modern Education] (Tokyo: Dojidai Raiburari).

———. 1997. *Gendai Shakai to Kyōiku* [Contemporary Society and Education] (Tokyo: Iwanami).

Hosmanek, John J. 1975. *A Descriptive Analysis of Trade Union Tactics and the Acceptability of Alternative Techniques for Resolving Teacher Union–School Board Disputes* (Unpublished Doctor of Education dissertation, Marquette University, Milwaukee, Wisconsin).

Hosokawa, Morihiro. 1993. *The Time to Act Is Now* (Tokyo: NTT Mediascope Inc.).

Hoye, Timothy. 1999. *Japanese Politics: Fixed and Floating Worlds* (Englewood Cliffs, NJ: Prentice-Hall).

Hrebenar, Ronald J. (ed.). 1992. *The Japanese Party System* (Boulder, CO: Westview Press).

———. 2000. *Japan's New Party System* (Boulder, CO: Westview Press).

Hyodo, Tsutomu. 1995. "Unifying the Labor Movement? The Birth of Rengo" in *Ampo Japan Asia Quarterly Review*, Vol. 26, No. 2.

Ichikawa, Shogo. 1984. "Japan" in J. R. Hough (ed.), *Education Policy: An International Survey* (London: Croom Helm).

———. 1991. "Financing Japanese Education" in Edward R. Beauchamp (ed.), *Windows on Japanese Education* (Westport, CT: Greenwood Press).

Inoguchi, Takashi. 1982. *Gendai Nihon no Seiji keizai* (Tokyo: Tōyō keizai shinpōsha).

———. 1991. "The Nature and Functioning of Japanese Politics" in *Government and Opposition*, Vol. 26, No. 2, Spring 1991 (London School of Economics and Political Science).

———. 1993. "Japanese Politics in Transition: A Theoretical Review" in *Government and Opposition*, Vol. 8, No. 4, Autumn 1993.

Iokibe, Makoto. 1997. "American Pre-surrender Planning, Japan's Surrender, and US Occupation Policy towards Japan" in Gerhard Krebs and Christian Oberlander (eds.), *1945 in Europe and Asia: Reconsidering the End of World War II* (Munich: Iudicium).

Ironside, Mike and Seifert, Roger. 1995. *Industrial Relations in Schools* (London and New York: Routledge)

Ishikawa, Sachiko. 1985. *Nikkyōso ga Kuzuresaru Hi* [The Day of Nikkyōso's Destruction] (Tokyo: Zenhonsha).

Jain, Purnendra. 1989. *Local Politics and Policy-making in Japan* (New Delhi: Commonwealth Publishers).

James, Estelle and Benjamin, Gail. 1988. *Public Policy and Private Education in Japan* (London: Macmillan).

———. 1993. "Public and Private Schools and Educational Opportunity in Japan" in James J. Shields Jr. (ed.), *Japanese Schooling: Patterns of Socialization, Equality and Political Control* (University Park: Pennsylvania State University Press).

Japanese National Commision for UNESCO. 1966. *The Role of Education in the Social and Economic Development of Japan* (Tokyo: Ministry of Education).

Johnson, Chalmers. 1982. *MITI and the Japanese Miracle* (Stanford, CA: Stanford University Press).

———. 1995. *Japan: Who Governs?* (New York: Norton).

Johnson, Stephen. 1995. *Strategies for Realignment: Japanese Opposition Politics Under a One Party Dominant Regime 1955–1993* (Unpublished D.Phil. Degree Thesis, University of Oxford).

———. 1997. "Opposition Party Fragmentation under the 1955 System: An Organisational Imperative or the Rational Choice?" in *Japan Forum*, Vol. 9, No. 1, 1997.

———. 2000. *Opposition Politics in Japan: Strategies under a One-Party Dominant Regime* (London and New York: Routledge).

Kabashima, Ikuo. 1998. "The Upper House Election: How the LDP Went Down to Defeat" in *Japan Echo*, Vol. 25, No 5.

———. 1999. "An Ideological Survey of Japan's National Legislators" in *Japan Echo* Vol. 26, No. 4.

Karatsu, Rie. 1997. *Some Foreign Perceptions of Japanese Education* (Unpublished MSc Dissertation, Oxford University).

Kataoka, Tetsuya. 1991. *The Price of a Constitution: The Origin of Japan's Postwar Politics* (Stanford University: Hoover Institute).

Kato, Hiroshi. 1996. *Kyōiku Kaikakuron* [Education Reform Theory] (Tokyo: Maruzen Library).

Kato, Junko. 1994. *The Problem of Bureaucratic Rationality: Tax Politics in Japan* (Princeton, NJ: Princeton University Press).

Kawai, Hayao. 1992. *Kodomo to Gakō* [Children and Schools] (Tokyo: Iwanami Shinsho).

Kawanishi, Hirosuke. 1992. *Enterprise Unionism in Japan* (London and New York: Kegan Paul International).

Keidanren [Federation of Economic Organisations]. 1996. *Sōzōtekina Jinzai no Ikusei ni Mukete—Motomerareru Kyōiku Kaikaku to Kigyō no Kōdō* ["Towards the Fostering of Creative, Talented People: Desirable Education Reforms and the Actions of Business"] *Kikan Kyōikuhō*, March 1996.

Kerbo, Harold K. and McKinistry, John A. 1995. *Who Rules Japan? The Inner Circles of Economic and Political Power* (Westport, CT: Praeger).

Kerchener, Charles Taylor and Mitchell, Douglas E. (eds.). 1988. *The Changing Idea of a Teachers' Union* (London, New York, Philadelphia: The Falmer Press).

Khan, Yoshimitsu. 1997. *Japanese Moral Education Past and Present* (Fairleigh Dickinson University Press. London: Associated University Presses).

Kishimoto, Koichi. 1997. *Politics in Modern Japan: Development and Organisation* (Tokyo: Japan Echo Inc.).

Knoke, David et al. 1996. *Comparing Policy Networks—Labor Politics in the U.S., Germany and Japan* (Cambridge: Cambridge University Press).

Kobayashi, Tetsuya. 1976. *Society, Schools and Progress in Japan* (Oxford and New York: Pergamon Press).

Kobayashi, Victor. 1978. "Japan Under American Occupation" in E. R. Beauchamp (ed.), *Learning to be Japanese* (Hampden, CT: Linnet Books).

Kogan, Maurice. 1975. *Educational Policy-Making: A Study of Interest Groups and Parliament* (London: George Allen and Unwin).

———. 1978. *The Politics of Educational Change* (London: Fontana)

———. 1986. *Education Accountability: An Analytic Overview* (London: Hutchinson).

———. 1994. "Researching the Powerful in Education and Elsewhere" in Geoffrey Walford (ed.), *Researching the Powerful in Education* (University College London Press).

Komisarof, Adam, M. 1998. *An Exploration of the Divergence and Convergence of Membership Criteria Between American JET Program Participants and Their Japanese Colleagues* (Unpublished M.A. Dissertation, Antioch University).

Kume, Ikuo. 1998. *Disparaged Success: Labor politics in Postwar Japan* (Ithaca, NY: Cornell University Press).

Kyoiku No Sengoshi Henshu Iinkai [Editorial Committee for the Postwar History of Education]. 1986. *Kyōiku no Sengoshi I: Sengo Kyōiku Kaikaku to sono Hōkai e no Michi* [The Postwar History of Education, Volume One: Postwar Education Reforms and the Road to their Collapse] (Published by the Editorial Committee for the Postwar History of Education, Tokyo).

———. 1986. *Kyōiku no Sengoshi II: Minshu Kyōiku e no Kōgeki to Teikō* [The Postwar History of Education, Volume Two: The Struggle For and Against Democratic Education] (Published by the Editorial Committee for the Postwar History of Education, Tokyo].

———. 1986. *Kyōiku no Sengoshi III: Kōdō Keizai Seichōshita no Kyōiku* [The Postwar History of Education, Volume Three: Education at a Time of High Economic Growth], (Published by the Editorial Committee for the Postwar History of Education, Tokyo).

———. 1987. *Kyōiku no Sengoshi IV: Arata na Kyōiku Kaikaku o Motomete* [The Postwar History of Education, Volume Four: Demanding New Education Reform] (Published by the Editorial Committee for the Postwar History of Education, Tokyo).

Langar, Paul F. 1972. *Communism in Japan, A Case of Political Naturalisation* (Stanford, CA: Hoover Institution Press).

Lanham, Betty B. 1986. *Ethics and Moral Precepts Taught in Schools of Japan and the United States* in Takie Sugiyama Lebra and William P. Lebra (eds.), *Japanese Culture and Behaviour* (Honolulu: University of Hawaii Press).

Lawn, Martin. 1985. *The Politics of Teacher Unionism: International Perspectives* (Croom Helm Ltd.).

Lawn, Martin and Whitty, Geoff. 1995. "England and Wales" in Bruce S. Cooper (ed.), *Labour Relations in Education, An International Perspective* (Westport, CT: Greenwood Press).

Leestma, Robert and Walberg, Herbert J. (eds.). 1992. *Japanese Educational Productivity* (Ann Arbor: University of Michigan).

LeTendre, Gerald. 1994. "Guiding Them on: Teaching, Hierarchy, and Social Organization in Japanese Middle Schools" in *The Journal of Japanese Studies*, Vol. 20, No. 1, Winter 1994.

Lewis, Catherine C. 1995. *Educating Hearts and Minds: Reflections on Japanese Preschool and Elementary Education* (Cambridge: Cambridge University Press).

Lieberman, Myron. 1997. *The Teacher Unions: How the NEA and AFT Sabotage Reform and Hold Students, Parents, Teachers, and Taxpayers Hostage to Bureaucracy* (New York: The Free Press).

Lincicome, Mark E. 1995. *Principle, Praxis and the Politics of Educational Reform in Meiji Japan* (Honolulu: University of Hawaii Press).

Livingstone, George. 1999. "Teachers' Professional Organisations" in T.G.K. Bryce and W.M. Humes (eds.), *Scottish Education* (Edinburgh: Edinburgh University Press).

Locke, Michael. 1974. *Power and Politics in the School System: A Guidebook* (London and Boston: Routledge and Keegan Paul).

Loveless, Tom (ed.). 2000. *Conflicting Missions? Teachers Unions and Educational Reform* (Washington, DC: Brookings Institution Press).

Marshall, Byron K. 1994. *Learning to be Modern, Japanese Political Discourse on Education* (Boulder, CO: Westview Press).

Martin, Curtis H. and Stronach, Bruce. 1992. *Politics East and West: A Comparison of Japanese and British Political Culture* (New York: East Gate).

Masuzoe, Yōichi. 1991. "The Upheaval Threatening the Liberal Democrats" in *Japan Echo*, Vol. XVIII, Special Issue, 1991.

———. (ed.). 2000. *Years of Trial: Japan in the 1990s* (Tokyo: Japan Echo Inc.)

Matsuzaki, Tetsuhisa. 1991. "Breaking Up the LDP's Family Business" in *Japan Echo,* Vol. XVIII, Special Issue, 1991.

Mayo, Marlene J. 1980. "Psychological Disarmament: American Wartime Planning for the Education and Re-education of Defeated Japan 1943–1945" in T. W. Burkman (ed.), *The Occupation of Japan, Educational and Social Reform* (Norfolk, VA: Gatling Printing and Publishing Co.).

McConnell, David L. 2000. *Importing Diversity: Inside Japan's JET Program* (Berkeley: University of California Press).

McNamara, Dennis. 1996. "Corporatism and Cooperation among Japanese Labor," in *Comparative Politics,* Vol. 28, No. 4.

McVeigh, Brian J. 1998. *The Nature of the Japanese State: Rationality and Rituality* (London and New York: Routledge).

Michels, Robert. 1962. *Political Parties: A Sociological Study of the Oligarchical Tendencies of Modern Democracy* [Translation by Eden and Cedar Paul from the original in German, first published 1911] (New York: The Free Press).

Ministry of Education. 1994. *Education in Japan: A Graphic Presentation* (Tokyo: Gyosei).

———. 1995. *Japanese Government Policies in Education, Science and Culture 1994: New Directions in School Education: Fostering Strength for Life* [Official English translation of *Wagakuni no Bunkyō Shisaku* published in 1994] (Published by the Printing Bureau, Ministry of Finance, Tokyo).

———. 1997. *Japanese Government Policies in Education, Science and Culture 1996: Priorities and Prospects for a Lifelong Learning Society: Increasing Diversification and Sophisticaion* [Official English translation of *Wagakuni no Bunkyō Shisaku* published in 1996] (Published by the Printing Bureau, Ministry of Finance, Tokyo).

———. 1998. *Statistical Abstract of Education, Science Sports and Culture* (Published by the Printing Bureau, Ministry of Finance, Tokyo).

———. 2000. *Japanese Government Policies in Education, Science, Sports and Culture 1999: Educational Reform in Progress* [Official English translation of *Wagakuni no Bunkyō Shisaku* published in 1999] (Published by the Printing Bureau, Ministry of Finance, Tokyo).

Miyamoto, Masao. 1994. *Straightjacket Society* (Tokyo: Kodansha).

Mochizuki, Mike. 1993. "Public Sector Labour and the Privatisation Challenge: The Railway and Telecommunications Unions" in G. D. Allinson and Y. Sone (eds.), *Political Dynamics in Contemporary Japan* (Ithaca and London: Cornell University Press).

Mochizuki, Muneaki. 1987. *Nikkyōso Kōsō no Ura no Ura* [Behind the scenes of Nikkyōso's Struggle] (Tokyo: Mainichi Shimbunsha).

———. 1989. "Munakata Seiya [1908–1970]" in Benjamin C. Duke (ed.), *Ten Great Educators of Modern Japan* (Tokyo: University of Tokyo Press).

Morita, Yohji et al. 1999. "Japan" in P. K. Smith et al. (eds.) *The Nature of School Bullying: A Cross-National Perspective* (London and New York: Routledge).

Moses, John A. 1990. *Trade Union Theory from Marx to Walesa* (New York: Berg).

Muramatsu, Michio. 1993. "Patterned Pluralism Under Challenge: The Policies of the 1980s" in Gary D. Allinson and Sone Yasunori (eds.), *Political Dynamics in Contemporary Japan* (Ithaca, NY: Cornell University Press).

———. 1997. *Local Power in the Japanese State* (Berkeley: University of California Press).

Muramatsu, Michio and Krauss, Ellis. 1987. "The Conservative Policy Line and the Development of Patterned Pluralism" in Yamamura Kozo and Yasuba Yasukichi (eds.), *The Political Economy of Japan,* Vol. 1 (Stanford, CA: Stanford University Press).

Nakajima, Makoto. 1987. "JNR Dies, But the National Railway Workers' Union Survives" in *AMPO Japan Asia Quarterly Review,* Vol. 19, No. 2.

Nakano, Akira. 1989. *Moral Education in Modern Japan* (Tokyo: International Society for Educational Information Inc.).

Nakasone, Yasuhiro. 1999. *The Making of the New Japan: Reclaiming the Political Mainstream,* translated and annotated by Lesley Connors (London: Curzon).

Nikkyōso [Japan Teachers' Union]. 1975. *How to Reform Japan's Education* [Official English translation of Nikkyōso's Council on Education Reform] (Published by Nikkyōso, Tokyo).

———. 1982. *Heiwa Kyōiku Undōshi* [A History of the Peace Education Movement] (Published by Nikkyōso, Tokyo).

———. 1987. *Nikkyōso no Rekishi* [History of Nikkyōso] (Published by Nikkyōso, Tokyo).

———. 1989. *Nikkyōso no Tatakai* [Nikkyōso's Struggle] (Published by Nikkyōso, Tokyo).

———. 1995. *Toward the Century of Open Education: A Challenge for the Japan Teachers' Union* [Official English translation of the final report of the 21st Century Vision Committee] (Published by Nikkyōso, Tokyo).

———. 1997. *Nikkyōso Gojūnenshi* [Nikkyōso's Fifty Year History] (Published by Nikkyōso, Tokyo).

Nishi, Toshio. 1982. *Unconditional Democracy: Education and Politics in Occupied Japan 1945–52* (Stanford, CA: Hoover Institution Press).

Ogawa, Masahito. 1998. *Chihō Bunken Kaikaku to Gakō. Kyōikuiinkai* [Decentralization Reforms and Schools and Boards of Education] (Tokyo: Toyokan Shupansha).

Ohmi, Naoto. 1997. "The Public Sector and Privatisation" in M. Sako and H. Sato (eds.), *Japanese Labour and Management in Transition* (London: Routledge).

Okada, Akito. 1998. *Equality of Opportunity in Postwar England and Japan: A Comparative Study of Educational Policy, 1944–1970* (Unpublished D.Phil. Thesis, Department of Educational Studies, Oxford University).

———. 1999. "Secondary Education Reform and the Concept of Equality of Opportunity in Japan" in *Compare*, Vol. 29, No. 2.

Okano, Kaori and Tsuchiya, Motonori. 1999. *Education in Contemporary Japan: Inequality and Diversity* (Cambridge: Cambridge University Press).

Ota, Haruo. 1993. "Political Teacher Unionism in Japan" in James J. Shields (ed.), *Japanese Schooling, Patterns of Socialization, Equality and Control* (University Park: Pennsylvania State University Press).

Ozawa, Ichirō. 1994. *Blueprint for a New Japan* (Tokyo: Kodansha International).

Park, Cheol Hee. 1997. "Electoral Reform and the 1996 Election" in *Asia-Pacific Review*, Vol. 4, No. 2, Fall/Winter.

Passin, Herbert. 1965. *Society and Education in Japan* (New York: Columbia University Press).

Pempel, T. J. 1978. *Patterns of Japanese Policy-making: Experiences from Higher Education* (Boulder, CO: Westview Press).

———. (ed.). 1990. *Uncommon Democracies—The One-Party Dominant Regimes* (Ithaca, NY: Cornell University Press).

———. 1998. *Regime Shift: Comparative Dynamics of the Japanese Political Economy* (Ithaca and London: Cornell University Press).

Pempel, T. J. and Tsunekawa, Keichi. 1979. "Corporatism Without Labor? The Japanese Anomaly" in Phillippe C. Schmitter and Gerhard Lehmbruch (eds.), *Trends Toward Corporatist Intermediation* (London: Sage).

Peterson, Bob and Charney, Michael. (1999). *Transforming Teacher Unions: Fighting for Better Schools and Social Justice* (Milwaukee: Rethinking Schools).

Pimlott, Ben and Cook, Chris. 1991. *Trade Unions in British Politics, The First 250 Years* (London: Longman).

Phillips, David. 1998. *British Interest in Education in Japan: Some Aspects Bearing Upon the Purposes of Comparative Studies* [UK-Japan Education Forum Monograph No. 4] (Published by the UK-Japan Education Forum, Waseda University, Tokyo).

Reed, Steven J. 1986. *Japanese Prefectures and Policymaking* (Pittsburgh: University of Pittsburgh Press).

Richardson, Bradley. 1974. *The Political Culture of Japan* (Berkeley: University of California Press).

———. 1997. *Japanese Democracy: Power, Coordination and Performance* (New Haven and London: Yale University Press).

Roesgaard, Marie H. 1994. *Rhetoric in Japanese Education Reform* (Unpublished Ph.D. Thesis, University of Aarhus, Denmark).

Rohlen, Thomas P. 1977. "Is Japanese Education Becoming Less Egalitarian? Notes on High School Stratification and reform" in *The Journal of Japanese Studies,* Vol. 3 No. 1.

———. 1983. *Japan's High Schools* (Berkeley: University of California Press).

———. 1984. "Conflict in Institutional Environments: Politics in Education" in Ellis S. Krauss et al. (eds.), *Conflict in Japan* (Honolulu: University of Hawaii Press).

Rohlen, Thomas P. and LeTendre, Gerald K. 1996. *Teaching and Learning in Japan* (Cambridge: Cambridge University Press).

Rubinger, Richard. 1992. "Education in Wartime Japan, 1937–1945" in Roy Lowe (ed.), *Education and the Second World War: Studies in Schooling and Social Change* (London and Washington, DC: The Falmer Press).

Sagara, Tadaichi. 1986. *Nikkyōso Shisuru Koto Nakare* [Nikkyōso Will Not Die], (Kyōiku Kaihatsu Kenkyūjo, Tokyo).

Saikōkyō [Saitama High School Teachers' Union]. 1995. *Saikōkyō Yonjūnenshi* [Saitama High School Teachers' Union: A Forty Year History] (Published by *Saikōkyō,* Urawa, Saitama).

Saitama Board of Education. 1994. *Education in Saitama: A Brief Outline* (Published by Saitama Prefectural Board of Education, Urawa, Saitama).

Sato, Seizaburo. 1997. "Is One-Party Dominance Reemerging in Japan? in *Asia-Pacific Review,* Vol. 4, No. 1.

Schoolland, Ken. 1990. *Shogun's Ghost, The Dark Side of Japanese Education* (New York: Bergin and Garvey).

Schoppa, Leonard J. 1991a. *Education Reform in Japan: A Case of Immobilist Politics* (London: Routledge).

———. 1991b. "Zoku Power and LDP Power: A Case Study of the Zoku Role in Education Policy" in *Journal of Japanese Studies,* Vol. 17, No. 1 Winter.

Scribner, Jay D. and Layton, Donald H. (eds.). 1995. *The Study of Educational Politics* (Washington, DC and London: The Falmer Press).

Shields, James J. (ed.). 1993. *Japanese Schooling: Patterns of Socialization, Equality and Political Control* (University Park: Pennsylvania State University Press).

Shiki, Moriya. 1993. "Keidanren's Proposals for Academia" in *Economic Eye: A Quarterly Digest of Views from Japan,* Spring 1993 (Keizai Koho Centre, Tokyo).

Shimahara, Nobuo K. and Sakai, Akira. 1995. *Learning to Teach in Two Cultures* (New York: Garland)

Shinoda Toru. 1997. "Rengō and Policy Participation: Japanese Style Neo-coporatism?" in Mori Sako and Hiroki Sato (eds.), *Japanese Labour and Management in Transition* (London and New York: Routledge)

———. 1997b. "Heisei Labour Politics: a Long and Winding Road" in Purnendra Jain and Takashi Inoguchi (eds.), *Japanese Politics Today: Beyond Karaoke Democracy?* (Melbourne: Macmillan).

Smethurst, Richard J. 1967. *The Origins and Policies of the Japan Teachers' Union 1945–56* (Ann Arbor: University of Michigan Press).

———. 1978. "The Army, Youth and Women" in E. R. Beauchamp (ed.), *Learning to be Japanese* (Hampden, CT: Linnet Books).

Stevenson, Harold W. and Stigler, James W. 1992. *The Learning Gap* (New York: Touchstone).

Stockwin J. A. A. 1992. "The Japan Socialist Party: Resurgance After Long Decline" in Ronald J. Hrebenar (ed.), *The Japanese Party System* (Boulder, CO: Westview Press).

———. 1994. "On Trying to Move Mountains: The Political Career of Doi Takako" in *Japan Forum* (Oxford University Press), Vol. 6, No. 1, April.

———. 1997. "Reforming Japanese Politics: Highway to Change or Road to Nowhere?" in Purnendra Jain and Takashi Inoguchi (eds.), *Japanese Politics Today: Beyond Karaoke Democracy?* (Melbourne: Macmillan).

———. 1999. *Governing Japan: Divided Politics in a Major Economy* (Oxford: Blackwell Publishers).

Stockwin J.A.A., et al. 1988. *Dynamic and Immobilist Politics in Japan* (London: Macmillan).

Sumino, Takanori. 1999. "Hinomaru, Kimigayo Hōseika Mondai to Kenpō" [The Problem of the Legalization of the National Flag and Anthem, and the Constitution] in *Hō to Minshushugi* [the Journal of the Japan Democratic Lawyers' Association], No. 340, July.

Suwa, Testuji et al. 1998. "Crisis in the Schools: A Colloquium of the Group of Pro Teachers." In *Japan Echo*, Vol. 23, No. 3 (June 1998) reprinted in Masuzoe Yōichi (ed.), 2000, *Years of Trial: Japan in the 1990s* (Tokyo: Japan Echo, Inc.).

Takabatake, Michitoshi. 1994. "Japanese Politics Since the Period of High Growth" in *The Journal of Pacific Asia*, Vol. 1, 1994 (Committee for Research on Pacific Asia, Tokyo).

Takenaga, Koichi. 1998. "Tokorozawa Kōkō no Sotsugyo Kinensai" [Tokorozawa High School's Graduation Memorial Service] in *Ningen to Kyōiku*, No. 19, pp. 83–91.

Takihara, Toshihiko. 1981. *Nikkyōso ni Kodomo o Makaserareruka* [Can We Entrust our Children to Nikkyōso?] (Nihon Kōgyō Shimbunsha, Tokyo).

Thurston, Donald R. 1973. *Teachers and Politics in Japan* (Princeton, NJ: Princeton University Press).

———. 1989. "The Decline of the Japan Teachers Union" in *Journal of Contemporary Asia*, Vol. 19 No. 2, pp. 186–205.

Trainor, Joseph C. 1983. *Educational Reform in Occupied Japan: Trainor's Memoir* (Tokyo: Meisei University Press).

Tsuchimochi, Gary H. 1993. *Education Reform in Postwar Japan: The 1946 U.S. Education Mission* (Tokyo: University of Tokyo Press).

Tsujinaka, Yutaka. 1993. "Rengō and its Osmotic Networks" in G. D. Allinson and Y. Sone (eds.), *Political Dynamics in Contemporary Japan* (Ithaca and London: Cornell University Press).

Turner, Christena L. 1995. *Japanese Workers in Protest: An Ethnography of Consciousness and Experience* (Berkeley: University of California Press).

Umesao, Tadao. 1991. "Nikkyōso Kyōkenshūkai Bōchōki" [An Observer's Record of Nikkyōso's Study Meeting] in *Umesao Tadao Chosakushū* [The Collected Works of Umesao Tadao] (Tokyo: Chuō Kōron-sha).

Van Wolferen, Karel G. 1993. *The Enigma of Japanese Power* (Tokyo: Tuttle).

Vogel, Ezra. 1979. *Japan as Number One* (Cambridge: Harvard University Press).

Walford, Geoffrey. 1994. *Researching the Powerful in Education* (London: University College London Press).

Watanabe, Ben. 1989. "The Japanese Labor Movement: Toward Total Dissolution?" in *Ampo Japan Asia Quarterly Review,* Vol. 20, No. 4, & Vol. 21, No. 1.

Weathers, Charles. 1994. "Reconstruction of Labour-Management Relations in Japan's National Railways" in *Asian Survey,* Vol. XXXIV, No. 7, July (Berkeley: University of California Press).

Weiner, Michael (ed.). 1997. *Japan's Minorities: The Illusion of Homogeneity* (London: Routledge).

White, Merry. 1987. *The Japanese Educational Challenge: A Commitment to Children* (New York: Free Press).

———. 1993. *The Material Child: Coming of Age in Japan and America* (Berkeley: University of California Press).

Williamson, Hugh. 1994. *Coping with the Miracle: Japan's Unions Explore New International Relations* (London: Pluto Press).

Woodiwiss, Anthony. 1993. "A Revolution in Labour Law? The Fate of the Trade Union Act in Post-war Japan" in Ian Neary (ed.), *War, Revolution and Japan* (Sandgate, Folkestone, Kent: Japan Library, Folkestone).

Woronoff, Jon. 1980. *Japan: The Coming Social Crisis* (Tokyo: Yohan).

———. 1997. *The Japanese Social Crisis* (London: Macmillan).

Wray, Harry, 1996, "Education Policy Formation for the Allied Occupation of Japan" in *Nanzan Review of American Studies,* Vol. 18 (Nagoya: Nanzan University).

———. 1997. "Attitudes among Education Staff during the Occupation of Japan" in *Nanzan Review of American Studies,* Vol. 19, No. 2 (Nagoya: Nanzan University).

Yagura, Hisayasu. 1993. "Redesigning Schools for the International Era" in *Economic Eye,* Spring 1993 (Tokyo: Keizai Koho Center).

Yamaguchi, Jiro. 1993. *Seiji Kaikaku* [Political Reform], (Tokyo: Iwanami Shinsho).

———. 1997. *Nihon Seiji no Kadai: Shin Seiji Kaikaku Ron* [Current Issues in Japanese Politics: A New Approach to Political Reform] (Tokyo: Iwanami Shinsho).

———. 1998. *Igirisu no Seiji, Nihon no Seiji* [British Politics, Japanese Politics], (Tokyo: Chikuma Shinsho).

Yamazaki, Masaoto. 1986. *Jimintō to Kyōiku Seisaku* [The LDP and Education Policy] (Tokyo: Iwanami).

Yamazaki, Tomoo. 1998. "Tokorozawa Kōkō: Hinomaru, Kimigayo ha naze ikenai" [Tokorozawa High School: Why are the Hinomaru and Kimigayo Banned?] in *Bungeishunju,* June 1998, pp. 194–200.

Yamazumi, Masaoto. 1986. *Nihon Kyōiku Shōshi* [A Brief History of Japanese Education] (Tokyo: Iwanami).

Yanaga, Chitoshi. 1968. *Big Business in Japanese Politics* (New Haven, CT: Yale University Press).

Yayama, Taro. 1983. "The Newspapers Conduct a Mad Rhapsody over the Textbook Issue" in *The Journal of Japanese Studies,* Vol. 9, No. 2, Summer.

Yokobori, Shōichi. 1988. *Nikkyōso Saisei: Nakamatachi ni Meseeji* [The Revival of Nikkyōso: A Message to Colleagues] (Tokyo: Tsumie Shobō).

Yoneyama, Shoko. 1999. *The Japanese High School: Silence and Resistance* (London: Routledge).

Yoshikawa, Tsuneo. 1999. "'Hinomaru.Kimigayo' no Hōseika ni Hantaisuru" [Opposing the legalisation of the Hinomaru and the Kimigayo] in *Hō to Minshushugi* [the Journal of the Japan Democratic Lawyers' Association], No. 340, July.

Zenkyō [All Japan Teachers and Staff Union]. 1993. *This is Zenkyō* (Published by Zenkyō, Tokyo).

———. 1997. *Kyōshokuin Kumiai Undō no Rekishi* [The History of the Teachers' Union Movement] (Published by Zenkyō. Tokyo).

INTERVIEWS

National Level

Amano Ikuo (Professor, Centre for National University Finance; former Professor of Education, Tokyo University), interview, 5 June 1996.

Baba Masashi (Member of Central Executive Committee, Zenkyō), interview 19 September 1998.

Hemmi Kazuka (Ministry of Education, International Affairs Division), interview 21 November 1996.

Ichikawa Shōgo (Director of Research Department, Centre for National University Finance), interview, 5 June 1996.

Imai Hiroshi (Shinshinto Diet member; former Mayor of Soka city, Saitama), interviews, 5 December 1995 and 26 May 1996.

Hatayama Hidetaka (Zenkyō, National Executive member), interview 16 June 1993.

Horio, Teruhisa (Professor of Education, Chuō University), interview 18 September 1998.

Juppe, Robert (Ministry of Education, International Exchange and Teaching Advisor), interview 23 February 1996.

Morishima Michio (Professor of Economics, London School of Economics; previously Professor at University of Kyoto), interview 19 August 1997.

Newman, Kevin (Programme Co-ordinator, Centre for Local Authorities and International Relations, Tokyo), interview, 1 May 1996.

Niisato Masao (Ministry of Education, Senior Curriculum Specialist), interviews 24 October 1995 and 6 August 1996.

Nishizawa Kiyoshi (Vice Chairman, Nikkyōso), interview 23 July 1996.

Ogawa Masahito (Associate Professor of Education, University of Tokyo), interview, 12 August 1996.

Oyama Shinnosuke (Ministry of Education, Planning Director of the Elementary and Secondary Education Bureau), interview, 30 May 1996.

Ueda, Takeo (Professor of Education, Nagoya University), interview, 18 September 1998.

Urano Toyokazu (Head of the Department of Education, University of Tokyo), interview, 25 October 1995.

Prefectural and City Level

Kono Toshinori (Member of Chiba Prefectural Assembly), interview, 5 December, 1995.

Mori Jun (Chairman Meikōkyō–Nagoya City High School Teachers' Union affiliated with Nikkyōsō) 7 January 1999.

Nakaoka Masahiro (Supervisor, High School Education Division, Kanagawa Prefectural Board of Education), interview, 23 May 1996.

Numata Yoshitaka (Secretary, Tokyo Metropolitan Prefecture Teachers' Union affiliated with Zenkyō), interview, 31 May 1996.

Seki Tarō (Supervisor, School Education Division, Kuki City Board of Education, Saitama), interview, 24 July 1996.

Takahashi Sanaru (Chairman of Executive Committee, Aikōkyō-Aichi Prefecture High School Teachers' Union affiliated with Zenkyō), interview, 17 January 1999.

Udagawa Tsutomo (Senior Teacher Consultant, Saitama Prefectural Board of Education), interview, 3 October, 1995.

Yoneura Tadashi (Secretary, Saitama High School Teachers' Union affiliated with Zenkyō), interview, 22 March 1996.

School Level

(Names have not been given for interviewees at this level).

One teacher and Juku owner, Saitama, interview, 2 August 1996.

One ex-union member, a Saitama special school for the handicapped, interview, 21 July 1996.

One ex-union member, a Saitama high school, interview, 19 July 1996.

One union member of Zenkyō-affiliated union, a Saitama commercial high school, interview 18 July 1996.

One non-union teacher, a Saitama high school, interview 13 August 1996.

The Principal of a Saitama high school, interview, 21 February 1996.

The Principal of a Saitama junior high school, interview 21 September 1995.

One union member Zenkyō-affiliated union, a Saitama commercial high school, interview 20 September 1995.

One School union representative for Nikkyōso-affiliated union, a Saitama commercial high school, interviews 20 September 1995 and 18 July 1996.

One union member, Zenkyō-affiliated union, a Saitama commercial high school, interviews 20 September 1995 and 18 July 1996.

One union member, a Nagoya City high school, 27 September 1998.

INDEX